WMC

WITHDRAWN

Sir Thomas Elyot

TUDOR HUMANIST

Thomas Elyot, drawing by Hans Holbein the Younger.
*(From the collection of Her Majesty the Queen at Windsor Castle.
Crown Copyright reserved)*

Sir Thomas Elyot

TUDOR HUMANIST

By Stanford E. Lehmberg

UNIVERSITY OF TEXAS PRESS, AUSTIN

Library of Congress Catalog Card No. 59–12858
© 1960 by the University of Texas Press

Manufactured in the United States of America
by the University of Texas Printing Division

God is my juge, I wryte neyther for glory, rewarde, nor promotion, only I desyre men to
deme wel myne intent, sens I dare assure them
that all that I have writen in this boke, I have
gathered of the moste princypall wrytars. . . .
Which beinge throughly studied and well re-
membrid, shalbe profitable (I doubt not)
unto the reder, and nothynge noyousse to
honest [scholars], that doo measure theyr
study with moderate lyvinge and Christian
charity.

SIR THOMAS ELYOT, "Proheme" to
The Castel of Helth (1541).

Preface

No single aspect of early sixteenth-century England has received more attention, from both historians and literary scholars, than the growth of Humanism: the new surge of interest in the writings, ideas, and stylistic techniques of the ancient Greeks and Romans. In this movement Sir Thomas Elyot was one of the chief forces; his Latin-English dictionary, for instance, made a solid contribution to knowledge, and his *Boke named the Gouernour* was among the most popular of the age. It is surely, then, surprising that this is the first full-scale biography to attempt an analysis of Elyot's life and works.

Modern study of Elyot's writings dates from 1880, when H. H. S. Croft published a two-volume edition of *The Boke named the Gouernour*. Besides annotating the *Governor* thoroughly, Croft prefaced the book with a rather long account of the Elyot family. Croft had seen most of the manuscripts which can be used in reconstructing Elyot's life, and he printed most of Elyot's extant correspondence at full length. Since only the first few volumes of the *Letters and Papers of Henry VIII* had appeared, Croft was unable to give a full account of Elyot's governmental services, and he did not use all of the pertinent family wills—in fact, inexplicably, he failed to find Sir Thomas's own testament, though he examined other wills in the same repository. Croft's real weakness, however, lay not in his lack of material, but rather in his want of critical perception and historical curiosity. He examined Elyot, as it were, in a vacuum.

This might not have been a serious defect in studies of certain other writers. With Elyot, however, it was nearly disastrous for several reasons. First, the pertinent manuscripts which have withstood the ravages of time are disappointingly meager, so inadequate that every jot of evidence must be drawn from Elyot's published works if we are to have anything like a full account of his life. His works must be studied carefully in the light of events contemporary with their composition, and use must be made of all asides and allusions, as well as of dedicatory prefaces. There is a further difficulty. During the latter part of his life Elyot was in disfavor at court and in disagreement with some of the King's policies; had he stated his views openly and unambiguously his head might have rolled on Tower Green. Yet he was not to be silenced. He camouflaged his criticisms of Henry VIII's divorce and of the King's councilors in "Platonic" dialogues and spoke his own views from the lips of characters borrowed from antiquity. This reflected his love of the classics, something which Croft recognized fully, but it did much more. Unfortunately the hidden meanings eluded Croft, and so he failed to emphasize one of the salient facts of Elyot's life: his lasting interest in public affairs and his bitterness at being excluded from the government just when he felt that his advice was most sorely needed.

Other recent studies concerning Elyot, all of them fragmentary, may be mentioned briefly. The article by Sir Sidney Lee in the *Dictionary of National Biography* follows Croft closely. More valuable contributions have been made in dealing with certain of Elyot's works. Leslie C. Warren's unpublished dissertation, "Humanistic Doctrines of the Prince from Petrarch to Sir Thomas Elyot: A Study of the Principal Analogues and Sources of *The Boke named the Gouernour*" (University of Chicago, 1937), carries further the analysis of the sources of the *Governor* begun by Croft; it is valuable, although I do not agree with all of its conclusions. In several articles and in his excellent book *Renaissance Dictionaries,* DeWitt T. Starnes has studied Elyot's Latin-English dictionary and its far-reaching influence. A number of German dissertations have been concerned with Elyot: Kurt Schroeder has written on Platonism in Elyot's thought, Josef Schlotter on Elyot's indebtedness to Patrizi, Cornelie Benndorf and Helmuth Exner of Elyot's view of education, and Emil Grether on Shakespeare's use of the *Governor.* Professor Starnes has also published a note on Elyot and Shakespeare. A chapter in Fritz Caspari's *Humanism and the Social Order in Tudor England* discusses Elyot's social and political ideas in rather general terms. Full data on these and other related works will be found in the bibliography, which attempts to list all significant writings concerning Elyot.

My interest in Sir Thomas Elyot began when I was doing research at Cambridge University under a Fulbright grant. It is a pleasure to acknowledge the kindness of Mr. Christopher Morris and Dr. D. E. D. Beales, both of whom read early drafts of this book. Professor C. S. Lewis, Dr. G. R. Elton, Mr. S. T. Bindoff, and Mr. M. M. Willcock were good enough to discuss certain aspects of my work with me. It was Professor William Gilbert, of the University of Kansas, who first kindled my interest in Tudor studies. Professor Starnes, of the University of Texas, kindly allowed me to use some of the books, photographs, and notes which he has gathered during a lifetime of interest in Elyot's writings. My former colleague, Mr. E. L. Cannan, discussed certain aspects of this study with me and made helpful comments. Probably none of these scholars would agree with all of my judgments, for which—together with all errors—I am alone responsible. I was fortunate to have the expert secretarial service, during the various stages in the preparation of the manuscript, of the Cambridge University Typewriting Service, Mrs. F. R. Holland, and Mrs. Frank Bertram.

I am grateful to Her Majesty Queen Elizabeth II for gracious permission to reproduce the Holbein drawings, now at Windsor Castle, of Sir Thomas and Lady Margaret Elyot; to the trustees of the British Museum for leave to reproduce a page from one of Elyot's letters; and to Mr. H. R. Creswick, the librarian of the University Library, Cambridge, for permission to reproduce pages from several early books in the collection of that library. The editors of the *Archiv für Reformationsgeschite* have kindly given permission to reproduce fragments from my article "Sir Thomas Elyot and the English Reformation." My thanks go also to members of the staffs of the University Library and the Seeley Historical Library, Cambridge; the British Museum; the Public Record Office; the Principal Probate Registry, Somerset House; the Bodleian Library; the Newberry Library; the Library of the University of Kansas; and finally the Library of the University of Texas, together with its Rare Books Collection. All have been unfailingly cooperative.

In conclusion, a word about my handling of sixteenth-century texts. Thinking Elyot's own vigorous prose far more interesting than any modern paraphrase or analysis of it, I have quoted at length from his letters and books. I have preserved the original spelling with one general exception: in order not to confuse the reader by writing—for instance—*vuula* for *uvula*, I have brought the distinction between *i* and *j* and *u* and *v* into conformity with modern practice (Tudor writers rarely, if ever, began a word with a *j* or *u*). I have expanded abbreviations and have modified the punctuation and capitalization where I thought it desirable. In the full titles of books the original orthography has been entirely preserved, even to *i*'s and *u*'s, but short titles are completely modernized. Thus Elyot's most famous work will be called *The Boke named the Gouernour* and also the *Governor*.

S. E. L.

December, 1958
Austin, Texas

Contents

Illustrations

Sir Thomas Elyot

TUDOR HUMANIST

CHAPTER ONE

By Nature Inclyned to Knowledge

THOMAS ELYOT can scarcely be called one of the forgotten men of the early Tudor age. His work as a political theorist and as a lexicographer has attracted considerable attention, as recent studies of *The Boke named the Gouernour* and of his Latin-English dictionary testify. His hygienic guide, *The Castel of Helth*, immensely popular in his own century, still interests historians of medicine, and it was accorded the honor of a new edition in 1937, the first since 1610. The *Governor* and the dialogue, *Of the Knowledeg that Maketh a Wise Man*, have also received republication in the twentieth century.

This continued interest in some of Elyot's works is by no means unmerited. Elyot lived at an important stage in the course of English intellectual development, and he played a significant role in that evolution himself. Although he was not the first Englishman to rediscover the Latin and Greek classics, it was perhaps he more than anyone else who made for them the home in his native isle to which they have clung for so long. In the fifteenth century Duke Humphrey had collected classical texts, and isolated pioneers—Flemmyng and Tiptoft, Gunthorpe and Grey—had traveled to Italy, absorbed its culture, and brought fragments of it back with them to England. These efforts made possible the work, under the first two Tudor monarchs, of Linacre and Colet, Erasmus and More, men whose Humanistic writings, though brilliant, were intended for scholars and were, significantly, in Latin. It remained for such men as Thomas Elyot and his friend Roger Ascham to communicate the results of the New Learning to their fellow countrymen in their vernacular. They did much to prepare the ground for the great flowering of Elizabethan literature and thought.

An injustice is done Elyot, however, when he is remembered solely as a Humanistic writer. Though primarily a scholar, Elyot was a man of action as well as a man of contemplation. He knew nearly all the great men of his day. He was a friend of Thomas Wolsey and Thomas Cromwell, the giants of Henry VIII's government. He was a pupil of Sir Thomas More and probably of Thomas Linacre. After serving for years in the law courts, he acted as chief clerk of the King's Council from about 1523 to 1530 and subsequently as ambassador to the Emperor Charles V during the strain of Henry's divorce proceedings. Moreover, Elyot was a leading member of the gentry, appropriately serving as a sheriff, a justice of the peace, and a member of numerous *ad hoc* commissions. He sat in the Parliament that completed the dissolution of the monasteries. He was involved in several vexing law suits; he acted as guardian for his relative, the great John Pym's grandfather. Clearly the breadth of Elyot's activities is more notable than the depth of his knowledge in any single area, and he will have less than his due unless the full range of his interests is considered.

WE KNOW LITTLE about the first years of Thomas Elyot's life. The earliest extant document to mention his name records his admission to the Middle Temple, one of the Inns of Court, in 1510; it also notes that he was then serving as clerk to the Justices of Assize on the Western Circuit, a position he held until Cardinal Wolsey had him resign from it about 1526 so that he could devote his full attention to the King's Council.[1] There is no record of the date of Thomas's birth; it has usually been assumed that he must have been of age before he began

[1] C. H. Hopwood (ed.), *Middle Temple Records* (London, 1904), p. 34.

his legal studies and his clerkship, and so his birth has been fixed at about 1490. This may, however, be too early, for boys sometimes went up to the Inns, as to the Universities, when they were still quite young, and there would be nothing very surprising in a minor's acting as clerk to a group of judges that included his father. Nor do we know the place of Elyot's birth; it was almost certainly in the west of England, probably in Wiltshire, where his father, Richard, held the manors of Chalk and Winterslow.

It was natural that Thomas Elyot should enter the legal profession, for his father was a distinguished jurist and Middle Templer. Richard Elyot was already a member of the Temple in 1501, the year of the Inn's earliest surviving records; probably he had spent the last years of the fifteenth century studying law there. In 1503 he was made a bencher, or member of the Inn's administrative body, and as reader for that year's Autumn "Vacation," or term of instruction, he was responsible for the education of youths studying law in the Inn.[2]

Richard Elyot was chosen reader, the records say, because he had just been raised to the dignity of King's Serjeant-at-Law. The position of the ordinary serjeant-at-law was "a state no less worshipful and solemn than the degree of Doctors," as Fortescue had written, and only the most distinguished of the serjeants were created King's Serjeants.[3] Richard Elyot received the honor in an elaborate series of ceremonies which began on November 10, 1503, and lasted for four days. His son, Thomas, was probably not permitted to see the festivities himself, but he must have been told of the proceedings in the Middle Temple, where Richard had been urged to favor members of his own Inn while acting in his new capacity; in the Archbishop's chapel at Lambeth, where there were speeches by the new King's Serjeants and by the Chief Justice of the King's Bench; and in Westminster Hall, where the serjeants were presented to the Justices of the Court of Common Pleas, the Chancellor, and the Treasurer. Finally, breakfast had been served in the Middle Temple hall for the King, members of his household, and members of the Inn—about a thousand

[2] Sir Henry F. MacGeagh and H. A. C. Sturgess (eds.), *Register of Admissions to the Honourable Society of the Middle Temple* (London, 1949), I, 1.

[3] W. S. Holdsworth, *A History of English Law* (5th ed., London, 1931), II, 486 f.

in all, according to the unusually full account in the Inn's records.[4]

The festivities in the Middle Temple were in a sense a farewell, for serjeants gave up membership in their old Inns and were admitted to Serjeants' Inn, across Fleet Street in Chancery Lane. It was not unusual, however, for them to retain chambers in their former Inns, and it is probable that Richard Elyot's professional and social life continued to center in the Temple. During the first years of the sixteenth century a number of Elyot's relatives and associates were members of the Middle Temple. William Fetiplace, a brother-in-law of Richard Elyot's second wife, was admitted to the Inn in 1504; William's brother, Sir Thomas, was probably the Fetiplace known to have been a member before 1501 and to have been fined for refusing to be steward for the Inn's Christmas feast in 1502.[5] Lewis Pollard, who like Elyot came from a good West Country family and who rode the Western Assizes with him from 1506 to 1516, was a member of the Middle Temple before 1501, became a bencher in 1503, and was promoted with Elyot to Serjeants' Inn later that year.[6] Just before Elyot's promotion Thomas Empson, son of the great Sir Richard, was admitted to the Middle Temple and was assigned to Elyot's chambers. The senior Empson, chancellor of the Duchy of Lancaster and later executed together with Edmund Dudley as a scapegoat for Henry VII's stringent financial policies, was a bencher of the Inn and probably another of Richard Elyot's close friends.[7]

Of greater interest is the connection of the More family with the Inns of Court, since Thomas Elyot was later to be a friend and pupil of Sir Thomas More. John More, father of the great Humanist, was made a member of Lincoln's Inn in 1470 in reward for years of faithful service as the Inn's steward. His son Thomas, born in 1478, came down from Oxford when he was twenty-three to study law in New Inn, one of the Inns of Chancery loosely connected with the Middle Temple. He was made a bencher of the Middle Temple in 1506 and was chosen reader for the Lent Vacations of 1506 and 1511; he was

---

[4] Hopwood, *op. cit.*, pp. 5–9. The unusual detail in the account is probably due to the fact that this was the first such ceremony after the Inn began keeping records.

[5] *Ibid.*, pp. 1, 4, 11.

[6] MacGeagh and Sturgess, *op. cit.*, I, 3.

[7] Hopwood, *op. cit.*, p. 5.

treasurer of the Middle Temple from 1512 to 1517. Thomas More's brother-in-law, John Rastell, was also a member of the Middle Temple, although he is better remembered as a publisher than as a jurist.[8] Enlightened gentry, trained in the law, accustomed to help govern their country: these were the men with whom Sir Richard Elyot lived and worked; this was the class of "governors" into which his son was born.

The public activities of Richard Elyot himself were numerous. He had served the Crown in minor capacities for a decade before his appointment as King's Serjeant. His earliest recorded service, in 1493, was as a member of two commissions to inquire about "concealed" royal lands—fiefs which should have escheated to the king at the death of their holder but which had illegally passed to an heir—in Wiltshire, Somerset, Dorset, Devon, and Cornwall.[9] He was named to the Commission of Gaol Delivery for Old Sarum, near Salisbury, as early as 1496 and again in 1506; in 1502 he was commissioned to deliver the jail of Colchester Castle.[10]

The position in which Sir Richard Elyot made his greatest contribution, however, was that of Justice of Assize for the Western Circuit, which included Hampshire, Wiltshire, Oxfordshire, Dorset, Somerset, Devon, and Cornwall. He was first named one of the justices in 1506 and probably served continuously until his death.[11] The courts of the justices of assize possessed a limited jurisdiction in civil cases, but they frequently handled quite difficult matters and were in fact only slightly inferior to the central common-law courts. Justices of assize were ex officio members of the Commissions of Oyer and Terminer and of Gaol Delivery for their circuit, and in this capacity they also had a limited criminal jurisdiction; because of the complexity of their duties they were always, like Elyot, trained lawyers.[12] As a King's

[8] R. W. Chambers, *Thomas More* (London, 1938), pp. 52 f., 20; MacGeagh and Sturgess, *op. cit.*, I, 3.

[9] *Calendar of Patent Rolls, Henry VII* (London, 1914–16), I, 476, 479.

[10] *Ibid.*, II, 50, 487, 289.

[11] *Ibid.*, II, 501; *Calendar of Letters and Papers, Foreign and Domestic, Henry VIII* (London, 1864–1932), I, 804 (36), 1083 (8), 1316 (14), 1662 (28), 2137 (11), 2684 (62), 3107 (34); II, 154, 693, 1537, 2163, 2919, 3467, 3949, 4317; III, 102, 347, 405, 644, 933, 1186, 1451. There is a hiatus in the records for 1508–11. Records of the Commission of Gaol Delivery for 1507 and 1508 are extant and imply that Elyot was acting as a justice then.

[12] Holdsworth, *op. cit.*, I, 278–285. As a member of the Commission of Gaol

Serjeant, Richard Elyot was summoned to the Parliaments of 1510, 1512, and 1515,[13] and his name appears in the list of those granted scarlet and red cloth for the coronation of Henry VIII in 1509.[14] Finally, in 1513, he was raised to the bench in the Court of Common Pleas;[15] he was knighted in 1517.[16]

Although busy in the Assizes and in Common Pleas, Richard Elyot continued to serve in a number of relatively minor positions. As a royal judge he was automatically a justice of the peace; specific commissions reveal that, at one time or another, he acted as a justice of the peace for Wiltshire, Dorset, Somerset, Oxfordshire, Essex, Berkshire, Hampshire, Devon, Cornwall, and the city of Oxford.[17] He was repeatedly commissioned to inquire into Crown lands in the West Country,[18] and from 1498 to 1511 he was Crown receiver for the manor of Wanborough, near Swindon in Wiltshire.[19]

He also held considerable lands in his own right. From his father, Simon Elyot, he had inherited the manors of Chalk and Winterslow, both near Salisbury. He had himself acquired land at Long Combe, Oxfordshire, and additional territory came into the Elyot family as a result of his two marriages. Both of his wives were widows when he married them, and both connected him with families considerably more wealthy and important than his own.[20] His first wife, Alice Dela-

---

Delivery for the Western Circuit, Elyot helped deliver the jails of Old Sarum, Dorchester, Ilchester, Exeter, Winchester, and Launceston (see *Cal. Pat. Rolls*, II, 547, 651; *L.P.*, I, 833 [2], 1316 [3], 1662 [1], 2055 [114]; II, 1441; III, 2074. Specific documents exist only for 1507–16 and 1522). In 1520 he was further commissioned to deliver all the jails of London and Middlesex and to try prisoners in them (*L.P.*, III, 1081).

[13] *L.P.*, I, 205, 963, 3464 (2).

[14] *Ibid.*, 82.

[15] *Ibid.*, 1836 (14).

[16] Commissions begin to refer to him as "Richard Elyot, Kt." in 1517.

[17] According to *Cal. Pat. Rolls*, II, and *L.P.*, I–III (patents too numerous for individual citation), Elyot was named to the following commissions: Wiltshire, 1494–1507, 1515; Dorset, 1515, 1519/20; Somerset, 1515, 1521; Oxfordshire, 1509, 1515; Oxford town, 1510–12; Essex, 1501–09; Devon, 1515, 1519; Cornwall, 1515, 1520/21; Berkshire, 1515; Hampshire, 1515.

[18] *Cal. Pat. Rolls*, II, 181, 188, 263, 507, 582.

[19] Chancery Inquisitions post Mortem, Hants. and Wilts., Public Record Office, C 142/75/144.

[20] A genealogical table will be found in Appendix I, together with detailed information concerning the public services of Elyot's relatives.

mere, was descended from the Finderns of Derbyshire. One branch of the Findern family had acquired lands in Berkshire only to have them confiscated during the Wars of the Roses, when the family had supported the Lancastrians. But Alice's cousin, Sir William Findern, eventually succeeded in gaining both the favor of Henry VII and extensive lands near Cambridge, lands which passed to Sir Thomas Elyot after the extinction of one of the Findern lines. Alice Delamere was, by her first marriage, the great-great-grandmother of John Pym, the seventeenth-century Parliamentary leader, and it was because of this relationship that Thomas Elyot later served as guardian for Pym's grandfather. Alice's first husband, Thomas Daubridgecourt, died in the year of Bosworth Field (not, so far as we know, in battle), and Alice was married again, probably about 1487, to Richard Elyot. She was the mother of his two children, Thomas and Margery. We do not know when she died; it must have been about 1510.

Soon after her death Richard Elyot married again. His second wife, Elizabeth, was a member of the Bessels family and the widow of Richard Fetiplace. Her father, William Bessels (or Besiles), was a Berkshire gentleman, holder of a manor at Besselsleigh, which eventually came to the Elyots. Although Elizabeth and Richard Elyot had no children, she had borne her first husband at least four sons and three daughters. Later we will find Thomas Elyot dedicating one of his translations to Susan Fetiplace Kingstone, one of his stepsisters.

Since Richard Elyot and his West Country relatives lived close to each other, they probably met often; certainly their duties to the Crown brought them together occasionally. For instance, the Commission of the Peace for Berkshire which was named on December 4, 1515, included Richard Elyot, William Bessels, Sir Thomas Fetiplace, John Fetiplace, William Fetiplace, Lewis Pollard, and Guy Palmes.[21] The Fetiplaces were all Elizabeth Elyot's brothers-in-law except John, who was her son. Pollard and Palmes were colleagues of Richard Elyot's in the Middle Temple and in the assizes. Here again one catches a glimpse of those West Country gentry among whom Thomas Elyot grew to maturity.

[21] *L.P.*, II, 1247.

UNTIL HIS ENTRY in the Middle Temple, young Thomas Elyot was educated at home. Years later, defending himself against the charge that he was not sufficiently learned to compile a Latin-English dictionary, he admitted that he had received his early training in his father's house and that he was virtually self-taught, both in liberal arts and philosophy. His statement, from the Preface to the first edition of his dictionary, is our only source of information about his early life:

> You may think among yourselves that this work has been undertaken by an unlearned British knight, seeing that he was educated in his father's house and not instructed by any other teacher from his twelfth year, but led by himself into liberal studies and both sorts of philosophy. This is far from the truth, as I might say boastingly; but no doubt (since, thanks to God, this my book will be useful not only to me but also to others) other men may undertake equal or greater works, profiting by the richer benefit of my example.[22]

It is curious that Elyot, refuting the implied charge that he was an ignorant knight, did not cite his studies in the Middle Temple and later at Oxford. When he entered the Middle Temple in 1510 he began the best training for public life that young men of his day could have. The Universities of Oxford and Cambridge were still primarily interested in educating men for the Church, but the Inns of Court aimed at preparation for careers in the law and in government. As Pollard has written, "It was not then a metaphor to call them an university: they had professors of law; they conferred the degrees of barrister and serjeant, analogous to the degrees of bachelor, master and doctor,

---

[22] Cogitetisque apud vosipsos, id operis iam coeptum ab equite britanno, barbarissimo scilicet, utpote in paternis tantum aedibus educato, nec ab anno aetatis duodecimo ab altero quopiam preceptore literis instructo, sibi ipsi nimirum duce tam in scientiis liberalibus, quam in utraque philosophia: quod procul abest, ut ostendando dicam vel arroganter: sed ut gratiis DEO OPT. MAX. cum a me tum ab his quibus hic meus liber fuerit utilis, utrinque reditis: ilii musarum uberiori benefitio freti, meo quidem exemplo, parem aut maiorem operam aggredi, pro sua Republica non dubitarent.—*The Dictionary of Syr Thomas Elyot knyght* (London, 1538), fol. A v^r.

The dictionary also contains, under *gigas* (giant), a rare glimpse into Elyot's youth. He relates an unusual occurrence of about 1508: while he and his father were visiting Ivy Church, near Salisbury, workmen digging stone unearthed what Elyot took to be a human skeleton thirteen feet long.

bestowed by universities; and every man, before he became a barrister, was subjected to examination, and obliged to defend a thesis."[23]

Although Elyot was admitted to clerk's commons by the Inn in November of 1510, there is no evidence that he was ever called to the bar or that he ever actually practiced law. Probably he was too busy acting as clerk, first to the Justices of Assize and then to the King's Council, to complete his legal studies. Some comments in *The Boke named the Gouernour* make it clear that he did not particularly enjoy whatever training he received in the Middle Temple.[24] The English legal system was difficult to understand, for all law is "founded on the depest parte of raison, and, as I suppose, no one lawe so moche as our owne; and the deper men do investigate raison the more difficile or harde muste nedes be the studie." Legal French, used with little change since the days of the Norman Conquest, struck him as an unnecessary stumbling block: that "barbarouse . . . langage . . . voyde of all eloquence, . . . beynge seperate from the exercise of our lawe onely, it serveth to no commoditie or necessary purpose, no man understandyng it but they whiche have studyed the lawes." Elyot complained in vain; it was nearly a century before Sir Edward Coke began to write legal expositions in English, and he was at pains to justify the novelty even then.

Elyot expressed horror that youths of fourteen or fifteen were set at legal studies, as he may have been himself. Such lads either "do abandone the lawes and unwares to their frendes do gyve them to gamyng and other (as I mought saye) idle busynesse nowe called pastymes," or else they understand only a small part of the law and are amazed when, years later, they realize that it is not the whole. "They no lasse be astonied than if commyng out of a darke house at noone dayes they were sodaynly striken in the eyen with a bright sonne beame." How much better for these youths to begin with a sound Humanistic education:

I thinke verily if children were broughte uppe as I have written, and continually were retayned in the right studie of very philosphy untyll they

---

[23] A. F. Pollard in *The Times* [London], October 1, 1932.

[24] *The Boke named the Gouernour*, I, Chap. 14. (All references herein to the *Governor* will be by chapter, not page, so that they may readily be located in any edition of the book.)

passed the age of xxi yeres, and than set to the lawes of this realme (being ones brought to a more certayne and compendiouse studie, and either in Englisshe, Latine, or good French, written in a more clene and elegant stile) undoughtedly they shuld become men of so excellent wisedome that throughout all the worlde shulde be founden in no commune weale more noble counsaylours, our lawes nat onely comprehendyng most excellent raisons, but also beyng gadred and compacte (as I mought saye) of the pure mele or floure syfted out of the best lawes of all other countrayes, as somwhat I do intende to prove evidently in the nexte volume, wherin I wyll rendre myne offyce or duetie to that honorable studie wherby my father was advaunced to a juge, and also I my selfe have attayned no lytle commoditie.

Without proper early training, the young lawyer's learning will become corrupted by the involuted nonsense of medieval glosses:

Example we have at this present tyme of divers excellent learned men, bothe in the lawes civile as also in phisike, whiche being exactly studyed in all partes of eloquence, bothe in the Greeke tonge and Latine, have nat witstanding radde and perused the great fardelles and trusses of the most barbarouse autours, stuffed with innumerable gloses, wherby the moste necessary doctrines of lawe and phisike be mynced in to fragmentes, and in all wise mens opinions, do perceyve no lasse in the said lernynges than they whiche never knewe eloquence, or never tasted other but the fecis or dragges of the sayd noble doctrines.

This is Elyot's clearest statement of his esteem for the New Learning and of his disgust at the "fardelles and trusses" of scholasticism.

ALTHOUGH ELYOT thought that youths should study philosophy before attempting legal training, the pattern was reversed in his own formal education, for he entered Oxford University in 1516, six years after his admission to the Middle Temple. Despite the disruption caused by a virulent outbreak of the sweating sickness in Oxford during 1517, he took the degree of B.A. in 1519. Then in 1523 he supplicated for the degree Bachelor of Civil Law; the grace granted by the Congregation on June 26 states that he had completed three years' study of arts and three years of civil law. This suggests that he was not in Oxford continuously between Lent, 1519, and June, 1523, for he claims only three years' study during the period of more than four years. No doubt his duties with the Justices of Assize prevented continuous residence. For some reason Elyot did not actually take his B.C.L. until August 1, 1524.[25]

We do not know Elyot's college, though Anthony à Wood recorded a tradition that he was a member of St. Mary's Hall, a small house under the control of Oriel College.[26] Jesus College, Cambridge, has also claimed Elyot; C. H. Cooper wrote in his *Athenae Cantabrigienses* of "good evidence" that Elyot "was really educated in Jesus college in

[25] H. H. S. Croft concluded that Elyot did not attend a university (see the Introduction to his edition of *The Boke named the Gouernour*, I, xxiii–xxvi, xxxvii–xxxix), and later writers have followed him. But I believe that the following entries in *Registrum H (Registrum Congregationis 1518–1536)* of the Oxford University Archives refer to our Thomas Elyot: (1) fol. 1^r, "Eodem die [June ?, 1518] admissi sunt ad lecturam alicuius libri facultatis artium . . . dns' Thomas Eliett"; (2) fol. 14^v, "Sequuntur nomine determinantium hac quadragesima [March ?, 1519] . . . dns' Thomas Eyllyett"; (3) fol. 111^v, "Eodem die [June 26, 1523] supplicat Thomas Elyett, scholaris facultatis iuris civilis, quatenus studium 3^m annorum in artibus et 3^m annorum in eodem iure sibi sufficiat [*sic*] ut admittatur ad lecturam alicuius libelli Institutionum. Hec gratia est concessa, sic quod solvat iij^s. iiij^d. ad reparationem baculi inferioris bedelli theologie in die admissionis"; (4) fol. 123^v, "Admissiones in iure canonico et civili anno Christi 1524°. . . . Eodem die [August 1] admissi sunt ad lecturam libelli Institucionum . . . d' Thomas Elyott." Entries (1) and (2) mean that Elyot took the degree of B.A.; the normal formalities of being admitted to the degree began with (1) admission "to lecture on any book of the faculty of Arts" and had to be completed by (2) "determining," or taking part in certain disputations during the following Lent. Elyot was admitted B.A. in June, 1518, and determined in Lent, 1519. Entries (3) and (4) mean that he took the degree of Bachelor of Civil Law; the formula for this was being "admitted to lecture on any book of the Institutes." Everyone wishing to take any degree had to "supplicate" for a "grace," giving details of the length of residence and amount of study he had fulfilled or hoped to fulfill by the time he took the degree. Entry (3) gives the actual grace for Elyot's B.C.L., in which he specifies three years' study of arts and three years of civil law. The grace was granted in June, 1523, but for some reason Elyot did not take the degree (4) until August, 1524. I am indebted to Mr. W. A. Pantin, of Oriel College, keeper of the Oxford University Archives, for sending me a transcript and explanation of these entries. The grace and admission for Elyot's B.A. have not survived, nor is there any record that he was excused from residence requirements, though I suspect that his duties with the Assizes, nominal as they may have been, made such exemption necessary.

[26] Anthony à Wood, *Athenae Oxonienses* (London, 1813), I, col. 150; C. E. Mallet, *A History of the University of Oxford* (London, 1924), I, 260.

this university, and here proceeded M.A. 1507," a year which could be harmonized with Elyot's other activities on the assumption that he was born before 1490 and studied in Cambridge before he went to the Middle Temple. But Cooper does not cite his evidence, and neither the College nor the University possesses records which substantiate his statement.[27]

Elyot's years in Oxford did not come at a good time for the University, which was beset with pestilence and poverty. The despondent authorities wrote to Sir Thomas More in 1523:

We are of the poor. Once we had each our yearly grant, some from noblemen, some from those who support monasteries, many from priests who have country livings. Now, however, those who ought to give assistance refuse to do so. Abbots fetch their monks home, noblemen send for their children, and priests for their relations. So is the number of scholars diminished. So our halls fall down. So all liberal customs grow cold. The Colleges alone persist.[28]

Nor was the curriculum probably very inspiring. Enthusiasm for scholasticism had waned; but despite the influence of such Oxonians as Grocyn, who had taught Greek, and Colet, who had instilled a fresh spirit into the study of St. Paul's epistles, students were still expected to spend their time conning Aristotle and Duns Scotus. Such New Learning as did creep in was officially discouraged: Bishop Longland, chancellor of the University from 1532 to 1547, warned Oriel College that disputations must not be neglected, that the classics must not oust older learning, and that the study of theology must be perpetuated.[29]

NOT CONTENT with his rather old-fashioned training in logic and civil law at Oxford, Elyot pursued the newer Humanistic studies under the guidance of Thomas More and was probably also taught Greek and medicine by Thomas Linacre.

[27] C. H. Cooper and Thomas Cooper, *Athenae Cantabrigienses* (London, 1858), I, 89. Cooper's statement appears to be based on a list of notable Jesus alumni presented to Queen Elizabeth when she visited Cambridge in 1564; see Wood, *op. cit.*, col. 152.

[28] Quoted in Mallet, *op. cit.*, I, 411.

[29] *Ibid.*, 262.

Elyot himself nowhere mentions studying with More the Humanist, but he was later at some pains to excuse his association with More the condemned traitor. In a letter written after More's execution Elyot urged Thomas Cromwell to "lay apart the remembraunce of the amity betwene me and Sir Thomas More, which was but *usque ad aras*, as is the proverb, consydering that I was never so moche addict unto him as I was unto truthe and fidelity towards my soveraigne lord, as Godd is my juge."[30] It is difficult to see exactly what Elyot meant when he said that he and More had been friends only "up to the altars." He probably referred to Erasmus' interpretation, in the *Adagia*, of the proverb *usque ad aram amicus sum*; Erasmus had urged his readers not to give false evidence even for a friend.[31] The context suggests that Elyot wished to draw a distinction between a private friendship based upon common literary interests and the sort of friendship which might have influenced his performance of public duties; although Elyot did not deny his friendship with More, the whole explanation seems ungracious, a bit like some of More's own less fortunate comments on Wolsey after the Cardinal's fall. Elyot's eagerness to reassure Cromwell about the nature of the relationship suggests that he and More had been widely known as rather close friends, although the idea of their intimacy should not be pushed too far. It may be significant that Elyot is nowhere mentioned in More's extensive correspondence.

There is, however, fairly reliable evidence of the association between the two Humanists. More's earliest biographer, his son-in-law William Roper, clearly knew Elyot, and so did a number of More's other friends. Roper related that Elyot was first told of More's execution by the Emperor Charles V, who said that he would rather have lost his best city than such a counselor. Although this story is unreliable in date and detail, as we shall see later, there is no reason to doubt Roper's statement that Elyot himself reported Charles's admiration for More "to my self, to my wife, to maister Clement and his wife,

[30] Elyot to Cromwell, [1537?], Cotton MS. Cleopatra E. IV, fol. 260, British Museum.

[31] The proverb is supposedly Plutarch's answer to Pericles, who had been asked to perjure himself for a friend. See Erasmus' *Adagia* (Venice, 1517), p. 490.

to maister John Haywood and his wife, and unto divers other his freinds."[32] John Clement had married More's foster daughter, Margaret Gigs, and was himself reader in Greek at Oxford and later court physician; John Heywood, the dramatist and wit who was a favorite of Queen Mary's, had married More's niece, Joan Rastell.

Roper's assertion of Elyot's association with More's circle is corroborated by the more specific statement of Thomas Stapleton, whose biography of More was published at Douai in 1588. Stapleton had access to manuscripts brought to Douai by Dorothy Colly, the former maid to More's daughter Margaret Roper and the wife of More's old secretary, John Harris. Her manuscripts may have mentioned Elyot, or Dorothy may have remembered him herself and told Stapleton. In any case, Stapleton wrote that among More's "friends and companions in the pursuit of polite literature . . . was Thomas Eliot, a well-known English writer, whose wife also gave herself to the study of literature in Sir Thomas More's school."[33]

Of course, Elyot could not have been a regular member of the "school" in the sense that More's own children were; he was considerably older than Margaret, Elizabeth, Cecily, and young John More; he had presumably already been given a thorough grounding in Latin; and he was occupied with legal studies and duties. It is unlikely, too, that his wife was a regular member of the school; there is no contemporary evidence to support Stapleton's statement. What is more probable is that the Elyots were frequent guests in More's home, first in Bucklersbury and then in Chelsea, during the years between 1510 and 1530, and that he guided their study of Humanistic texts.

Thomas Elyot's marriage to Margaret à Barrow (or Abarrow) probably took place about the time his association with More began. Like her husband, Margaret came from good West Country stock; her

---

[32] William Roper, *The Lyfe of Sir Thomas Moore*, ed. E. V. Hitchcock (London, 1935), pp. 103 f.

[33] Thomas Stapleton, *Tres Thomae* (Douai, 1588), Pt. III, 52. Trans. from the Latin by P. E. Hallett, *The Life and Illustrious Martyrdom of Sir Thomas More* (London, 1928), p. 44. The biography of More by "Ro. Ba." follows Stapleton in including the Elyots among More's friends (Ro. Ba., *The Lyfe of Syr Thomas More*, ed. E. V. Hitchcock and P. E. Hallett [London, 1950], p. 100). These sources are discussed and evaluated in the first chapter of Chambers, *op. cit.*

The Lady Eliot.

Margaret Elyot, drawing by Hans Holbein the Younger.
*(From the collection of Her Majesty the Queen at Windsor Castle.
Crown Copyright reserved)*

❧THE PROHEME
OF SYR THOMAS ELY-
ot knyght vnto his booke, called the
Castell of helthe.

ALENE THE
mooste excellent physition ceassed, that in wrytynge a compen-
dyous doctrine for the curynge
of sickenesse, he shoulde loose
all his labour, for as moche as
no man amonate broode endeuour hym selfe to
the studyenge of truthe, but that all men dyd soo
moche esteme prickes, possessions, authoritie, and
pleasures, that they supposed them, whiche were
studyous in any parte of sapience, to be madde
or, best, at of diuers wittes, for as moche as they
dyd that theyr sapience, whiche is in knowlege
of thynges belongynge as well to good as to man,
to bnic no beurge. Seing this noble matter founde
that lacke in that tyme, in that there foure floryssh in
studye countraves a great multitude of men excellent in all kyndes of lernyng, do it not bothe appere in some of theyr workes, why shoulde I be
countray doo to compart me, for my laboure take
without hope of temporall rewarde, onely for the
ferrente affection, whiche I haue euer borne towarde the publyke weale of my countrey? I wol-
dly matter say the one, syr Thomas Elyot is become a physition, and wrytethe in physicke, whiche
she besemeth not a knyght, he mought haue ben

B iii
mocke

father was Sir Maurice Barrow, who held land at North Charford, Hampshire, and Downton, Wiltshire.[34] Barrow may have known Richard Elyot well, for both had manors near Salisbury. They served together on the Commission of Gaol Delivery for Old Sarum in 1495 and on the Commission of the Peace for Wiltshire from 1494 to 1515.[35] Barrow was also appointed to numerous *ad hoc* commissions and was among the knights named to attend the King at the Field of Cloth of Gold, along with Sir Richard Elyot and Sir Thomas Fetiplace.[36] Perhaps he anticipated that the trip might be too strenuous for him; he made his will on February 4, 1520, shortly before the expedition sailed, and he must have died not long after it returned, since the will was proved on May 1, 1521. Aside from her association with More's school, we know almost nothing about Margaret herself. One is tempted to think that she did share her husband's literary interests and gave him intellectual companionship unusual in the age. Elyot left us no comment on his life with her.

During their visits at More's home Thomas and Margaret Elyot may have met the best scholars of the time. Grocyn, Colet, Linacre, William Lily, William Mountjoy, Hugh Latimer, Thomas Lupset, John Croke, Reginald Pole, Edward Lee, John Fisher, and Cuthbert Tunstall were all among More's friends.[37] And so, of course, was Erasmus, who was first drawn to England in 1499 by Mountjoy and who wrote his *Moriae Encomium*—the very title was a play on his host's name—while a guest in More's home in 1509. We do not know whether Elyot ever met Erasmus, but certainly he was a member of the chorus who sang

[34] Wills of Sir Maurice Barrow (Mores Barowe), Prerogative Court of Canterbury, MS. 9 Maynwaryng, and of his wife, Dorothy, MS. 12 Thower. Croft (I, lxii) said that Margaret was the daughter of John Abarrow, and other writers have copied the statement. But Maurice's will is clear: he refers to "Margaret Elyot my doughter" and bequeaths her a gilt cup with a cover. She was in fact related to two men named John Abarrow, or à Barrow: one was Sir Maurice's brother, the other his eldest son. Since neither was of any importance in governmental service, it is desirable to get it clear who Margaret's father was. Croft took his information from William Berry, *County Genealogies: Pedigrees of the Families of Hants.* (London, 1883), p. 265. Berry did not know Margaret's Christian name; his pedigree is inaccurate in other respects also.

[35] *Cal. Pat. Rolls*, II, 50, 664; *L.P.*, I, 1546; II, 196, 1125, 1200.

[36] *L.P.*, III, 703.

[37] Stapleton, *op. cit.*, tr. Hallett, pp. 43–46.

the praises of the "moste excellent divine Erasmus Roterodamus," whose *Institutio principis Christiani* (Elyot wrote) "can nat be so moche praysed as it is worthy."[38] It was to be one of the sources for *The Boke named the Gouernour*.

Regular members of More's school studied Latin and Greek literature, logic, philosophy, theology, mathematics, and astronomy. They had frequent exercises in Latin translation; More anticipated Roger Ascham's double-translation system by having one daughter turn Latin to English and another translate the English back into Latin.[39] Thomas Elyot probably discussed these same subjects when he visited the school. His interest in translating Latin and Greek classics into good English no doubt stems from his association with More, as do his Platonism and his interest in Pico della Mirandola, St. Cyprian, and Lucian—More and Erasmus were much interested in Lucian's works—and Elyot was probably the translator of one of Lucian's dialogues which was printed by Thomas Berthelet about 1528.[40] More's liberal method of education

[38] *Governor*, III, Chap. 11.

[39] Stapleton, *op. cit.*, tr. Hallett, pp. 98 ff.; Chambers, *op. cit.*, p. 181.

[40] An English translation of Lucian's *Cynicus* was printed, undated, by Thomas Berthelet as *A dialogue betwene Lucian and Diogenes of the life harde and sharpe, and of the life tendre and delicate*. Elyot's name does not appear in the book, but the translation has, probably correctly, been ascribed to him (e.g., in James Wortham, "Sir Thomas Elyot and the Translation of Prose," *Huntington Library Quarterly*, XI [1948], 219–240). More and Erasmus translated several of Lucian's dialogues into Latin; their joint efforts were published at Paris in 1506 and reprinted more than forty times before 1550 (see C. R. Thompson, *The Translations of Lucian by Erasmus and St. Thomas More* [Ithaca, N.Y., 1940], pp. 1–3, 20). Perhaps Elyot caught their enthusiasm and tried turning the Greek text into English. The fact that Berthelet was the original printer of all of Elyot's later works adds strength to this hypothesis. Since in this dialogue Berthelet uses virgules instead of commas much more often than in the *Governor* or in his other later publications, it is probably safe to assume that the translation was published before the *Governor*, possibly before John Rastell's edition of Lucian's *Necromantia* (1530?). If so, Berthelet's edition of the *Cynicus* is the earliest printed version of Lucian in English. The Bodleian and the Huntington Library have the only two copies of the book now known to exist.

It is possible that Elyot was the author of an original dialogue written in imitation of Lucian. Constance W. Bouck has recently suggested (see "On the Identity of Papyrius Geminus Eleates," *Transactions* of the Cambridge Bibliographical Society, Vol. II, Pt. V [1958], 352–358) that Papyrius Geminus

was certainly one of the things which influenced Book I of the *Governor*; it probably also led Elyot to agree with Plutarch's treatise on the education of children, which he later translated. And More's unorthodox practice of providing Humanistic training for his daughters was probably one of the roots of Elyot's praise of philosophical learning for women in *The Defence of Good Women*.

It was doubtless in More's house in Chelsea that the portrait drawings of the Elyots by Hans Holbein the Younger were made.[41] Holbein lived in More's household in 1526 and 1527, sketching portraits of old John More, Sir Thomas, young John, Cecily Heron, Anne Cresacre, and Margaret Gigs, as well as of Thomas and Margaret Elyot. He also made the drawing, now in the Basel Museum, which served as a guide for part of the composite portrait of the More family now in the National Portrait Gallery in London.[42] The drawing of Thomas Elyot shows us a man staring sadly and dreamily into space, as if contemplating some philosophical problem; Margaret has a more down-to-earth expression, but she too is sober and unsmiling.

Eleates, author of the *Hermathena* published by John Siberch at Cambridge in 1522, was Thomas Elyot. The similarity in the names is obvious: "Geminus" is a Latin form of "Thomas," and "Papyrius" may be regarded as denominative or descriptive. Furthermore, the *Hermathena* is dedicated to Richard Pace, the King's secretary, whom Elyot almost certainly knew; one dedication, at the beginning of the book, is dated at London, February, 1522, and the other, at the end, reads "Comi pridie Nonas Septembr. M.D.XXII." Elyot was certainly in London during part of 1522, and if we translate "Comi" as "at Combe" it too points to Elyot, for he held the manor of Long Combe near Oxford. Papyrius Geminus Eliates (spelled this time with an *i*) also contributed the Preface to an anti-Lutheran tract, the *Propugnaculum*, written by Edward Powell, canon residentiary of Salisbury, and printed in Pynson in 1523. Elyot's own anti-Lutheran leanings will be touched on below, in Chap. Ten.

[41] The drawings, reproductions of which face the title page and p. 16, are in the Royal Library at Windsor Castle. An engraving of the portrait of Thomas Elyot was made by Francesco Bartolozzi.

[42] Croft (I, xliii) attributed this painting to Holbein and thought that it might have been in the possession of Elyot at Besselsleigh before it passed to Burford Priory. But the picture was not painted until 1593 and includes More's great-grandson, who was not yet born when Elyot died. The painting, by an unknown artist, was made for Thomas More's grandson and was subsequently owned by Thomas Lenthall, speaker of the Long Parliament. According to the catalogue of the National Portrait Gallery, it was bequeathed to the Gallery by Mr. E. J. Horniman, of Burford Priory, in 1933.

If Sir Thomas More was one of the men who significantly influenced the formation of Thomas Elyot's interests, another was probably Thomas Linacre.

Our knowledge of Elyot's studies with Linacre is even less precise than our information about his association with More. In the case of Linacre the sole source is the "Proheme" or Preface to the 1541 edition of *The Castel of Helth*, where Elyot defends his competence to write of medical matters:

Whan I wrate fyrst this boke, I was not all ignorante in phisycke, [for] before . . . I was twenty yeres old, a worshypfull phisition, and one of the most renoumed at that tyme in England, perceyving me by nature inclyned to knowledge, radde unto me the workes of Galene of temperamentes, naturall faculties, the Introduction of Johannicius, with some of the Aphorismes of Hippocrates.[43]

It has usually been assumed that Elyot's "worshypfull phisition" was Linacre, who was easily the most renowned physician of the day. His Latin translation of Proclus's *De sphaera* had attracted the attention of the court and led to his appointment as tutor to Prince Arthur. After the untimely death of his royal student, Linacre was physician to Henry VIII and the first president of the Royal College of Medicine. The works of Galen and Hippocrates, cited by Elyot, were precisely the ones in which he was most interested; he translated many of Galen's works from Greek into Latin. A fellow of All Souls, Oxford, he had taken his M.D. in Padua and had studied Greek under Chalcondyles in Florence along with the sons of Lorenzo the Magnificent. He lived in London from 1501 until his death twenty-three years later and was a close friend of Sir Thomas More. He probably met Elyot at More's home.[44]

---

[43] *The Castel of Helth* (London, 1541, octavo ed.), fol. A iiii^r.

[44] Croft (I, cviii), W. H. Woodward (*Studies in Education during the Age of the Renaissance* [Cambridge, 1906], p. 268), and L. C. Warren ("Humanistic Doctrines of the Prince from Petrarch to Sir Thomas Elyot" [unpublished dissertation, University of Chicago, 1937], p. 88 n.) concur in the identification of the "worshypfull phisition" with Linacre. J. M. Berdan (*Early Tudor Poetry* [New York, 1920], p. 304 n.) has dissented: "The passage was written to justify Elyot's right to authorship of a book on medicine. As Linacre had been appointed royal physician, and as his reputation was very great, surely, had Elyot studied with him, he would have emphasized that fact here. Since he does

We do not, unfortunately, know how long Elyot's studies with the worshipful physician lasted. It is quite possible that they continued, sporadically, until Linacre's death, though Elyot's statement suggests that the concentrated work was done about 1510. To the association with Linacre, if indeed he was Elyot's mentor, we can probably trace Elyot's continuing interest in medicine, culminating in his *Castel of Helth;* his knowledge of Greek; and his desire to translate Greek works into a language more commonly understood. We shall see more of each of these themes as we examine Thomas Elyot's later life.

---

not, certainly the presumption is contrary to the usual statement." I do not think that this argument is very convincing, especially if one considers the facts, ignored by Berdan, which make the identification with Linacre likely. It is possible, as Warren has suggested, that Elyot did not name Linacre because he did not want to lessen the physicians' respect for Linacre's memory. A simpler explanation is that Elyot was writing the *Castle* primarily for a popular audience of people who would not necessarily have heard of Linacre; he had been dead for seventeen years when the book appeared.

CHAPTER TWO

Unthankfull Travayle

URING the two decades between his first Crown appointment and the publication of his *Boke named the Gouernour*, Thomas Elyot witnessed the death of his father and experienced his own rise in the governmental hierarchy from clerk of the Western Assizes to clerk of the King's Council.

He was named clerk to the Justices of Assize for the Western Circuit, probably at his father's request, in 1510, and he continued to serve until about 1526, four years after his father's death. The patents do not differentiate between the justices and their clerks; the theory was still held that the record resided in the breast of the justices, and so the fiction of associating the clerks with the justices rather than actually calling them clerks was invoked. This has sometimes caused confusion, but in Elyot's case the situation is clear. Obviously Thomas could not have been a justice in 1511, for he was probably barely of age and had little if any legal training; he was in fact never made a serjeant-at-law, and only serjeants were eligible for the bench.[1] Besides, we have Elyot's

[1] W. S. Holdsworth, *A History of English Law* (5th ed., London, 1931), II, 484 ff.

own statement that he was "clerk of the Assizes Westward" and that the post was worth 100 marks, or about 67 pounds, a year.[2] As clerk, Thomas joined his father on the Commission of Gaol Delivery for the circuit.[3]

Sir Richard Elyot died early in 1522, either while he and his son were actually riding the circuit or shortly after they had completed it. His will, made on October 9, 1520, was proved by Thomas Elyot in the Prerogative Court of Canterbury, Lambeth, on May 26, 1522.[4] It is an interesting document, and its list of Elyot's properties is impressive. Thomas was named executor and was principal heir, but there were a number of bequests to others. Sir Richard left his manor at

[2] Elyot to Cromwell, December 8, [1532]. B.M., Cotton MS. Titus B. I, fols. 376–377.

[3] There is no patent granting Elyot the clerkship before 1511, but Middle Temple records speak of him as clerk in November, 1510 (C. H. Hopwood, *Middle Temple Records* [London, 1904], p. 34). For the five years beginning in 1511, Thomas Elyot and Thomas Fitzhugh were clerks to Richard Elyot and Lewis Pollard (*L.P.*, I, 804 [36], 1083 [8], 1316 [14], 1662 [28], 2137 [11], 2684 [62], 3107 [34]; II, 134, 693, 1537, 2163). After 1515, the justices managed with only one clerk, perhaps because Thomas Elyot had become more experienced. John Ernley replaced Pollard as one of the justices in 1517; he served until 1519, when Thomas Pigott was appointed. Pigott was succeeded by John Broke in 1520. In 1521 there were two clerks—Thomas Elyot and Richard Matthew—but only one justice, Richard Elyot, was named (*ibid.*, II, 2919, 3467, 3949, 4317; III, 102, 347, 405, 844, 933, 1186, 1451). After 1522, Richard's place was taken by John Fitzjames, who had been a bencher of the Middle Temple with Richard from 1504 and who later presided at the trials of More and Fisher. Broke served with Fitzjames in 1522. Robert Norwich was probably Fitzjames's colleague on the bench in 1523—the records for that year have been lost—and certainly in 1524 and 1525. Fitzjames and Pollard served in 1526 (*ibid.*, III, 2415; IV, 546 [11], 1136 [12], 2002 [3]; J. D. Williamson, *The Middle Temple Bench Book* [London, 1937], pp. 52 f.). Thomas Pigott and John Broke were also Middle Temple benchers before 1501 (*ibid.*, pp. 47, 50). Norwich was a member of Lincoln's Inn from 1503 (*Records of the Honourable Society of Lincoln's Inn* [London, 1896], I, 30). The clerks of the assizes, as well as the justices, were ex officio members of each Commission of Gaol Delivery for their territories. Thus the Elyots and Pollard were named to the Commission of Gaol Delivery for the Western Circuit from 1511 until 1516; the Elyots, Broke, and Matthew were appointed in 1522; Thomas Elyot, Fitzjames, and Norwich served from 1523 until 1525; Elyot, Fitzjames, Pollard, and John Dyer were commissioned in 1526 (*L.P.*, I, 833 [2], 1316 [3], 1662 [1], 2055 [114]; II, 1441; III, 2074; IV, 2002 [12]).

[4] P.C.C., MS. 24 Maynwaryng; printed in Croft, I, Appendix B, with minor errors.

Long Combe, Oxfordshire, and lands at Long Combe and Wooton to his rather distant relative Thomas Findern of Carlton, Cambridgeshire, with the stipulation that these lands should revert to Elyot's heirs if Findern died without children. This happened in 1523, when Thomas Elyot received both his father's former lands in Oxfordshire and also Findern's extensive estates.[5]

Sir Richard directed that the profits of his land at Chalk, Berkshire, should be expended in good works "for my soule and my frendes soules and all Christen soules." The manor at East Shefford, once the seat of Elizabeth Elyot's first husband, Richard Fetiplace, was to go to John Fetiplace, who was also given the option of purchasing the cattle and sheep at East Shefford and at Petwick. Thomas Elyot was to have the use of his father's other "landes, tenementes, rentes, and services"; they included land at Besselsleigh and Winterslow, other lands in Berkshire, Wiltshire, and Dorset, property in Salisbury, and houses near the Temple, London, and at Staines, Middlesex.[6] Since lands could not, strictly speaking, be bequeathed, Richard Elyot had adopted the usual means of evasion: he had arranged that a continuing group of feoffees be seised with his lands to the use of his heirs. "Be it knowen to al men," he wrote, "that all my manours, londes, and tenementes stande in feoffees handes or in the handes of recoverers, to the use of me and of myn heires." He directed that "the feoffementes . . . be renewed as ofte as . . . the feoffees therof be decessed to the nombr of vi survivours, . . . they to make astate in fee to two other discrete persones, and forthwith to take astate ageyn to theym and to xii moo, wherof viii be of the citie of Newe Sarum [Salisbury], suche as have ben mayres of the same citie or be . . . likely to be maires there." With the fief legally in the hands of such a group of men there was no need for it to revert to the Crown at the death of the gentleman who had enjoyed its profits.

Should Thomas Elyot die without heirs, his sister, Margery Puttenham, was to receive all of Sir Richard's property not otherwise specifi-

---

[5] This was in accordance with the will of Sir William Findern (P.C.C., MS. 36 Holder). He and Richard Elyot agreed that Long Combe should pass to the Finderns and that, in return, Richard's heirs should inherit the Cambridgeshire lands if the Findern family died out.

[6] The property in Staines had belonged to William Bessels.

cally bequeathed. She was also granted in her own right a number of cattle, some linen and drapery, furniture, certain pieces of silver—"ii lesse gilt saltes with a cover of the newe facion, ii standyng cuppis gilte with ii covers, ii litell gilt pottes for ale with ii covers, ii playn bolles of silver with a cover, ii nuttes garnyshed with silver and gilt, ii gilt sponys, and vi silver sponys"—and all her father's English books, including a "faire great prymer with silver clapse." Thomas was to have the Latin and French books as well as "my fair great Sawter written [manuscript Psalter], and my prymer that I wrote my self, and my litell prymer that I occupie daily." It would be interesting to know what other books Sir Richard owned, but he did not catalogue them; perhaps they were mostly legal works. Sir Richard made other specific bequests to his stepchildren—John, Edmund, Anthony, Thomas, and Eleanor Fetiplace; to his uncle James Bryce; to his nephews Richard Crouche and John Gilpurne; to his cousin John Michell (or John Elyot); and to John Barrow, presumably the brother of Thomas Elyot's wife.

Richard Elyot directed that his body be buried in Salisbury Cathedral beneath a "flat stone with convenyent writing" and that "placebo, dirige, and masse" should be said for him there. The monument, if it was ever erected, does not remain. The cathedral was granted money for repairs to the fabric, as were the churches of St. Thomas, St. Edmund, and St. Martin, all in Salisbury; St. Dunstan's, Fleet Street; and the parish churches of Long Combe and East Shefford. Sir Richard also made gifts to the fellows of Lincoln and All Souls Colleges, Oxford; to the master of the Temple Church; to the "Freres Observantes" of London and Greenwich, and to the "Freres Prechours, Mynours, Carmelites, and Austyns" of London, Oxford, Salisbury, and Fisherton. These bequests, so typical of pre-Reformation wills, were presumably to be paid, at least in part, out of the revenues of the land at Chalk.

Carrying out his father's requests must have kept Thomas Elyot busy in 1522; during the next year he was further troubled by a suit challenging his right to inherit the Findern properties near Cambridge. These included the manors of Weston Colville, Weston Moynes, and Little Carlton or Loppams, with numerous other lands in the eastern part of the county and with the advowson of the church at Weston Colville. Although the line of Cambridgeshire Finderns had come to an end with the death of young Thomas Findern, the senior branch in Derbyshire still flourished. It was represented by another Thomas Findern and by his son George, who had married the daughter of John Port, a serjeant-at-law and later a justice of the King's Bench. Their suit claiming the Cambridgeshire lands was unsuccessful but it was expensive for Elyot, as he later complained to Thomas Cromwell:

Soon after the decesse of my poure father the lande that I now have in Cambridgeshyr fell unto me not moche lokid for. But to tempre that sodayne joye I was furthwith assaultid with trouble by them which made title withoute ryght or goode consyderation. And allthowgh my Lorde Cardinall [Wolsey], whome Godd pardone, knowing my title to be perfect and suer, as having it enrollid bifore him, and at the first beginning hiering him self the mutuall covenaunte bytwene my fader and by cosen Sir William Fynderne, whoes fader was my mothers unkle, by his good justice gave me goode comfort, yet then having agayne me many grete personages, by the meanes of Mr. Porte the justice, I was constrayned to retayne so many lernyd men and so to applie my busyness that the saide sute contynuyng one yere and an half, stoode me above one hundred poundes.[7]

Records of Chancery proceedings preserved in the Public Record Office confirm that the suit was a long and complex one. Findern had set up trusts to be enfeoffed with his estates so that he could bequeath the use of them. Dr. Edmund Natures, master of Clare College, Cambridge, was the principal member of the trusts; Elyot had to petition twice to have him examined regarding the Findern will. The Prior of Christ Church within Aldgate, London, was charged with detaining certain deeds relating to the manors, possibly at Port's behest, and these had to be produced before the case could be settled.[8]

RICHARD ELYOT may have died disappointed in his son's progress. Thomas, after all, was about thirty-two, yet he had not become a barrister or a justice. The position as clerk of the assizes was a good steppingstone, no doubt; it paid well enough. But it was hardly the one which an ambitious father would want his son to hold for life. It may

[7] Elyot to Cromwell, December 8, [1532].
[8] P.R.O., C 1/499/59, C 1/501/29, C 1/501/32, C 1/501/33, C 1/501/34, C 1/631/18.

be that Richard was skeptical about his son's literary interests and thought that they kept Thomas from devoting sufficient attention to his legal career.

If these were indeed Richard's last thoughts, they were unnecessarily pessimistic ones: about two years after his death, Thomas was named to the senior clerkship of the King's Council, the post which Lambarde, writing under Elizabeth, described as "the best Clarkeship of this Lande, unlesse you will call the Master of the Rols a Clarke againe."[9] The story of Elyot's services with the Council is somewhat complicated but was well told by Thomas himself in an important letter to Cromwell. Elyot wrote that after the conclusion of the suit over the Findern property

my sayde Lorde Cardinall, for some goode oppynion that he conceyved of me withoute by merites, advauncid me (as he supposid) to be Clerk of the Counsayle, withoute my sute or desyre. All be it afterward I was not ingrate as I will tell you hereafterward. Than was there newly delegate from the Steere Chamber all maters of the North partes and Wales, as ye know. Those fewe that remaynid were for the more parte the complaynts of beggars, which shortly perceyving, I, my clerks repugning, didd sett such a rate in fees ordinary as neither any man shold be excessifly grievyd, nor that I shold be seene to pik oute substance oute of other mennys povertie. But that mought I the better sustayne by raison that I was than allso Clerk of the Assizes Westward which was to me worth yerly one hundred marcs.

But by the solicitation of some men which yet doo lyve, my sayde lorde bearing me on hand that I was and sholde be so necessary to be continually attendant on the Counsayle that it shold be expedient for me to leve the office of the Assizes, promysing moreover that by his meanes the King shold otherwise promote me bothe to more worship and profite, finally willed me to resign my said office, takyng onely for it CC li. [200 pounds], which after long resistence finally I meist folow his pleasure to keepe him my goode Lorde.

That doone whan the yere was finisshed I suyd to him to optayne a patent for the office in the Counsayle, which his Grace didd as I herd say. But I could never com by it, Doctor Cleyburgh and other keping it from me. After, I suyd for the fee, which as I herd saye was fourti marcs by the yere, wherof I hadd promyse, but I never receyvid it. So by the space of six yeres

[9] William Lambarde, *Archeion*, ed. C. H. McIlwain and P. L. Ward (Cambridge, Mass., 1957), pp. 86–87.

27

and an half I servyd the King not in the Sterre Chamber onely, but in some thinges pertayning to the Clerk of the Croune, some to the Secretaries, and other travaile which I will not reherce leste ye sholde deeme me longe in praising my self, and all this time without fee, withoute reward more than the ordinarie: and that which more grevith me, withoute thank of the King which I deservyd as it wold appier if his Grace hadd ben truely infourmed of me, and my drawghtes seene which I devisid and made to my saide Lorde. In this unthankfull travayle I no thing gate but the colike and the stone, debilitating of nature, and allmoste contynuell destillations or rewmes, ministres to abbreviate my lif; which though it be of no grete importance, yet some wayes it mought be necessary.

Finally, after the deth of my saide Lorde, there was a former patente founde of the sayde office, and myn was callid in and cancellid, and I discharged withoute any recompence, rewarded only with the order of Knighthode, honorable and onerouse, having moche lasse to lyve on than bifore.[10]

The end of Elyot's clerkship is easily dated; a patent of April 20, 1530, granted the office to Richard and Thomas Eden in survivorship.[11] This was after Wolsey's fall but not, as Elyot said, after his death. It is less easy to say when Elyot began his duties with the Council. There is no evidence to controvert his statement that he had served for six and a half years: that would mean that he took the post in the last months of 1523. No patent was made at the time of his appointment; both Elyot and one of his colleagues, Richard Lee, seem to have been put into office by rather high-handed acts of Wolsey's, measures short-circuiting the usual procedure.[12]

Elyot resigned his clerkship in the assizes in 1526, or perhaps early in 1527, and he was subsequently able to devote all his time to the work of the Council.[13] His resignation was probably one of the few

[10] Elyot to Cromwell, December 8, [1532].

[11] *L.P.*, IV, 6490 (1).

[12] See A. F. Pollard, "Council, Star Chamber, and Privy Council under the Tudors: I, The Council," *English Historical Review*, XXXVII (1922), 347–349 *et passim*.

[13] The last patent for the Western Circuit of the assizes which mentions Elyot is that of February 12, 1525 (*L.P.*, IV, 546 [11]). The only patent for 1526, dated February 3, names Fitzjames and Pollard justices but does not list a clerk (*ibid.*, 2002 [3]). No patent for 1527 exists, probably because an epidemic of sweating sickness necessitated the adjournment of the assizes. Patents for the Commission of Gaol Delivery for the Western Circuit do, how-

tangible results of Wolsey's half-hearted endeavor, recorded in the Eltham Ordinances of January, 1526, to make the Council function with greater regularity.[14] Wolsey finally had a patent issued in 1528; it granted Elyot the clerkship of the Council with the same perquisites that his predecessors John Baldeswell, Robert Rydon, and Richard Eden had enjoyed. The salary was 40 marks a year, plus summer and winter livery and the usual fees from suitors in Star Chamber. These payments indicate that Elyot held the senior clerkship, for the junior clerk received only 20 pounds annually.[15] But a condition of the grant to Elyot was the surrender of a patent dated 1513 granting the clerk-ship to Richard Eden. Eden refused to relinquish his patent, and after Wolsey's death he reasserted his right to the office. He was finally successful in having it granted to him and his nephew in survivorship. Lines have been drawn through Elyot's grant on the patent roll, and a marginal note records its cancellation. Eden apparently continued to draw the salary while Elyot was doing the work.

Elyot's duties as clerk were probably as varied, if not so debilitating, as he claimed. His position as senior clerk was the one which later developed into the clerkship of the Star Chamber, but in his time the Council had not yet become differentiated into the Privy Council and the Court of Star Chamber.[16] Such specialization came only in the 1530's. Meanwhile Wolsey tried a different division of labor by dealing with administrative matters himself while delegating to the Lady Mary's council judicial cases pertaining to Wales and to the Duke of Richmond's council those arising in the North.[17] It was this which

---

ever, exist, and these commissions were normally composed of the justices and their clerks. They indicate that Elyot must have resigned his clerkship some-time between February, 1526, when he was named to the commission with Fitzjames, Pollard, and John Dyer, and June, 1527, when Fitzjames, William Shelley, and Robert Dacres were commissioned (*ibid.*, 2002 [12], 3213 [28]). Robert Dacres, who replaced Elyot as clerk, was a nephew of Dr. Taylor, master of the rolls. After Dacre's appointment to the assizes, Wolsey had him resign his reversionary interest in a post as one of the secretaries of the "comptes" in favor of William Marshall, who was supported by More and Elyot (*ibid.*, App., 133; n.d., probably 1527).

[14] See G. R. Elton, *The Tudor Revolution in Government* (Cambridge, England, 1953), p. 321.

[15] P.R.O., C 66/650, membrane 11.

[16] Elton, *op. cit.*, pp. 334–335, 59–65.

[17] Pollard, *op. cit.*, p. 359.

caused Elyot to complain that the remaining cases were but the complaints of beggars, on which he could make little profit.

Although Elyot's statement that he owed his advancement to Wolsey's favor is doubtless correct, it is not easy to say exactly how he came to the Cardinal's attention. It might have been through More's good offices; but even if we suppose that the friendship between Elyot and More was sufficiently close to make this likely, there is some question that More's recommendation would have carried much weight at the time. Wolsey was displeased with More's actions as Speaker of the House of Commons in 1523 and had said, "Wold to God you had bine at Rome, master Moore, when I made you Speaker."[18] It is more likely that Elyot ultimately owed his preferment to Thomas Cromwell. A Latin letter to Cromwell written by Elyot on the flyleaf of a presentation copy of his Latin dictionary (1538) says that they had been friends for nineteen years.[19] That would place their first meeting in 1519, probably while Cromwell was studying law in London. By the time of Elyot's appointment Cromwell was handling the legal details associated with Wolsey's new colleges at Oxford and Ipswich, and his influence with the Cardinal may already have been considerable.

There is additional evidence that Elyot was in Wolsey's favor. A dispatch written by Eustace Chapuys to Charles V on the eve of Elyot's embassy to the imperial court said that the new ambassador, "Maystre Vullyot," had been in the service of the Cardinal and then that of the Lady. Although he was quite incorrect in thinking that Elyot was attached to Anne Boleyn, perhaps we may accept the first part of his statement. Chapuys further reported that Elyot was expected to be named Master of the Rolls as soon as the incumbent retired.[20] Doubtless this was the position of "more worship and profite" for

[18] William Roper, *The Lyfe of Sir Thomas Moore*, ed. E. V. Hitchcock (London, 1935), p. 19.

[19] See below, Chap. Ten.

[20] "Maystre Vullyot . . . a este au cardinal et maintenant est [à] la dame, laquelle, ainsy que l'on m'a dit, la promen à ceste charge quant et luy partira le maystre des rolez, qu'est ung vieux docteur ecclesiastique que va en France pour successeur de Brian" (*Calendar of State Papers, Spanish*, IV, ii, 239 f.). The statement that Taylor was to succeed Francis Brian as ambassador to France turned out to be incorrect.

which Elyot hoped. But the Master of the Rolls, Dr. John Taylor, hung on until 1534, and then both Elyot and Dr. John Tregonwell, a Chancery official who also coveted the appointment, were disappointed: Cromwell himself succeeded Taylor.[21]

As Wolsey was responsible for Elyot's appointment, so his fall accounted for Elyot's dismissal. Thomas's failure to hold a governmental position of any importance for well over a year after his loss of the clerkship suggests that he had some difficulty dissociating himself from Wolsey's circle.

Considering the friendship between Elyot and Sir Thomas More, it seems rather strange that Wolsey's successor did not find a way to retain the clerkship for Elyot. More, however, was not a man to take extraordinary powers into his own hands, as Wolsey had done, and if he found the previous patent still legally valid he would doubtless have asserted its force, even against one of his best friends. Elyot's distinction between a private friendship and one which might influence public acts,[22] if it meant anything, was a two-edged sword which could cut against him as well as for him.

THOMAS ELYOT made Long Combe, near Oxford, his principal residence until 1530. He was intermittently named a justice of the peace for Oxfordshire and Wiltshire between 1515 and 1529,[23] and in 1527 and 1529 he was sheriff of Oxfordshire and Berkshire.[24] By the sixteenth century the duties of the sheriff, who was originally the king's chief agent in local government, had declined—the sheriffs had been too closely allied with the defunct feudal system—and the justices of the peace found their responsibilities correspondingly heavier. Members of the Commission of the Peace were charged with the trial, in quarter sessions, of all those criminal cases which were not of peculiar difficulty and thus reserved to the justices of assize; they were also the enforcement agents for a large and growing body of statutes, among

---

[21] See Elton, *op. cit.,* p. 122.

[22] See above, Chap. One.

[23] Wiltshire: 1515, 1525, 1526, 1529 (*L.P.,* II, 1125, 1200; IV, 1049 [12], 2002 [6], 5243 [28]); Oxfordshire: 1522, 1524–26 (*ibid.,* III, 2415; IV, 137 [12], 1049 [24], 2002 [11]).

[24] *Ibid.,* IV, 3581.

them those dealing with apprenticeship and wages, enclosures, livery and maintenance, and theft of swans' eggs. Under a statute of 1495 the justices of the peace could examine sheriffs suspected of extortion.

Despite the rise of the justices, each sheriff retained important duties. Although he had nothing to do with Parliamentary taxation, he still had to collect—and to account for in the Exchequer—various revenues, particularly debts to the king, farms of the counties, and the fee farms of cities and boroughs. He could settle civil cases involving less than 40 shillings, and his presence was essential for proper procedure in the Quarter Sessions and the Assizes. He was charged with providing hospitality for the justices of assize, distinguished foreign visitors, or the king and his retinue. Perhaps most important, the sheriff presided over the county court in which members of Parliament were elected, and it was to him that the writs authorizing the payment of wages and traveling expenses of members were directed: this is the reason that sheriffs were not eligible, during their terms of office, to sit in Parliament themselves. Until the creation of the lords lieutenants under Edward VI, the sheriff was also responsible for holding musters and controlling the local militia. It was not uncommon for two counties to share a single sheriff, as Oxfordshire and Berkshire did; among the nine pairs of shires usually so joined during the early Tudor age were Cambridge and Huntingdon, Norfolk and Suffolk, Bedfordshire and Buckinghamshire, and Somerset and Dorset. Each sheriff held office for a year and, unlike a justice of the peace, who might serve for decades, was not eligible for immediate reappointment.[25]

Unfortunately no information about Elyot's work in the Commission of the Peace has survived, and we have only a few fragmentary records to suggest some of his activities as sheriff. A letter written to Cromwell on March 25, 1528, says that he has ordered his undersheriff to bring certain men, probably those trying to conceal Crown lands, to a hearing before the escheator: a routine matter. More interesting is the familiarity with which Elyot signs himself "your lovyn companyon" and asks Cromwell to visit "yn my pour house if you make long abode in these partis, all be it I can nat make you suche chere

[25] On the duties of sheriffs and justices of the peace, see Kenneth Pickthorn, *Early Tudor Government: Henry VII* (Cambridge, England, 1949), pp. 59–73.

Elyot's writing and signature, from a letter to Cromwell, December 8, 1532.
(Cotton MS. Titus B. I, fol. 377, British Museum)

PERISCELIDIS ✠ VERA EFFIGIES THOMÆ CROMWELL ☙ ESSEXIÆ COMITIS EQVITIS

H. Holben pinxit. *R. White sculpsit.*

Natus 1490
Regis vicarius
Generalis 1536

Eques Periscelidis
1537.
Capite truncatus
July. 18:th 1540.

Printed for Richard Chiswell at the Rose and Crowne in St Pauls Churchyard.

Thomas Cromwell, engraving by R. White, based on a painting by Hans
Holbein the Younger. From Gilbert Burnet,
History of the Reformation of the Church of England.
(London, Richard Chiswell, 1681)

as you have yn Oxford [where Cromwell was attending to Wolsey's affairs], but onely hartily welcom."[26]

Later in the year Elyot had to settle a hunting fray near Woodstock. It seems to have run out of hand; Elyot was accused of magnifying it into a riot and of nearly undoing the poor men of Woodstock by summoning them to London at their own expense.[27] He was also involved in the rather interesting case of John Macy, or John Chaffcombe, abbot of the Cistercian Abbey of Bruern, who complained to Cromwell that certain persons had acted riotously against his abbey and that the local justice of the peace had taken inadequate action. The Abbot enclosed a letter of Elyot's which suggested that he would be turned out of his monastery, and he rather brazenly offered to pay for Cromwell's favor. His opponents had boasted, he said, that they would spend 100 pounds to evict him.[28] It should not have surprised him that his office might go to the highest bidder, for he himself had obtained the abbacy by giving Wolsey 250 marks and 280 oaks "of the greatest and best of all the woods of the monastery" for use in the new Cardinal's college at Oxford.[29] In order to retain his post Macy pawned the abbey's plate, using the money for bribes; a monk sent to London in 1530, ostensibly to redeem the plate but more likely to repawn it for a larger sum, was accused of having stolen the monastery's seal as well as the silver.[30] The neighboring gentry, doubtless including Elyot, at length persuaded the Duke of Suffolk to force the heads of the Cistercian Order in England to investigate Abbot Macy's conduct, and two other abbots came to Bruern to force his resignation. It came out that he had impoverished the monastery in order to satisfy his expensive tastes and female acquaintances. Although his successor did much to reform the abbey, its income in 1535 was only 124 pounds, and it was accordingly dissolved in 1536. In this, one of the most flagrant cases of monastic

[26] P.R.O., SP 1/235/242.

[27] John Knolles to Master Chamberlain, Calais, [June 7, 1528], *L.P.,* IV, App., 176. Knolles adds that Wolsey has made Elyot clerk of the Council; apparently he refers to the patent and not to the beginning of Elyot's service.

[28] *L.P.,* IV, 5373. March 11, [1529].

[29] G. Baskerville, *English Monks and the Suppression of the Monasteries* (London, 1937), p. 106, quoting the Longland MSS. at Lincoln.

[30] *L.P.,* IV, 6141. January 10, [1530].

corruption, Elyot had been obliged to act as sheriff and justice of the peace to preserve order, and it may be that he was instrumental in securing the reform.[31]

In 1528, Elyot obtained the wardship of his cousin, Erasmus Pym. Young Pym's father, Reginald or Reynold Pym, had married Mary Daubridgecourt, Sir Richard Elyot's stepdaughter. Since Reginald was one of the king's tenants-in-chief, his minor son and heir became a royal ward at the time of his death. It was uncommon, however, for the Master of the Wards to exploit wardships directly; they could more profitably be sold. Members of the ward's family, knowing that administration of lands by an outsider might result in financial disaster, frequently endeavored to buy such wardships. It was therefore only natural that Thomas Elyot, one of Erasmus Pym's closest surviving relatives, should become his guardian and should manage his estates, which consisted mainly of the manor of Brymore in Cannington, a village near Bridgewater in Somerset.[32] Elyot paid 80 pounds for the wardship and received, during Pym's minority, just over 40 pounds a year from the Pym lands.[33] He also had the right, often a valuable one, of arranging a marriage for his ward; we do not know whether he did in fact profit from it. It would be of considerable interest to know more about Thomas Elyot's connection with the grandfather of the great John Pym. Did Elyot, for instance, arrange the Humanistic education which would have been appropriate for a lad named Erasmus? Did Pym live in his guardian's home, as wards often did? Did he accompany Elyot on his embassy in 1531? The absence of records is exasperating.

In 1530, Elyot changed his principal residence from Long Combe to Carlton in Cambridgeshire, where he lived for the rest of his life. The move probably coincided with his dismissal as clerk of the Council, though it is difficult to see any connection between the two events since the two manors were about equally distant from Westminster.

[31] *Ibid.*, IX 457, 493; Baskerville, *op. cit.*, p. 63; D. Knowles and R. N. Hadcock, *Medieval Religious Houses: England and Wales* (London, 1953), p. 105.

[32] *L.P.*, IV, 4313 (14). May 14, 1528.

[33] *Ibid.*, 5508 (1). April, 1529. The MSS. pertaining to the guardianship are P.R.O., C 1/1016/62–64. I am indebted to Mrs. John Nurser for calling my attention to them.

In June of 1530 Elyot, now for the first time styled "Sir" Thomas, was appointed to the Commission of Gaol Delivery for Cambridge Castle and Oxford Castle, and in December he was named a justice of the peace for Cambridgeshire.[34] It was at Carlton that Sir Thomas, free from major responsibility in the English government for the first time in nearly twenty years, settled down to write *The Boke named the Gouernour*.

[34] *L.P.*, IV, 6490 (20), 6803 (6). The knighthood was no doubt a costless way of rewarding Elyot for his service with the Council.

CHAPTER THREE

The Boke named the Gouernour:
The Fourme of a Juste Publike Weale

SIR THOMAS ELYOT'S most important book, *The Boke named the Gouernour,* was published in 1531. It is an exceedingly interesting work, as its continued appeal testifies, but a rather strange one.

It is peculiar in several respects. First, it treats an amazing variety of subjects—political theory, education, physical training, ethics, history—and although all of them have something to do with the development of a prospective governor they still seem only tenuously related to each other. Furthermore, it is not clear at whom the book is aimed; Elyot seems to have been writing for different audiences at different times and to have found it difficult to harmonize his intentions.

These peculiarities in subject matter and tone will become apparent if we examine the organization of the *Governor's* three books. Book I begins with a foray into the field of political theory; its first two chapters describe how a "publike weale" is made up of a hierarchical order

of degrees of men. At the top of the hierarchy there must be a single
ruler, the king. Monarchy, therefore, is the only natural and proper
form of government; and since Elyot says that the king within his
realm is like God in His, he implies that the king's power is unlimited.
Sir Thomas proceeds in his third chapter to deal with magistrates,
whom the king must have to help him govern. These members of
the governing class, together with the king, are Elyot's "governors."

The remainder of the first book of the *Governor* is concerned with
the proper training, both mental and physical, for the child who is to
become a governor. In fact, Elyot neglects the supreme governor—the
king—and the discussion is aimed at country gentlemen. He says, for
instance, that the pride, avarice, and negligence of gentlemen have
caused the decay of learning, that "it is commendable in a gentilman
to paint and kerve exactly," and that he will "retourne to the order of
lernyng apt for a gentyll man."

Having covered such a variety of topics in Book I, Elyot in Books II
and III deals with virtues which governors should possess. His comments are couched in language applicable to all governors—both the
king and his magistrates—but the ideas expressed seem to be far more
appropriate for kings. It would hardly seem necessary, for example, to
tell members of the gentry that they should be merciful or allow liberty of speech to those under them or take adequate counsel before they
act. Since well over two-thirds of the space in these two books is devoted to examples taken from classical antiquity and from the Bible,
it is these examples which really set the tone of Books II and III—and
nearly all are stories about kings. The tone here differs from that in the
chapters on education, and it is also rather different from the tone of
the chapters praising monarchy: a king bound by all the virtues which
Elyot commended would find that his power to act, far from being unlimited, was in fact severely circumscribed.

These differences in tone and subject matter would be considerably
easier to understand if Elyot had not written all of the *Governor* at one
time—if, that is, he had changed his purpose or outlook at some stage
in its composition. And Elyot gives us reason to believe that this is precisely what happened. Let us examine one passage rather closely.

In the third chapter of Book I, Elyot writes that the sons of noble
men, provided that they are properly instructed, make better magis-

trates than poor men's sons. "Towarde the whiche instruction I have, with no litle study and labours, prepared this warke," he adds. "I *have* prepared": the chapters on education, Elyot is saying, were already written when he penned Chapter 3. Indeed, the passage which begins with this revealing statement sounds very much as if it has been transplanted. Was it not originally intended to serve as the preface dedicating to the gentlemen of England a book about education? Elyot wrote that he had

with no litle study and labours, prepared this warke, as almighty God be my juge, without arrogance or any sparke of vayne glorie: but only to declare the fervent zele that I have to my countrey, and that I desyre only to employ my poure lerning, that I have gotten, to the benefite thereof, and to the recreation of all the reders that be of any noble or gentill courage, gyvynge them occasion to eschewe idelnes, beynge occupied in redynge this warke, infarced throughly with suche histories and sentences wherby they shal take, they them selfes confessing, no lytell commodite if they will more than ones or twyse rede it. The first reding being to them newe, the seconde delicious, and every tyme after, more and more frutefull and excellent profitable.

This is not the sort of comment that a writer would be likely to put in the middle of his book, but he might not alter it if he subsequently added material which stood before it in the published version.

The chapters on education and physical training, then, were probably the first part of the *Governor* to be written, and they seem to have been addressed originally to all gentlemen, not alone to the king or to magistrates.

Elyot apparently wrote next the first three chapters of Book I. It is clear that they were written before the two books on virtues, and in fact when Elyot wrote his chapters on monarchy he contemplated a work of only two books, not three. He says in Chapter 2:

I wyll ordinately treate of the two partes of a publike weale, wherof the one shall be named Due Administration, the other Necessary Occupation, whiche shall be devided into two volumes. In the fyrst shall be comprehended the best fourme of education or bringing up of noble children from their nativitie, in suche maner as they may be founde worthy, and also able to be governours of a publike weale. The seconde volume, whiche, God grantyng me quietnes and libertie of mynde, I wyll shortly after sende forthe, it shall conteine all the reminant, whiche I can either by lernyng or experience fynde apt to the perfection of a juste publike weale.

He does not seem to have been sure just what his proposed second volume would contain. It eventually became Books II and III. They confirm that they were composed after Book I: Book II begins with a summary of the contents of the first book, and several paragraphs in Book III refer to statements in Book I.[1]

The conclusion, then, seems to be this. Elyot first wrote a treatise on the training of young gentlemen. He next composed two chapters praising monarchy. These he linked to his discussion of education by writing a chapter about magistrates. In order to equate these magistrates with the sons of gentlemen, about whose education he had already written, he had to discourage enlisting poor men's sons in the business of government, despite the fact that the two greatest administrators of his time—Wolsey and Cromwell—had sprung from the lower classes. Later Elyot added two books discussing the virtues which were desirable in all members of the governing class but particularly appropriate to the king.

IF WE ACCEPT this reconstruction of the way in which the *Governor* was written, is it possible to explain the difference in tone and subject between the chapters on education, those praising monarchy, and the books dealing with virtues? And is the order of composition of any real significance in understanding the *Governor*? In both cases the answer seems to be Yes. The explanation requires an examination of the Preface and the first two chapters of Elyot's book.

Elyot dedicated the *Governor* to Henry VIII in a "Proheme," or preface, which was in all probability written at the same time as the first three chapters of Book I. In it Sir Thomas says:

I late considering (moste excellent prince and myne onely redoughted soveraigne lorde) my duetie that I owe to my naturall contray with my faythe also of aliegaunce and othe, wherewith I am double bounden unto your majestie, more over thaccompt that I have to rendre for that one litle talent delivered to me to employe (as I suppose) to the increase of vertue,

[1] See the last paragraph of Book III, Chap. 3, and the beginning of Book III, Chap. 24.

I am (as God juge me) violently stered to devulgate or sette fourth some part of my studie, trustynge therby tacquite me of my dueties to God, your hyghnesse, and this my contray.[2]

He goes on to protest his patriotism—one of the most striking features of the *Governor*—and his resulting desire to write in the vulgar tongue for the benefit of his fellow countrymen:

And if, moste vertuous prince, I may perceyve your hyghnes to be herewith pleased, I shall sone after (God giving me quietenes) present your grace with the residue of my studie and labours, wherein your Hyghnes shal well perceive that I nothing esteme so moche in this worlde as youre royall astate, (my most dere soveraigne lorde), and the publike weale of my contray.

After this preface, Elyot begins the *Governor* itself with a discussion of political theory, and with a definition: "A publike weale," he writes, "is a body lyvyng, compacte or made of sondry astates and degrees of men, whiche is disposed by the ordre of equite and governed by the rule and moderation of reason."[3] He is careful to distinguish this from a common weal, which he defines in an unusual manner:

Men have ben longe abused in calling *Rempublicam* a commune weale. And they which do suppose it so to be called for that, that every thinge shulde be to all men in commune, without discrepance of any astate or condition, be thereto moved more by sensuality than by any good reason or inclination to humanite.

Clearly Elyot would not have wanted all things to be owned communally, as they were in More's Utopian state:

In myn oppinion *Plebs* in Latin is in Englisshe communaltie: and *Plebeii* be communers. And consequently there may appere lyke diversitie to be in Englisshe betwene a publike weale and a commune weale, as shulde be in Latin betwene *Res publica* and *Res plebeia*. And after that signification, if there shuld be a commune weale, either the communers only must be welthy, and the gentil and noble men nedy and miserable, or els excluding gentilite, al men must be of one degre and sort, and a new name provided. For as moche as *Plebs* in Latin, and comminers in Englisshe, be wordes only

---

[2] *The Boke named the Gouernour,* "Proheme."

[3] *Ibid.,* I, Chap. 1. Quotations from the *Governor* will be identified by footnotes only when their location is not clear from the text.

made for the discrepance of degrees, wherof procedeth ordre: whiche in thinges as wel naturall as supernaturall hath ever had suche a preeminence, that therby the incomprehensible majestie of God, as it were by a bright leme of a torche or candel, is declared to the blynde inhabitantes of this worlde.

This analogy leads Elyot directly to one of his most important assertions, that of the necessity of order and degree among men:

Take away ordre from all thinges, what shulde then remayne? Certes nothynge finally, except some man wolde imagine eftsones [again] Chaos: whiche of some is expounde a confuse mixture. Also where there is any lacke of ordre nedes must be perpetuall conflicte: and in thynges subjecte to Nature nothynge of hym selfe onely may be norisshed; but whan he hath distroyed that where with he dothe participate by the ordre of his creation, he hym selfe of necessitie muste than perisshe, wherof ensueth universall dissolution.

Elyot proceeds to give examples of established hierarchies. God has set degrees in all His glorious works. He is served by numberless ranks of angels. He has ordered the four elements, each in its own sphere: fire is the lightest and hence highest, followed by air and then water, with earth, the heaviest, at the bottom. God has also ranked all living creatures in order, "begynnyng at the moste inferiour or base," that is, herbs, "and assendynge upwarde" to birds, beasts, and fishes. Even within a single species there is "a peculier disposition appropered unto them by God, . . . so that in every thyng is ordre, and without ordre may be nothing stable or permanent; and it may nat be called ordre, excepte it do contayne in it degrees, high and base, accordynge to the merite or estimation of the thyng that is ordred."

The same hierarchical principle applies to the sorts and conditions of men:

Nowe to retourne to the astate of man kynde, for whose use all the sayd creatures were ordayned of God, and also excelleth them all by prerogatife of knowlege and wisedome, hit semeth that in hym shulde be no lasse providence of God declared than in the inferiour creatures; but rather with a more perfecte ordre and dissposition. And therfore hit appereth that God gyveth nat to every man lyke gyftes of grace, or of nature, but to some more, some lesse, as it liketh his divine majestie.

High in this human hierarchy stand men of understanding and virtue, who must govern those beneath them. Here

in this worlde, they whiche excelle other in this influence of understandynge, and do imploye it to the detaynyng of other within the boundes of reason, and shewe them howe to provyde for theyr necessarye lyvynge; suche oughte to be set in a more highe place than the residue where they may se and also be sene; that by the beames of theyr excellent witte, shewed throughe the glasse of auctorite, other of inferiour understandynge may be directed to the way of vertue and commodious livynge. And unto men of suche vertue by very equitie appertaineth honour, as theyr juste rewarde and duetie, whiche by other mennes labours must also be mainteined according to their merites.

This reasoning justifies the existence of the nobility and the gentry, or of the governors.

AND IT DOES MORE. The concept of degree and order justifies the authority of the prince also. Here Elyot comes to his real point:

Lyke as to a castell or fortresse suffisethe one owner or soverayne, and where any mo be of like power and authoritie seldome cometh the warke to perfection; or beinge all redy made, where the one diligently overseeth and the other neglecteth, in that contention all is subverted and commeth to ruyne. In semblable wyse dothe a publike weale that hath mo chiefe governours than one.

He insistently emphasizes that there must be a single ruler at the apex of the hierarchy:

Wherfore undoubtedly the best and most sure governaunce is by one kynge or prince, whiche ruleth onely for the weale of his people to hym subjecte: and that maner of governaunce is beste approved, and hath longest continued, and is moste auncient. For who can denie but that all thynge in heven and erthe is governed by one God, by one perpetuall ordre, by one providence? One sonne ruleth over the day, and one moone over the nyghte; and to descende downe to the erthe, in a litell beest, whiche of all other is moste to be marvayled at, I meane the bee, is lefte to man by nature, as it semeth, a perpetuall figure of a juste governaunce or rule: who hath amonge them one principall bee for theyr governour, who excelleth all other in greatnes, yet hath he no pricke or stinge, but in hym is more knowlege than in the residue. For if the day folowyng shall be fayre and drye, and that the bees may issue out of theyr stalles without peryll of rayne or vehement wynde, in the mornyng erely he calleth them, makyng a noyse as it were the sowne of a horne or a trumpet; and with that all the residue prepare them to labour, and fleeth abrode, gatheryng nothing but that shall be swete and profitable, all though they sitte often tymes on herbes and other thinges that be venomous and stynkinge. . . . I suppose who seriously beholdeth this example, and hath any commendable witte, shall therof gather moche matter to the fourmynge of a publike weale.[4]

Readers who wish to know more about the bees are referred to Vergil's *Georgics*, or to Pliny or Columella.[5]

Elyot further demonstrates the desirability of having a single ruler by examples from scripture and history: "Onely Moses conducted the [Israelites] through the redde see; he onely governed them fourtie yeres in deserte." Descending perilously near the ridiculous, Elyot adds, "And bicause Dathan and Abiron disdayned his rule, and coveyted to be equall with hym, the erthe opened, and fyre issued out, and swalowed them in, with all their holle familie and confederates, to the nombre of 14,700."[6] Moses was succeeded by Joshua, and "after the deth of Josue, by the space of 246 yeres, succeded, from tyme to tyme, one ruler amonge the Jewes." Elyot regarded the subsequent division of Judea into two kingdoms under Jereboam and Rehoboam as responsible for the decline of the Jews and the Babylonian captivity. There was a single ruler in the time of the Maccabees. Surely God willed that there should be monarchy.

Ancient history as well as the Bible provides Elyot with proof that monarchical governments are most successful. Athenian democracy was "a monstre with many heedes: nor never it was certeyne nor stable: and often tymes they banyssed or slewe the beste citezins." Democracy can never be satisfactory because those in authority become intoxicated

[4] *Ibid.*, Chap. 2.

[5] Allusions to bees were popular in Tudor England, perhaps partly as a result of Elyot's comments. Sir Edward Coke in his address as Speaker closing the Parliament of 1593 compared Parliament "to that sweet Commonwealth of the little bees . . . who have but one governor whom they serve" (Catherine Drinker Bowen, *The Lion and the Throne* [New York, 1957], p. 42, quoting D'Ewes). For Shakespeare's references to bees in *Henry V*, see below, p. 93.

[6] One of Botticelli's frescoes in the Sistine Chapel depicts the punishment of Dathan and Abiron. Although it is a crowded picture, it is able to show only a fraction of the 14,700 followers.

with power, incensed with ambition and desire for wealth and glory. They fight among themselves until few of them are left, and then these few oppress the people. Oppression cannot last long, however; rebellion will result. "Power that is practized to the hurte of many can nat continue," Elyot wrote. But if the masses revolt, then they "ordre every thynge without justyce, only with vengeance and crueltie: and with incomparable difficultie . . . be pacified and brought agayne in to ordre."

It was not difficult for Elyot to find cases where this had happened. "Beholde the astate of Florence and Gene [Genoa], noble cites of Italy, what calamite have they both sustained by their owne factions, for lacke of a continuall governour. Ferrare and the moste excellent citie of Venise, the one havyng a duke, the other an erle, seldome suffreth damage excepte it happen by outwarde hostilitie." But there was an example even closer home than that offered by the cities of Renaissance Italy:

After that the Saxons by treason had expelled out of Englande the Britons, whiche were the auncient inhabitantes, this realme was devyded in to sondry regions or kyngdomes. O what mysery was the people than in. O howe this most noble isle of the worlde was decerpt and rent in pieces: the people pursued and hunted lyke wolfes or other beastes savage: none industrie avayled, no strength defended, no riches profited. Who wolde than have desired to have ben rather a man than a dogge: whan men either with sworde or with hungre perisshed, havynge no profit or sustinance of their owne corne or catell, whiche by mutuall warre was continually distroyed? Yet the dogges, either takynge that that men coulde nat quietly come by, or fedynge on the deed bodies, whiche on every parte laye scatered plenteously, dyd satisfie theyr hunger.

Indeed, life in England would still be nasty, brutish, and short had not Edgar restored the power of the monarchy. Elyot waxes nearly as eloquent about his country's future glory under a strong monarch as about its past misery:

All be it it is nat to be dispaired, but that the kynge our soveraigne lorde nowe reignynge, and this realme alway havynge one prince like unto his highnes, equall to the auncient princis in vertue and courage, it shall be reduced (God so disposynge) unto a publike weale excellynge all other in preeminence of vertue and abundance of thynges necessary.

44

History shows what great things can be done under a single ruler as well as what discord results from the lack of one. The Greeks were wise, Elyot says, in placing Agamemnon in complete charge of the Trojan War, though Achilles and Ajax, Nestor and Ulysses were perhaps equally capable. The Romans were well governed under their kings (an extraordinary view!) but after the expulsion of the Tarquins the "communaltie" encroached more and more on the government and caused disorder:

And if the nobles of Rome had nat ben men of excellent lernynge, wisedome, and prowesse, and that the Senate, the moste noble counsaile in all the worlde, . . . I suppose verily that the citie of Rome had ben utterly desolate sone after the expellyng of Tarquine; and if it had been eftsones renewed it shulde have bene twentye tymes distroyed before the tyme that Augustus raigned: so moche discorde was ever in the citie for lacke of one governour.

This statement is in striking contrast to one in a later section of the *Governor* discussing the physical training of young gentlemen, where Elyot says that the ability of a Roman captain to swim "saved the citie of Rome from perpetuall servitude, whiche was likely to have ensued by the returne of the proude Tarquine."[7] Here we see at its clearest the difference in tone between these two sections of the *Governor*.

BUT WHY had Elyot's tone changed? Why did he add these chapters on monarchy to his treatise on education?

The most probable answer is that he wanted to ingratiate himself with Henry VIII. He needed to counteract the damning memory of his association with Wolsey. He must have known the King well enough to realize that praises of monarchy and statements of the exalted position of kings pleased him. They would be especially welcome in 1531, when it was becoming clearer and clearer that only some drastic assertion of the King's power could settle Henry's "great matter." And so, perhaps, Elyot took up a treatise on education which he had written previously—possibly while a member of the Humanistic circle centered about More—and added the dedication to Henry and the chapters concerning monarchy.

[7] *Governor*, I, Chap. 17.

45

If Elyot did write this part of the *Governor* in an attempt to regain royal favor, it was a successful attempt: in September, 1531, Henry appointed Elyot ambassador to the Emperor Charles V. Certainly Henry had good enough reason to be pleased with these chapters, for their statement of the king's authority, though vague, was unusually strong. Elyot did not say that the king held supreme power over the Church, or suggest that he was not bound to follow the pope, but his doctrine could be interpreted as implying both of these things. If the king sat in lonely eminence at the apex of a pyramidal hierarchy of men, he was superior to all other persons and powers, and hence his own authority was virtually unlimited. And, if the pubic weal was not to become a "monstre with many heedes," persons of lower degree could only obey and follow his lead.

In making the hierarchical principle do such service, Elyot was putting some very old wine in a new bottle. The classes of men had been carefully ordered in Plato's republic, and Aristotle had held that the principle of degree was a law of nature.[8] Aquinas traced it to the order of the universe as originally established by God.[9] The "great chain of being" was a commonplace idea for both scholastic theologians and Humanistic philosophers. Within England, and within the field of political theory, it had been used by Edmund Dudley in the treatise which he wrote while a prisoner in the Tower (1509/10), but in his hands it had justified the power and position of the nobles, not that of the king. Dudley's king was in fact circumscribed by his duty to his subjects; he had to uphold the *Tree of Commonwealth*,

that thing for which all trew Englisshe men have greate nede to pray to God that our lord and king will have a singuler regard and favour theron, for princypally by God and hym hit most be holpen. Therefore God had ordeuyned hym to be our king, and therto is every king bounden, for yt is his charge, for, as the subjectes are bounden to ther prince, so be all kinges bounden to ther subjectes by the comaundyment of God them to maynteigne and supporte as farre as in hym is his power. His welth and prosperite standith in the welth of his trew subjectes, for though the people be sub-

[8] *Politics,* II, 2; VII, 8, 9.

[9] *De regimine principum,* Chap. XIII. Aquinas was unwilling to accept all the logical implications of the doctrine. See A. O. Lovejoy, *The Great Chain of Being* (Cambridge, Mass., 1950), pp. 73–82.

jectes to the king yet are thei the people of God, and God hath ordeyned ther prince to protect them and thei to obey their prince.[10]

Elyot did something quite different with the old concept: he made it do new duty in emphasizing the importance of a single seemingly omnipotent ruler. He said nothing original; but he restated a commonplace at a time when it needed to be said.

Although Elyot repeated one commonplace, he omitted its corollary, one which we should normally expect to find in a discussion of monarchy. Nearly all other writers who said that monarchy was the best form of government hastened to add, following Aristotle, that its corrupted form—tyranny—was the worst possible sort of rule. Among those who point out its dangers are Castiglione and Erasmus, both of whom influenced Elyot in the composition of parts of the *Governor*.[11] Castiglione does not go into detail but merely says that "of these three ill governments (it is sure) the tyranny is worst of all, as it may be proved by many reasons."[12] Erasmus, however, dwells on the point in his *Institutio principis Christiani*. An evil prince is, he writes, an incarnation of the very devil.[13] Although he thinks that "a tyrant is such a monstrous beast that his like does not exist" on earth,[14] Erasmus proceeds to compare him to an imaginary fiend:

A frightful, loathsome beast, formed of a dragon, wolf, lion, viper, bear, and like creatures; with six hundred eyes all over it, teeth everywhere fearful from all angles, and with hooked claws; with never satiated hunger, fattened on human vitals, and reeking with human blood; never sleeping, but always threatening the fortunes and lives of all men; dangerous to everyone, especially to the good; a sort of fatal scourge to the whole world, on which everyone who has the interests of state at heart pours forth execration and hatred; which cannot be borne because of its monstrousness and yet cannot be overthrown without great disaster to the city because its maliciousness is hedged about with armed forces and wealth. This is the

---

[10] Edmund Dudley, *The Tree of Commonwealth,* ed. D. M. Brodie (Cambridge, England, 1948), p. 31.

[11] See below, Chap. Five.

[12] *The Courtier,* trans. Sir Thomas Hoby (1561), Everyman ed., p. 275.

[13] *The Education of a Christian Prince,* trans. L. K. Born (New York, 1936), p. 157.

[14] *Ibid.,* p. 150.

picture of a tyrant—unless there is something more odious which can be depicted.[15]

The absence of some such warning makes Elyot's chapters strikingly one-sided.

Elyot's statements in the first two chapters of the *Governor* imply half of another commonplace which was normally dual-winged. His analogies with God, the sun, and the "principall bee" suggest that the king's power is unlimited. It was usual enough to regard the king as absolute in his administrative governmental acts. Within the sphere of his *gubernaculum*, as McIlwain has written, "no act of his can be illegal, because within it his discretionary power is legitimate, complete, and shared by none. All government is the king's government and there is no other."[16] There was another sphere, however, in which the king was regarded as an individual and not as the supreme governor, and within this field of *jurisdictio* he was as much bound by legal right and judicial decision as his subjects. One of Stephen Gardiner's letters shows that this distinction was not forgotten under the Tudors. Bishop Gardiner is referring to Wolsey's fall:

Ded ye never knowe or here tell of any man, that for doynge that the Kynge our late soveraigne lorde willed, devysed, and required to be done, he that took paynes and commanded to do it, was fayne to sue for his pardon? . . . I have bene present when it hath bene reasoned that the doinge ageynst an acte of Parliament excuseth not a man even from the case of treason, all thoughe a man ded it by the Kynges commaundement.[17]

Sir Thomas More was willing to die rather than forswear his conviction that there was a sphere in which the king was not absolute. But Elyot did not make the distinction, and hence his assertion of the monarch's power had unusual strength.

It is, of course, taking undue liberty to read too much into Elyot's silence concerning tyranny and the limits of the king's power. We cannot be sure that he consciously omitted these commonplaces in order

[15] *Ibid.*, p. 163. Erasmus favored a limited, elective monarchy. On his political thought see C. R. Thompson, "Erasmus as Internationalist and Cosmopolitan," *Archiv für Reformationsgeschichte,* XLVI (1955), 167–195.

[16] C. H. McIlwain, *Constitutionalism, Ancient and Modern* (Ithaca, N.Y., 1947), p. 78.

[17] Quoted in *ibid.*, p. 101.

to assert the authority of the king with single-minded emphasis. Whatever his purpose, the result is the same: it is clear that Elyot's praise of
monarchy is far stronger than a discussion which included all the commonplaces could have been. In the opening chapters of the *Governor*
there is much which would have pleased Elyot's sovereign, nothing at
which he might have grumbled.

Elyot left his praise of monarchy short and vague, yet powerful.
"I do wel perceive," he wrote in conclusion, "that to write of the
office or duetie of a soveraigne governor or prince farre excedeth the
compasse of my lernyng, holy scripture affirmyng that the hartes of
princes be in Goddes owne handes and disposition."[18] That comment,
too, must have pleased Henry.

THERE IS an alternative possible explanation of Elyot's praises of
monarchy. He might have been "violently stered" by Thomas Cromwell to write these chapters as propaganda for Henry's cause. It is well
known that Cromwell used the printing press later in the decade to
influence men's opinions.[19] Elyot's chapters on monarchy were probably written sometime in the second half of 1530. This was the time
when Cromwell was beginning his climb to power; he had entered
Parliament in 1529, pledged to support Henry's policy. In 1530 he was
admitted to the Council, and in 1531 he became a member of its inner
ring and began to help direct governmental affairs. As we have seen,
Cromwell had known Thomas Elyot since 1519. Might he not have
suggested to his old friend in 1530 that they could rise to favor together if Elyot would write a book justifying the assertion of royal
power which Cromwell was going to propose to the King?

There is one piece of evidence which may fit in with this hypothesis.
Early in 1531, Cromwell carried on a correspondence with Stephen
Vaughan, the English resident in the Netherlands, concerning the pos-

[18] *Governor,* I, Chap. 2.
[19] See W. Gordon Zeeveld, *Foundations of Tudor Policy* (Cambridge, Mass.,
1948); Pierre Janelle, *L'Angleterre catholique à la veille du schisme* (Paris,
1935). Janelle's Chap. VI, "L'Expression intellectuelle du schisme" (pp. 232–
319), begins only with the pamphlets of 1533, though reference is made to the
earlier works of Tyndale. Franklin le Van Baumer (*The Early Tudor Theory
of Kingship* [New Haven, Conn., 1940]) gives (Appendix A) a useful and
convincing list of propagandistic documents issued between 1528 and 1539.

sibility of persuading William Tyndale to return to England and write for the government.[20] Tyndale had attracted attention in 1528 when his book ,*The Obedience of a Christen Man,* appeared as a defense against charges that he was urging disobedience to the civil government by circulating his translation of the New Testament. It "proved by Gods worde" that children should obey their elders, wives their husbands, servants their masters, and—most important—subjects their kings. Tyndale took as his text the thirteenth chapter of Paul's Epistle to the Romans and showed how it demanded obedience:

Let every soule submit him self to the auctoritie of the hyer powers. . . . The powers that be are ordeyned of God. Who so ever therfore resisteth the power resisteth the ordinaunce of God. . . . God hath made the kinge in every realme judge over all, and over him is ther no judge. He that judgeth the kinge judgeth God, and he that layeth handes on the kinge layeth hande on God, and he that resisteth the kinge resisteth God and damneth Gods lawe and ordinaunce. . . . If the kinge sinne he must be reserved to the judgement, wrath and vengaunce of God. And as it is to resiste the kinge, so is it to resiste his officer which is set or sent to execute the kinges commaundement. . . . Here by seist thou that the kinge is in this worlde without lawe and maye at his lust do right or wrong and shall geve accomptes but to God only.[21]

Both the laity and members of the ecclesiastical hierarchy were subject to the king's rule, Tyndale wrote. Well might Cromwell and Henry pay attention.

Tyndale unfortunately proceeded to doctrinal discussions and expressed views far too Lutheran to please the Defender of the Faith, but he had set out a political theory which would adequately justify any assertion of power that Henry might have to make. Could he be induced to return to England, lay aside his radical doctrinal views, and write propaganda?

It is not entirely clear where this idea originated. Perhaps Vaughan suggested it. More likely, however, Cromwell asked Vaughan to ascertain Tyndale's attitude. After several meetings between Vaughan and

[20] On Cromwell's interest in Tyndale, see R. B. Merriman, *Life and Letters of Thomas Cromwell* (Oxford, 1902), I, 99–101.

[21] William Tyndale, *The Obedience of a Christen Man . . . Newly Printed and Diligently Corrected* (Marburg, 1535), fols. xxix^r–xxxiii^r.

Tyndale, and numerous letters from Vaughan to Cromwell,[22] it came out that Tyndale was unalterably opposed to the King's divorce. So in the end the idea of using Tyndale was dropped; Vaughan was ordered to stop seeing him and on no account to persuade him to return to England, where he would only trouble the King by spreading seditious ideas.[23]

The significance of all this lies in the government's eagerness to secure a propagandist in 1531; it dovetails neatly with the hypothesis that Elyot's political views were put forth at Cromwell's request. The fact that the *Governor* was published by Thomas Berthelet, the King's printer who published the subsequent Henrician propaganda, also fits in with this view, though of course it may have been only a coincidence.

It is unfortunate that we have no direct statement of Elyot's purpose in writing about monarchy. The idea that these chapters are the earliest example of Cromwellian propaganda is intriguing but unprovable. Perhaps it remains more likely that Elyot wrote the chapters on his own initiative to curry royal favor. In any case the praise of monarchy in *The Boke named the Gouernour* stands as one of the earliest implicit justifications of the English Reformation.

[22] *L.P.,* V, 65, 153, 201.

[23] *Ibid.,* p. 248. On the negotiations between Cromwell and Tyndale, see also J. F. Mozley, *William Tyndale* (London, 1937), pp. 187–200.

CHAPTER FOUR

The Boke named the Gouernour:
Education and Vertue in Manners

SIR THOMAS ELYOT'S political theory, so applicable to the contemporary English situation, is the most significant part of *The Boke named the Gouernour.* Important out of all proportion to its length, it forms only a small fraction of the complete work— three chapters out of seventy-one. In the remaining sixty-eight chapters, to which we now turn, Elyot discusses "education and vertue in manners"; he tries to establish an ideal system of mental and physical training for young governors and then enumerates, at length, the virtues which gentlemen must seek and the vices which they should eschew.

Of this material the most interesting is the treatise on education. In it Elyot gives a thorough description of the objectives and methods of the Humanistic system of education. Although his ideas were not new, as we shall see in the next chapter, he was one of the earliest English writers to advocate applying in England the precepts developed in Renaissance Italy, and his views had considerable influence, both with gentlemen and with tutors. They are well worth examining in some detail.

Elyot thought that reform in English education was imperative. The "decay of lernyng amonge gentilmen" distressed him keenly, and he tried to discover why members of the English gentry were not so learned as the ancient Greeks and Romans had been.[1] He concluded that the pride, avarice, and negligence of parents were at fault. Pride made them scorn learning; gentlemen thought it "a notable reproche to be well lerned and to be called a great clerke,"[2] though being learned had been no humiliation to Henry I, Alexander the Great, Antoninus Pius, Hadrian, Julius Caesar, or Charlemagne. Avarice prevented gentlemen from sending their children away to good but costly schools. Many a gentleman lavished great care on the selection of falconers and cooks, not hesitating to pay them well, but if a schoolmaster was hired to teach at home, "to whom he will committe his childe, to be fedde with lernynge and instructed in vertue, whose lyfe shall be the principall monument of his name and honour, he never maketh further enquirie but where he may have a schole maister, and with howe litel charge."[3]

Even the few gentlemen who did provide good elementary training for their sons often assumed, through ignorance, that education could safely end at the age of fourteen, when the children were able to speak good Latin. In such cases the good early training was wasted: "If the elegant speking of Latin be nat added to other doctrine, litle frute may come of the tonge, sens Latine is but a naturall speche, and the frute of speche is wyse sentence [understanding], which is gathered and made of sondry lernynges." Universities often erred in the same way: "There be many nowe a dayes in famouse scholes and universities whiche be so moche gyven to the studie of tonges onely, that whan they write epistles, they seme to the reder that, like to a trumpet, they make a soune without any purpose." And so there were few good orators in England, since a true orator had to know not only a language but also "a heape of all maner of lernyng."

Elyot did not, however, blame parents alone, for schoolmasters themselves were at fault. "Lorde God," Sir Thomas broke out, "howe

[1] *The Boke named the Gouernour,* I, Chap. 13.
[2] *Ibid.,* Chap. 12.   [3] *Ibid.,* Chap. 13.

many good and clene wittes of children be nowe a dayes perisshed by ignorant schole maisters! Howe litel substancial doctrine is apprehended by the fewenesse of good gramariens!" Better masters would be forthcoming, he held, if society esteemed them more highly. His comments have a curiously modern ring:

Undoubtedly ther be in this realme many well lerned, whiche if the name of a schole maister were nat so moche had in contempte, and also if theyr labours with abundant salaries mought be requited, were righte sufficient and able to induce their herers to excellent lernynge, so they be nat plucked away grene, and er they be in doctrine sufficiently rooted. But nowe a dayes, if to a bachelar or maister of arte studie of philosophie waxeth tediouse, if he have a spone full of Latine, he wyll shewe forth a hoggesheed without any lernynge, and offre to teache grammer and expounde noble writers, and to be in the roome of a maister: he wyll, for a small salarie, sette a false colour of lernyng on propre wittes, whiche wyll be wasshed away with one shoure of raine.[4]

So much had learning decayed.

Elyot proposes a plan for its restoration. It is a detailed scheme of training for prospective governors, beginning with their birth and continuing until they come of age.

First, a proper supervisor must be provided for the child at every age. Even his nurse, who should be selected before the baby is born, has to meet a high standard; Elyot insists that she be between twenty and thirty, of a clean and perfect body, free from servile condition and notable vice, and of a sanguine complexion. This is not all. The child must have, besides the nurse, another woman of virtue, discretion, and gravity, and—so that he may not hear any wanton or unclean words— all men except the physician must be shut out of the nursery. Such elaborate precautions surely seemed as foolish to Tudor fathers as they do to us; Elyot was quite sure, however, that they were necessary. If the nurse is not virtuous the child will suck vice along with his milk:

I verily do suppose that in the braynes and hertes of children, whiche be membres spirituall, whiles they be tender, and the litle slippes of reason begynne in them to burgine, ther may happe by ivel custome some pestiferous dewe of vice to perse the sayde membres, and infecte and corrupt the

4 *Ibid.*, Chap. 15.

softe and tender buddes, wherby the frute may growe wylde, and some tyme conteine in it fervent and mortal poyson, to the utter destruction of a realme.[5]

In emphasizing the importance of the infant's early impressions Elyot anticipated one aspect of Freudian psychology.

The child must be kept away from the company of men until he is seven. After that age he must be excluded from association with women. Elyot allows him to have, for a year or two, an "auncient and sad matrone, attendynge on hym in his chambre," but the lad should be carefully kept away from all young women. Not, Elyot admits, that there is any "perille of offence in that tender and innocent age," but "in the tender wittes be sparkes of voluptuositie: whiche, norished by any occasion or objecte, encrease often tymes in to so terrible a fire, that therwith all vertue and reason is consumed."[6]

When the boy is withdrawn from the company of women he must be given a tutor—"an auncient and worshipfull man, in whom is aproved to be moche gentilnes, mixte with gravitie, and, as nighe as can be, suche one as the childe by imitation folowynge may growe to be excellent. And if he be also lerned, he is the more commendable."[7] This tutor should teach the boy the parts of speech in English; when he has learned them, it is time for his father to provide "suche a maister as is excellently lerned both in Greke and Latine, and therwithall is of sobre and vertuous disposition, specially chast of livyng, and of moche affabilitie and patience."[8] A diligent search for such a master may be necessary, but it will pay dividends in the long run.

Enlightened education theory must guide the master. He must not be too harsh, for a cruel master will dull the lad's wits; his charge must not be forced to learn but rather "swetely allured therto with praises and suche praty gyftes as children delite in."[9] The best method of learning Latin is the painless, conversational one; the master should tell

[5] *Ibid.,* Chap. 4.   [6] *Ibid.,* Chap. 6.
[7] *Ibid.*   [8] *Ibid.,* Chap. 9.
[9] *Ibid.,* Chap. 5. Although most Humanists advocated a similarly enlightened practice, this view was not universal. Lodovico Vives wrote, in a treatise commissioned by Catherine of Aragon, that he agreed with the sentiment "Never have the rod off a boy's back; specially the daughter should be handled without any cherishing. For cherishing marreth sons, but it utterly destroyeth daughters" (H. F. M. Prescott, *Mary Tudor* [London, 1952], p. 26).

the child the Latin names of familiar objects, and the boy should be encouraged to ask for things he wants in Latin. If the child is not particularly bright, he should first read books which will immediately appeal to his interests, "and therwith by litle and litle, as it were with a pleasant sauce," the master can "provoke him to have good appetite to studie."[10]

Children must be taught virtue as well as knowledge. Virtuous masters should set good examples, of course, but their duty does not end there. Elyot describes fully how they should proceed:

The office of a tutor is firste to knowe the nature of his pupil, that is to say, wherto he is mooste inclined or disposed, and in what thyng he setteth his most delectation or appetite. If he be of nature curtaise [courteous], piteouse [merciful], and of free and liberall harte, it is a principall token of grace (as hit is by all scripture determined). Than shall a wyse tutor purposely commende those vertues, extolling also his pupill for havyng of them; and therwith he shall declare them to be of all men mooste fortunate, whiche shall happen to have such a maister. And moreover shall declare to hym what honour, what love, what commodite shall happen to him by these vertues. And, if any have ben of disposition contrary, than to expresse the enormities of theyr vice, with as moche detestation as may be. And if any daunger have therby ensued, misfortune, or punisshement, to agreve it in suche wyse, with so vehement wordes, as the childe may abhorre it, and feare the semblable adventure.[11]

The tutor is also charged with careful regulation of the lad's daily life. The boy must not be allowed to eat too much meat, or to sleep more than eight hours a day, "for undoubtedly bothe repletion and superfluous slepe be capitall enemies to studie." And, of course, the boy must not drink wine unless it has been mixed with water, for it "fylleth the heed with fume."[12]

LEAVING no stone unturned in his attempt to prescribe good education for English gentlemen, Elyot passes to the question of curriculum and describes in considerable detail the studies appropriate to each age. He urges that boys be taught elementary Latin and grammar before they

[10] *Governor,* I, Chap. 9.
[11] *Ibid.,* Chap. 6.   [12] *Ibid.,* Chap. 11.

are seven; he notes that these subjects had become easier in his day than ever before because good introductory grammars in Latin and Greek were newly available.[13]

More serious studies are to begin when the boy reaches the age of seven. He may read Greek and Latin authors at the same time; but Elyot thinks it better to begin with Greek, since it is the more difficult. If a child "do begyn therin at seven yeres of age, he may continually lerne Greke autours thre yeres, and in the meane tyme use the Latin tonge as a familiar langage: whiche in a noble mannes sonne may well come to passe, havynge none other persons to serve him or kepyng hym company, but suche as can speake Latine elegantly."[14] Elyot must have realized that the less wealthy parents would find it difficult to provide servants who spoke Latin elegantly. At any rate, the boy must learn good Latin, and then he should begin French. Elyot thought it necessary to warn the master again "nat to detayne the childe to longe in that tedious labours, eyther in the Greke or Latyne grammer. For a gentyll wytte is therewith sone fatigate."

After the lad has learned the first rules of grammar, the master should read some of Aesop's fables to him in Greek, "in whiche argument children moche do delite." The fables chosen should reprove one of the boy's vices or praise one of his virtues. "The nexte lesson wolde be some quicke and mery dialogues, elect out of Luciane, whiche be without ribawdry, or to moche skorning, for either of them is exactly to be eschewed, specially for a noble man." Selections from Lucian must be chosen with care; it is better to read no Lucian than to read all of Lucian. If the master prefers the comedies of Aristophanes, these may be substituted for the dialogues.

Elyot thought he needed to defend the ancient poets and show "what profite may be taken by the diligent reding of [them], contrary to the false opinion that nowe rayneth, of them that suppose that in the warkes of poetes is contayned nothynge but baudry, (suche is their foule worde of reproche,) and unprofitable leasinges," or deceits. Although many suppose comedies to be but

a doctrinall of rybaudrie, they be undoubtedly a picture or as it were a mirrour of man's life, wherin ivell is nat taught but discovered; to the in-

[13] *Ibid.,* Chap. 5.   [14] *Ibid.,* Chap. 10.

tent that men beholdynge the promptnes of youth unto vice, the snares of harlotts and baudes laide for the yonge myndes, the disceipte of servantes, the chaunces of fortune contrary to mennes expectation, they beinge therof warned may prepare them selfe to resist or prevente occasion.[15]

Poets are not to be shunned even if they have written some wanton verses; Ovid himself, the most lascivious of the poets, left some noble and commendable sentiments. To abandon the poets because of their occasional dissolute writings would be, Elyot says, like avoiding a fair garden simply because one might be stung by a nettle.

Clearly, then, the young gentleman must read the poets. He ought to begin with Homer, "from whom as from a fountain proceded all eloquence and lernyng."[16] The *Iliad* and the *Odyssey* describe both war and politic governance excellently, and they inflame readers to imitate the virtues of the noble Greeks; Aristotle did well to begin his instruction of Alexander the Great with Homer. But Homer's works are admittedly long "and do require therfore a great time to be all lerned and kanned." For variety one would do well to read the *Aeneid* at the same time; Vergil is much like Homer, and "by the joynynge together of those autours, the one shall be the better understande by the other." Elyot was especially fond of Vergil:

verily . . . none one autour serveth to so divers witts as doth Virgile. For there is nat that affect or desire, wherto any childes fantasie is disposed, but in some of Virgils warkes may be founden matter therto apte and propise. For what thinge can be more familiar than his Bucolikes? . . . In his Georgikes, Lorde, what pleasaunt varietie there is . . . . If the childe have a delite in huntyng, what pleasure shall he take of the fable of Aristeus: semblably in the huntynge of Dido and Eneas, whiche is discrived moste elegantly in his boke of Eneidos. If he have pleasure in wrastling, rennyng, or other lyke exercise, where shall he se any more plesant esbatementes [diversions], than that whiche was done by Eurealus and other Troyans, whiche accompanyed Eneas? If he take solace in hearynge minstrelles, what minstrell may be compared to Jopas, whiche sange before Dido and Eneas? or to blinde Demodocus, that played and sange moste swetely at the dyner, that the kynge Alcinous made to Ulisses: whose dities and melodie excelled as farre the songes of our minstrelles, as Homere and Virgile excelle all other poetes.[17]

[15] *Ibid.*, Chap. 13.   [16] *Ibid.*, Chap. 10.   [17] *Ibid.*

After Homer and Vergil, the lad must read Ovid, for a knowledge of the fables he tells in the *Metamorphoses* is necessary for understanding other poets. But excessive time should not be spent on Ovid, because he does not teach virtuous manners or politics. For these it is well to bring in Horace, "in whom is contayned moche varietie of lernynge and quickenesse of sentence." Elyot adds that Lucian and Hesiod may also be read, and—surprisingly—he recommends Silius Italicus's poetic account of the Second Punic War, a work of no great merit.

Such studies should occupy the boy until he is fourteen. Then the second stage in his education should begin; it should be, Elyot notes, more serious and more varied. Now the pupil should be given a small dose of logic out of Cicero or Agricola.[18] Next should follow rhetoric, taught from Hermogines's Greek work or Quintilian in Latin. The master who prefers a shorter work may use the treatise that Cicero wrote for his son; "for him that nedeth nat, or doth nat desire, to be an exquisite oratour, the litle boke made by the famous Erasmus, (whom all gentill wittis are bounden to thanke and supporte), whiche he calleth *Copiam Verborum et Rerum*, that is to say, plentie of wordes and maters, shall be sufficient." The works of Isocrates are profitable and pleasant to read, and they encourage virtue—Elyot evidently had an especially high regard for the oration to Nicocles, for he later translated it.[19] Demosthenes and Cicero were, of course, the most eminent ancient orators; their writings teach eloquence, wisdom, gentle manners, virtue, and policy. Not only that:

The utilitie that a noble man shall have by redyng these oratours, is, that whan he shall happe to reason in counsaile, or shall speke in a great audience, or to strange ambassadours of great princes, he shall nat be constrayned to speake wordes sodayne and disordred, but shal bestowe them aptly and in their places.[20]

The next important study is history; but if the reader does not know about the countries and towns mentioned, the histories will be "tedious or els the lasse pleasant." Some knowledge of geography (Elyot calls it

---

[18] *Ibid.,* Chap. 11.
[19] See below, Chap. Eight.
[20] *Governor,* I, Chap. 11.

cosmography) "encreaseth an inexplicable delectation" for histories. Reference may be made to the tables of Ptolemy and to the new treatises on the spherical nature of the earth. This study is both pleasant and necessary, Elyot says:

for what pleasure is it, in one houre, to beholde those realmes, cities, sees, ryvers, and mountaynes, that uneth [hardly] in an olde mannes life can nat be journaide and pursued: what incredible delite is taken in beholding the diversities of people, beastis, foules, fisshes, trees, frutes, and herbes: to knowe the sondry maners and conditions of people, and the varietie of their natures, and that in a warme studie or perler, without perill of the see, or daunger of longe and paynfull journayes: I can nat tell what more pleasure shulde happen to a gentil witte, than to beholde in his owne house every thynge that within all the worlde is contained.[21]

Here Elyot gave away one of the significant characteristics of his own mind; he was obviously intensely curious about foreign lands and strange sights but too timid to travel to see them himself. He preferred reading about them in his warm parlor.

The gap between geography and history can be bridged, Sir Thomas continues, by reading a writer like Strabo, who commingles the two. And then the serious study of history must begin. The young ought to be allured to history by being told of its delights:

the mayster in the mooste pleasant and elegant wise expressinge what incomparable delectation, utilitie, and commodite shal happen to emperours, kinges, princis, and all other gentil men by reding of histories: shewinge to hym that Demetrius Phalareus, a man of excellent wisdome and lerninge, and whiche in Athenes had ben longe exercised in the publick weale, exhorted Ptholomee, kyng of Egipt, chiefly above all other studyes, to haunte and embrace histories, and suche other bokes, wherin were contayned preceptes made to kynges and princes: sayng that in them he shule rede those thinges whiche no man durst reporte unto his persone. Also Cicero, father of the Latin eloquence, calleth an historie the witnesse of tymes, maistres of life, the lyfe of remembrance, of trouthe the lyght, and messager of antiquite.

It is best to start with Livy, for he describes the beginning of Rome, and his eloquence flows like a fountain of sweet milk. Xenophon

21 Ibid.

should follow, and Quintus Curtius may well be read at the same time; the life of Alexander the Great should be carefully marked, since he excelled all other rulers in "wysedome, hardynes, strength, policie, agilite, valiaunt courage, nobilitie, liberalitie and curtaisie." The orations in Tacitus repay attention. Julius Caesar and Sallust should probably be deferred until the lad is a bit older, because they require "an exact and perfect jugement" and because they lack variety. For the older student, however, Caesar is invaluable—his book is "studiously to be radde of the princes of this realme of Englande and their counsailors; considering that therof maye be taken necessary instructions concernynge the warres agayne Irisshe men or Scottes, who be of the same rudenes and wilde disposition that the Suises and Britons were in the time of Cesar." Caesar's tactics were still thought valid in the sixteenth century.

Elyot emphasizes that histories have a very practical value; no other study can be so profitable:

In the lerning of these autors, a yonge gentilman shal be taught to note and marke, nat only the ordre and elegancie in declaration of the historie, but also the occasion of the warres, the counsailes and preparations on either part, the estimation of the capitaines, the maner and fourme of theyr governance, the continuance of the bataile, the fortune and successe of the holle affaires. Semblably out of the warres in other dayly affaires, the astate of the publike weale, if hit be prosperous or in decaye, what is the very occasyon of the one or the other, the forme and maner of the governance therof, the good and evyll qualities of them that be rulers, the commodities and good sequele of vertue, the discommodies and evyll conclusion of vicious licence.

Elyot concludes that "there is no studie or science . . . of equal commoditie and pleasure." His was one of the first and most sincere of the Tudor encomiums of history.[22]

The coping stone of Elyot's house of learning is moral philosophy. Seventeen is the right age at which to begin this study, he thinks, and it is best to start with the first two books of Aristotle's *Ethics*. They ought to be studied in the original Greek; Elyot calls the translations then available "a rude and grosse shadowe of the eloquence and wise-

[22] *Ibid.* See S. E. Lehmberg, "The Divine Art and Its Uses," *The Historian,* XX (1957), 24–38.

dome of Aristotle." Cicero's *De officiis* should follow, together with Plato's works. Elyot is really more enthusiastic about Plato than about Aristotle, as were nearly all the Humanists.[23] Nor can the Bible be neglected. The Proverbs, Ecclesiastes, and Ecclesiasticus, together with the historical books, should be studied by the mature gentleman, but the New Testament ought to be regarded with awe and reverence, "havynge the chiefe interpretour of those bokes trewe and constant faithe." The *Institutio principis Christiani,* that "lytell boke of the most excellent doctour Erasmus Roterodamus," should on no account be forgotten: "There was never boke written in Latine that, in so lytle a portion, contayned of sentence, eloquence, and vertuous exhortation, a more compendious abundaunce." With the *Institution* Elyot ends his long list of recommended texts. The governor who completed Sir Thomas's curriculum would have been well educated indeed.

BUT ELYOT did not think that young Englishmen should spend all their time in serious studies. His aim was rather the well-rounded, "complete gentleman" of the Italian Humanists and, later, the Elizabethan courtesy books; he thought that governors could not neglect physical training and that they should practice the fine arts as recreation.

Elyot praises the study of music at length, even suggesting that some knowledge of music is necessary for the proper understanding of grammar, which includes the study of meters and harmonies.[24] Music is wonderfully soothing, and gentlemen should try to emulate David, who calmed Saul's vexed spirits with his harp. But they ought not to copy Nero, who delighted in music so much that he attended to nothing else; it is better for the governor to know no music than to let too great love of it distract him from his duties to the public weal. Tutors should emphasize the proper role of music in the life of a gentleman:

that is to say, that it onely serveth for recreation after tedious or laborious affaires; and to shewe him that a gentilman, plainge or singing in a com-

---

[23] "Lorde God," Elyot wrote, "what incomparable swetnesse of wordes and mater shall he finde in the saide warkes of Plato and Cicero: wherin is joyned gravitie with dilectation, excellent wysedome with divine eloquence, absolute vertue with pleasure incredible."—*Governor,* I, Chap. 11.

[24] *Ibid.,* Chap. 15.

mune audience, appaireth his estimation: the people forgettinge reverence, when they beholde him in the similitude of a common servant or minstrell. Yet, natwithstanding, he shall commende the perfecte understandinge of musike, declaringe howe necessary it is for the better attaynynge the knowlege of a publike weal: whiche, as I before have saide, is made of an ordre of astates and degrees, and, by reason therof, conteineth in it a perfect harmony: whiche he shall afterwarde more perfectly understande, whan he shall happen to rede the bokes of Plato, and Aristotle, of publike weales: wherin be written divers examples of musike and geometrye.[25]

It is commendable for the young gentleman to learn painting and sculpture also, if they interest him; but here again he must not become absorbed in them. "They [shall] nat be by him exercised, but as a secrete pastime, or recreation of the wittes, late occupied in serious studies."[26] Some knowledge of drawing can, however, be useful to governors; they can sketch models of "engynes for the warre" and make maps of the regions they rule. Hence—and because princes of antiquity did not disdain painting and sculpture—children inclined to these arts ought to be taught by the best artists obtainable.

To complete the training of young governors Elyot recommends a number of suitable physical exercises. For, he writes,

continuall studie without some maner of exercise shortly exhausteth the spirites vitall, and hyndereth naturall decoction and digestion, wherby mannes body is the soner corrupted and brought into divers sickenessis, and finallye the life is therby made shorter; where contrayrye wise by exercise, whiche is a vehement motion (as Galene prince of phisitions defineth) the helthe of man is preserved, and his strength increased: for as moche the membres by mevyng and mutuall touching, do waxe more harde, and naturall heate in all the body is therby augmented. Moreover it maketh the spirites of a man more strong and valiant, so that, by the hardnesse of the membres, all labours be more tollerable.[27]

Elyot's reference to Galen and his citation, a bit later, of Linacre's "wonderfull eloquent" translation of Galen's *De sanitate tuenda* show

[25] *Ibid.*, Chap. 7. The last sentence was probably inserted when Elyot added his first three chapters. For a survey of the attitude toward amateur musicians in sixteenth- and seventeenth-century England, see W. L. Woodfill, *Musicians in English Society* (Princeton, N.J., 1953), pp. 201–239.

[26] *Governor,* I, Chap. 8.   [27] *Ibid.,* Chap. 16.

that he was interested in the preservation of health some years before he wrote his own *Castel of Helth*. Indeed Elyot's whole attitude toward exercise is the utilitarian one of a physician; he recommends sports because they strengthen the body or purge an excess of one of the humors or give training that would be valuable in war. It did not occur to him, apparently, that sports might be enjoyable, that their best justification might be their pleasantness.

Since different exercises serve different purposes, Elyot thought it necessary to inform tutors about them at length. Youngsters of fourteen may well be set at wrestling, trying "with strengthe and agilitie to throwe downe eche other." They will find running "a good exercise and laudable solace." Although swimming can be "right profitable in the exstreme daunger of warres," it was not in favor during Elyot's time (he complains) because it seemed dangerous to learn. Nevertheless Sir Thomas recommends it, commenting that Alexander the Great called himself the unhappiest man of his time because he had never learned to swim.[28] Tennis, played occasionally and for short periods, is a good exercise for young men.[29] Games of bowls, pins, or quoits are to be "utterly abjected of al noble men," and so is football, "wherin is nothinge but beastly furie and exstreme violence; wherof procedeth hurte, and consequently rancour and malice do remaine with them that be wounded; wherfore it is to be put in perpetuall silence." It is better, and more useful, to learn how to handle various weapons, particularly the sword and battle-ax, while the most honorable exercise of all is riding "suerly and clene on a great horse and a roughe." Expert horsemanship is not only necessary in war but also useful to a governor in time of peace, since it "importeth a majestie and drede to inferiour persones, beholding him above the common course of other men, dauntyng a fierce and cruell beaste."[30]

Historical reasons, always of great importance to Elyot, led him to praise hunting. It "may be an imitacion of batayle, if it be suche as was used amonge them of Persia, wherof Xenophon [writeth;] . . . and in that fourme beyng used, it is a laudable exercise."[31] Noble Greeks and Romans were also fond of hunting. The more like battle, the better the hunt. It is more commendable to seek deer than foxes; only women

[28] *Ibid.*, Chap. 17.
[30] *Ibid.*, Chap. 17.
[29] *Ibid.*, Chap. 27.
[31] *Ibid.*, Chap. 18.

and sedentary scholars should stoop to taking hares. Although Elyot was unable to find any mention of hawking in antiquity, he reluctantly admits that it too may be a "right delectable solace."[32]

But the best exercise of all is shooting with a longbow; it "incomparably excelleth all other exercise."[33] Here again Elyot's sense of history, together with his patriotism, comes out. He recalls that "a fewe Englisshe archers have ben seene to prevayle agayne people innumerable," probably a reference to Henry V's success on St. Crispin's Day. "This is the feate," he adds, "wherby Englisshe men have ben moste dradde and had in estimation with outwarde princes, as well enemies as alies." But, Elyot laments, interest in shooting had seriously declined in his own day:

O what cause of reproche shall the decaye of archers be to us nowe livyng? Ye, what irrecuperable damage either to us or them in whose time nede of semblable defence shall happen? Whiche decaye, though we all redy perceive, feare, and lament, and for the restauryng therof cesse nat to make ordinances, good lawes, and statutes, yet who effectuelly puttethe his hande to continual execution of the same lawes and provisions? or beholdyng them dayly broken, wynketh nat at the offendours? O mercifull God, howe longe shall we be mockers of our selfes? Howe longe shall we skorne at our one calamitie? whiche, bothe with the eien [eyes] of our mynde, and also our bodily eien, we se dayly imminent, by neglectyng our publike weale, and contemnynge the due execution of lawes and ordinaunces.

Elyot's friend Roger Ascham tried to encourage archery by publishing a book of instructions, called *Toxophilus, the Schole of Shootinge*, slightly more than a decade after the *Governor* first appeared.

Forms of recreation which do not provide exercise for the body are not so commendable, Elyot thinks. Games of dice are the worst; they do not even call for wit or cunning, and they lead to "vehement chidyng and braulyng, horrible othes, cruell, and sometyme mortall, menacis. . . . O why shulde that be called a playe, whiche is compacte of malice and robry?"[34] Card games are somewhat better, since they demand more skill and involve less chance. But chess is the most commendable of the games not providing bodily exercise; it sharpens the wit and quickens the memory, "and it is the more commendable . . . if

[32] *Ibid.,* Chap. 24.   [33] *Ibid.,* Chap. 27.   [34] *Ibid.,* Chap. 26.

the players have radde the moralization of the chesse," that is, Caxton's *The Game and Playe of the Chesse*, first printed in 1475.[35]

There remains but one form of recreation or exercise which Elyot recommends: dancing. His chapters praising it—there are seven of them—are the most curious part of the *Governor*. Elyot admits that Augustine condemned dancing, but he explains that dances in the Saint's time were idolatrous or wanton or both.[36] He rehearses several tales of the origin of the dance, more for their "mery fantasie" than because he believes them.[37] He tells how ancient rulers and philosophers commended the dance and how ancient dancing expressed the virtues in allegorical form. Then he urges that English dances also be allegorized, and he goes so far as to suggest a version of the popular French *basse danse*, in which the steps signify such virtues as love of God, industry, prudence, circumspection, and modesty.[38]

Instruction in allegorized dances completes the mental and physical training which Elyot prescribed for young governors. It is, basically, a Humanistic education in the classics, with ample play for the interests of the student if he seeks recreation in music, painting, or sculpture, and with a variety of exercises to make his body perfect. And it was far in advance of any educational system common in Elyot's England.

THE LAST TWO BOOKS of the *Governor* are of considerably less interest than the first. They are devoted to a discussion of the virtues which Elyot thought members of the governing class should possess. His framework of ethical philosophy is thin and weak, however; he is generally satisfied with a definition of each virtue, and his main interest is in giving historical examples to show how each virtue was commended in antiquity.

Although both books deal with the virtues, their tone is rather different, probably as a result of the differing sources which Elyot followed. Sir Thomas flatly admitted that part of Book II was "nat of myn owne

[35] Caxton translated his book from Jehan de Vignay's French version of Jacobus de Cessolis's *Ludus Scaccorum.*

[36] *Governor,* I, Chap. 19.

[37] *Ibid.,* Chap. 20.

[38] *Ibid.,* Chap. 21. For a description of the form of the *basse danse* without the allegory, see Thoinot Arbeau (pseud. of Jean Tabourot), *Orchesographie* (Langres, 1588).

heed [head] devised, but excerped or gathered as well out of holy scripture as out of the warkes of other excellent writars of famouse memorie, as they shall sone perceive whiche have radde and perused good autours in Greke and Latine."[39] In our next chapter we shall see how true Elyot's confession was; here it will be sufficient to indicate the topics on which he wrote in Books II and III and to examine briefly some of the more significant points raised.

Book II, after a list of considerations which a governor should premeditate—for instance, that "the most sure fundation of noble renome is a man to be of suche vertues and qualities as he desireth to be openly publisshed"—proceeds to define and praise majesty, nobility, affability, placability, mercy, humanity, benevolence, liberality, and friendship. Elyot's comments on nobility are quite pointed, for he thought that its true nature was often misunderstood. It depends more on virtue than birth. Elyot admits that "where vertue joyned with great possessions or dignitie hath longe continued in the bloode or house of a gentilman, . . . there nobilitie is mooste shewed," but he exposes the "errour and folye" of those who "thinke that nobilitie may in no wyse be but onely where men can avaunte them of auncient lignage, an auncient robe, or great possessions."[40] In asserting that the most noble blood might in time be corrupted, Elyot helped justify the rise of the new commercial aristocracy; but he was careful to emphasize that if the vital element was not ancestry, neither was it money. Virtues made nobles.

Indeed, all true gentlemen must be virtuous; Elyot exhorts them particularly to be affable, placable, and merciful. Those who think "with a loke to subdue all the worlde" are far from the mark; "Lorde God, how they be sore blinded which do wene that haulte countenance is a comelynesse of nobility."[41] The virtue of placability was notably exhibited by Henry V. Elyot tells how one of Prince Hal's servants had been taken to stand trial for a felony; the prince tried to intervene and to forcibly carry his servant away; the courageous judge committed Hal to prison for contempt of court; the prince was abashed; and the king rejoiced that he had a judge not afraid to minister justice and a son willing to obey. For this tale, which is found in both Hall's chronicle

[39] *Governor*, II, Chap. 1.
[40] *Ibid.*, Chap. 4. [41] *Ibid.*, Chap. 5.

and Shakespeare's play, the *Governor* is our earliest known source. No one has yet discovered how Elyot came by it.[42]

After chapters on benevolence, beneficence, and liberality, Elyot concludes his second book with a lengthy discussion of friendship. He was ashamed to admit that true friendship "is nowe so infrequent or straunge amonge mortall men, by the tyrannie of covetise and ambition, whiche have longe reigned, and yet do, that amitie may nowe unethe [hardly] be knowen or founden throughout the worlde, by them that seeke for her . . . diligently." Perhaps there was, indeed, no example of friendship as Elyot defined it, for he thought that it could exist only between virtuous men and only between men of the same class; there can be no real friendship "betwene him whiche is elevate in authoritie and another of very base astate or degree."[43] The best that Elyot could do was to recount the fictional tale of an ideal friendship. He chose that between Titus and Gisippus, first described in the *Decameron*; his version is the earliest known translation of Boccaccio into English, and it forms the longest chapter in the *Governor*.[44]

A member of the governing class must be particularly careful in his choice of friends, Elyot writes, for he is likely to tell them important secrets. He will be surrounded by flatterers, who are very hard to distinguish from true friends. Since flatterers are "mortall enemyes of noble wittes," Elyot thought they should be tortured publicly, as an example to others.[45] This is only one of the passages scattered throughout his works in which he speaks bitterly about flatterers; it was a Humanistic commonplace to warn rulers of them, but Elyot's comments also suggest strongly that he thought Henry VIII was not so discriminating as he should have been in his choice of associates and that this was the cause of his failure to reward Elyot properly for his services in the Council. The same dissatisfaction was probably rankling behind Sir Thomas's pointed comment that "the moste damnable vice

[42] *Ibid.*, Chap. 6. See Croft's note (I, 60–71) and L. W. Vernon Harcourt, "The two Sir John Fastolfs," *Transactions* of the Royal Historical Society, 3d ser., IV (1910), 47–62.

[43] *Governor*, II, Chap. 11.

[44] *Ibid.*, Chap. 12; from *Decameron*, Day 10, Tale 8. Elyot probably worked from the Latin version of Philip Beroaldo (? Leipzig, 1495).

[45] *Governor*, II, Chap. 14.

and moste agayne justice" is ingratitude, or failure to reward faithful service.[46]

The last book of the *Governor* is more closely organized than Book II, since it deals with the cardinal virtues. Its unity is not immediately apparent, however, for Elyot discusses also a number of subsidiary virtues more or less closely allied to wisdom, courage, justice, and temperance.

He begins with justice, "a wille perpetuall and constaunt, whiche gyveth to every man his right." It is so necessary for governors that "without it none other vertue may be commendable, ne witte or any maner of doctrine profitable."[47] But justice is often perverted by fraud and deceit. Elyot's comments on these perversions are particularly interesting because they appear on first view to be directed against Machiavelli's *Prince*. Even the analogy with the fox is there: "Injurie, which is contrary to justice, is done by two meanes, that is to say, either by violence or by fraude; fraude semeth to be proprely of the foxe, violence or force of the lyon; the one and the other be farre from the nature of man, but fraude is worthy moste to be hated."[48] Elyot laments that deceit was "at this present tyme so communely practised, that if it be but a litle, it is called policie, and if it be moche and with a visage of gravitie, it is than named and accounted for wisedome." Obvious danger may be resisted by power or avoided by treaty, but

where it is by craftie engynne imagined, subtilly prepared, covertly dissembled, and disceytefully practysed, suerly no man may by strength withstande it, or by wisedome eskape it, or by any other maner or meane resiste or avoyde it. Wherfore of all injuries that which is done by fraude is moste horrible and detestable, nat in the opinion of man onely, but also in the sight and jugement of God.[49]

Deceit is a sin which evil councilors are guilty of: "To councell any thynge whiche thou knowest, to the intent that for thyne owne profite thou woldest that another who shall take any damage or benefite therby shulde nat knowe it, is . . . the act . . . of a persone crafty, ungentill,

---

[46] *Ibid.*, Chap. 13.
[47] *Ibid.*, III, Chap. 1.   [48] *Ibid.*, Chap. 4.
[49] Cf. *Il Principe,* Chap. XVIII, "How Princes Are to Keep Faith. . . ."

subtille, deceytefull, malicious, and wilie."[50] So common was the failure to keep faith in Elyot's time that "all the lerned men in the lawes of this realme . . . can nat . . . devise so sufficient an instrument to bynde a man to his promyse . . . but that there shall be some thinge therein espied to brynge it in argument if it be denyed."[51] Sir Thomas, after his years with the assizes, should have known. Whether his hatred of fraud and deceit is an early example of anti-Machiavellianism is a question which we shall examine, if not solve, in the next chapter.

Elyot does not discuss the virtue of courage as a whole, but breaks it down into fortitude, contempt of death, diligence, patience, magnanimity, abstinence, and continence. None of his comments are of unusual significance. Turning to temperance and, specifically, to moderation in daily life, Elyot gives suggestions for proper diet, and comments that he has "knowen men of worshippe in this realme, whiche durynge their yongth have dronken for the more parte water. Of whome some yet lyveth in great auctorytie, whose excellencie as well in sharpnesse of wytte as in exquisite lernynge, is all redy knowen throughe all Christendome." The reference is clearly to Sir Thomas More; editions of the *Governor* printed after his execution omit the second sentence.[52]

Finally Elyot writes of wisdom or sapience, "because in governaunce be included disposition and ordre, whiche can nat be without soveraigne knowlege, procedynge of wisedome, in a more elegant worde called sapience."[53] He accepts a neo-Platonic view of knowledge and of the soul, in which there are "certayne spices, or as it were sedes of thynges and rules of artes and sciences." A teacher is only a midwife bringing into the open knowledge which was present, but latent, in the student's mind. That is why Socrates said, "Never man lerned of me anythinge, allthoughe by my company he became the wiser." Like Pico della Mirandola, of whose works he had some knowledge,[54] Elyot tried to fuse the Aristotelian entelechy with the Platonic idea; he seems not

---

[50] *Governor,* III, Chap. 4.

[51] *Ibid.,* Chap. 7.

[52] *Ibid.,* Chap. 22. Erasmus' letter to Ulrich von Hutten confirms that More drank only water or small beer; see P. S. Allen, ed., *Opus Epistolarum Des. Erasmi Roterodami* (Oxford, 1905–47), IV, 15.

[53] *Governor,* III, Chap. 23.

[54] See below, Chap. Eight.

to have realized the difficulties of such a position, and he admits that he discusses Aristotle "principally to thentent to ornate our langage with usinge wordes in their propre signification."

Elyot then adds a view not consistent with his neo-Platonic episte-mology: wisdom, he writes, proceeds from experience. Experience may come vicariously, from reading histories—and Sir Thomas again praises them at length—or it may be gained directly in our own lives.[55] "No operation or affaire may be perfecte, nor no science or arte may be complete, except experience be thereunto added, whereby knowlege is ratified and (as I mought saye) consolidate." Governors should travel about their realms gaining knowledge of their subjects, but of course no ruler can have sufficient experience himself. Hence—again— the need for trustworthy counselors. On the familiar note that they must place the "universall astate of the publike weale" above any private considerations Elyot concludes his analysis of the cardinal vir-tues.

His final paragraph stresses the usefulness of his book:

Nowe all ye reders that desire to have your children to be governours, or in any other authoritie in the publike weale of your contrey, if ye bringe them up and instructe them in suche fourme as in this boke is declared, they shall than seme to all men worthye to be in authoritie, honour, and noblesse, and all that is under their governaunce shall prospere and come to perfection. And as a precious stone in a ryche ouche [setting] they shall be beholden and wondred at, and after the dethe of their body their soules for their endevour shall be incomprehensibly rewarded of the gyver of wisedome, to whome onely be gyven eternall glorie. Amen.[56]

The Boke named the Gouernour was to be a catholicon for rulers.

[55] *Governor,* III, Chaps. 25, 26.
[56] *Ibid.,* Chap. 30.

CHAPTER FIVE

The Boke named the Gouernour:
Nat of Myn Owne Heed Devised

N O STUDY of *The Boke named the Gouernour* would be complete without an examination of the sources from which Elyot drew his material. He himself admitted that part of the volume was "nat of myn owne heed devised"; it is interesting to see what truth his statement has, and significant to discover which writers of classical antiquity and of the Italian Renaissance he followed.

It would be unfair to Elyot, however, to discuss his sources without having first examined the ideas in the *Governor* as if they were his own, as we have done in the last two chapters. For in a real sense they are his—that is, they express his views—whether he originated them or not. Several facts need to be recognized in this connection: first, that none of the Renaissance Humanists were very original. They uniformly sought the authority of the ancients, and when they conceived new ideas they tried to conceal their novelty by clothing them in classical garb. Moreover, there are a limited number of possible ideas about political theory, education, and ethics; it is difficult to see how any writer can express an idea which is entirely new. Not alone the *Governor*, but indeed any book, might be broken down into its component sources. It is easy to forget that even derivative writers must be selective, must consciously choose their ideas from the mass of commonplaces; often a writer who adopts one idea might just as easily have repeated its opposite. Elyot borrowed only those ideas with which his own mentality and experience led him to sympathize. He followed no source slavishly, but selected those things which he thought Tudor Englishmen needed to be told. If the *Governor* appears unoriginal, that is perhaps one of its attractions; we can see through to its sources more easily.

THE FIRST THREE chapters of the *Governor*—those which deal with political theory—are the least transparent part of Elyot's book. The problem is not that his ideas are original, even if his use of them was novel, but rather that they were so common that it is difficult to pin them down. Although most of Sir Thomas's views can be traced back to Plato and Aristotle, they were so much in the air during the sixteenth century that it is impossible to be sure where he discovered them.

Still, it is worth trying to see what sources he turned to. The conception of an ordered hierarchy of men, with an appropriate division of labor, obviously goes back to Plato's *Republic*, and the view that monarchy, if it can be kept from degenerating into tyranny, is better than aristocracy or democracy stems from Aristotle's *Politics*. Elyot no doubt knew these works directly, but he may also have found the ideas readily available in the works of Aquinas. Since the hierarchical principle embodied in the "great chain of being" was a commonplace even before Aquinas codified it in his *Summa Theologiae,* we need not suppose that Elyot was dependent on the *Summa*; it was, in fact, just the sort of work which he condemned for its "fardelles and trusses." But as he wrote he may well have consulted the short treatise *De regimine principum*, most of which is now thought to be by Aquinas. There are some notable similarities; consider this passage from Aquinas:

Whatever is in accord with nature is best: for in all things nature does what is best. Now, every natural governance is governance by one. In the multitude of bodily members there is one which moves them all, namely, the heart; and among the powers of the soul one power presides as chief, namely, the reason. Even among bees there is one queen (*rex*) and in the whole universe there is One God, Maker and Ruler of all things. And this is reasonable. For every multitude is derived from unity. Wherefore, artificial things imitate natural things and since a work of art is better according as it attains a closer likeness to what is in nature, it necessarily follows that it is best, in the case of a human multitude, that it be ruled by one person.[1]

Other chapters of the *Governor* suggest that Elyot knew the *Education of a Christian Prince* by Erasmus and Castiglione's *Courtier*, and it is likely that these books, too, were at his side when he wrote of monarchy. Elyot came very near to Erasmus' words that "God placed a beautiful likeness of himself in the heavens—the sun. Among mortal men he set up a tangible and living image of himself—the king."[2] Erasmus differed from Elyot in thinking that a prince of only average ability and morality should be kept in check by aristocratic and democratic elements lest tyranny creep in; Elyot may indeed have thought that members of the governing class should perform such a function, but he could hardly say so in a book designed to please Henry. Defense of monarchy by analogy with bees is also to be found in the *Education*,[3] but it is impossible to trace so common an idea to a single source. Castiglione and Patrizi, as well as Columella and Vergil, were among the writers who made use of the analogy in works which Elyot must have known.

Possibly Elyot was introduced to the *Courtier* by his friend Cromwell, for we know that Cromwell obtained a copy soon after its publication in Venice in 1528.[4] In the *Courtier*, Castiglione has one of his characters, Octavian Fregoso, set forth the Aristotelian view of the perfect and corrupt forms of monarchy, aristocracy, and democracy. "It followeth . . . that of the three good, the kingdom is best," Octavian says, "because it is contrarie to the worst, for (as you know) the effects of contrarie causes, they be also contrarie among themselves." Mon-

---

[1] *De regimine principum,* I, Chap. 2; trans. Gerald B. Phelan as *On the Governance of Rulers* (Toronto, 1935), pp. 38 f.

[2] *Institutio principis Christiani,* trans. L. K. Born as *The Education of a Christian Prince* (New York, 1936), p. 157.

[3] *Ibid.,* pp. 147, 165, 208.

[4] In 1530, Edmund Bonner, preparing for an embassy to Italy, asked Cromwell to lend him "the boke called Cortigiano in Ytalion" (Sir Henry Ellis, *Original Letters Illustrative of English History,* 3d ser. [London, 1846], II, 177 f.). See also Pearl Hogrefe, "Elyot and the 'Boke Called Cortegiano in Ytalion,'" *Modern Philology,* XXVII (1930), 303–311.

archy is "agreeable to nature" since deer, fowls, and bees follow a single leader and since the heart rules all the body; it is a form "like unto God's," for He "one and alone governeth the universall."[5] God has ordained, concluded both Castiglione and Elyot, that there should be a monarch to rule and subjects to obey.

Although Erasmus' *Education* includes a chapter on magistrates, Elyot's discussion does not resemble it. It is obvious that monarchs must be assisted by magistrates or inferior governors, and we need not suppose that Elyot, unoriginal as he was, needed any literary source for his third chapter. In any case his aim was not to discuss magistrates in any detail. The chapter serves merely to link the defense of monarchy with the treatise on the education of governors.

ELYOT'S CHAPTERS on education of the mind and body follow two principal sources. Again both were ancient writers—Plutarch and Quintilian—and again both were very popular with the Humanists. Elyot repeats most of the ideas in Plutarch's *Discourse Touching the Training of Children*, and we know that he was familiar with the work because he later translated it into English from the Latin version by Guarino da Verona.[6] Plutarch emphasized the importance of choosing carefully the child's associates, particularly nurses and teachers; he thought learning was better than riches and that it was the responsibility of a father to see that his son was well trained in both virtue and knowledge. But he "would not have fathers of an over-rigid and harsh temper, but so mild as to forgive some slips of youth, remembering that they themselves were once young"; and masters should avoid corporal punishment, since "praise and reproof are more effectual upon free-born children than any such disgraceful handling."[7] Plutarch also urged that young students be allowed recreations and gymnastic exercises, though he did not discuss them so thoroughly as did Elyot.

If Elyot took most of his ideas on education from Plutarch, he added details from the longer *Institutio oratoria* of Quintilian. Quintilian's

---

[5] *The Courtier,* trans. Sir Thomas Hoby (1561), Everyman ed., pp. 273 ff.

[6] Guarino's translation of *De liberis educatione* was first printed in 1497; it is included in *Plutarchi Chaeronei opuscula quaedam* (Mainz, 1522), pp. 287–319. On Elyot's translation, see below, Chap. Seven.

[7] *Plutarch's Morals,* ed. W. W. Godwin (London, 1870), I, 30, 20.

work was by far the most important ancient influence on Renaissance education. During the Middle Ages it was known only in a fragmentary and corrupt text, but an authoritative version was discovered by Poggio in 1416 at the Abbey of St. Gall and it was printed at Rome in 1470. It profoundly influenced the ideas of such Renaissance writers as Guarino, Vittorino da Feltre, P. P. Vergerius, Matteo Palmieri, L. B. Alberti, Aeneas Sylvius, Francesco Patrizi, Rudolf Agricola, Erasmus, Vives, and Melanchthon.[8] Sir Thomas probably knew Quintilian's treatise at first hand, perhaps in the fine Aldine edition of 1514; he recommended that "the arte of rhetorike" be taught "out of Quintilian in Latine, begynnyng at the thirde boke."[9] Elyot's adherence to Quintilian's opinion that Greek should be taught before Latin was seriously studied probably indicates that he had the *Institutio* before him, for most of the Humanistic writers on education thought Quintilian's procedure impracticable. It is impossible to determine how much else in the *Governor* comes directly from Quintilian; Humanistic treatises, in particular those by Erasmus and Patrizi, appear to have acted as intermediaries from which Elyot took Quintilian's ideas at second hand. The problem of tracing Quintilian's influence is further complicated by the similarity of his ideas to Plutarch's. Both, for instance, were concerned about the character of nurses and tutors, and both held an enlightened attitude toward punishment.[10]

Erasmus' *Institutio principis Christiani* is one of the treatises embodying Quintilian's ideas which Elyot knew, but his *De ratione studii* and *De pueris instituendis* are more important in this connection. In the *De ratione,* written at Cambridge and first printed at Paris in 1511, Erasmus admits that "it seems a mere impertinence in me to handle afresh a subject which has been made so conspicuously his own by the great Quintilian."[11] He follows the ancient writer most closely in

---

[8] See W. H. Woodward, *Studies in Education during the Age of the Renaissance* (Cambridge, England, 1906), pp. 8 ff., and R. R. Bolgar, *The Classical Heritage and Its Beneficiaries* (Cambridge, England, 1954), pp. 255–264, 338, 346, *et passim.*

[9] *The Boke named the Gouernour,* I, Chap. 11.

[10] On early education, see Quintilian, *Institutio oratoria,* I, Chaps. 1, 3; on qualifications and duties of masters, see II, Chap. 2.

[11] *De ratione studiis,* trans. W. H. Woodward in *Desiderius Erasmus concerning the Aim and Method of Education* (Cambridge, England, 1904), p. 166.

urging a conversational approach to the study of Latin and Greek, with the gradual introduction of syntax. He repeats these recommendations in his treatise *De pueris instituendis*, which was published in 1529 at Basel. In the *De pueris* Erasmus also sets out the duties of parents, particularly in selecting good nurses and masters. (It is perhaps a significant comment on the influence of Quintilian and Plutarch that the Humanists so often discuss the seemingly unimportant matter of wetnurses: Erasmus devotes an entire dialogue to it.[12]) Erasmus makes it clear that he would have the child "beguiled, not driven to learning." A chapter on the evil conditions of schools in Erasmus' time may have suggested Elyot's complaint about the decay of learning.[13] Erasmus' comments, however, are quite different from Elyot's; Erasmus complains primarily about corporal punishment and monastic schools, subjects which were joined in his own experience. There are other significant differences between the ideas of Erasmus and Elyot—Elyot was, for instance, nationalistic, while Erasmus was perhaps the greatest cosmopolitan of all time; Elyot was far more interested in physical training than was Erasmus.[14] And Erasmus' ideal was a *Christian* prince, whereas Elyot, because he idealized the ancients, never escaped a certain pagan element in his outlook.

Quintilian's ideas on education are also present in the works of Francesco Patrizi, one of which at least Elyot knew. Elyot's indebtedness to Patrizi requires examination more because recent studies of Elyot's sources have centered around Patrizi's writings than because of their intrinsic importance. H. H. S. Croft, the first writer to show interest in analyzing Elyot's sources, wrote that "it appears . . . as if the

---

[12] *Puerpera*, trans. N. Bailey as "The Lying-In Woman" in *The Colloquies of Erasmus* (London, 1878), I, 441–464.

[13] *De pueris instituendis*, trans. W. H. Woodward in *Desiderius Erasmus concerning the Aim and Method of Education*, p. 204.

[14] Born, *Education of a Christian Prince*, p. 184: "If Homer was right when he said that the prince, to whom so many thousand souls and so many burdensome tasks are entrusted, should not sleep through the whole night, . . . whence, I ask you, does the prince get the leisure time . . . to waste the greatest part of his life in playing at dice, in dancing, in hunting, in associating with utter fools, and in [other forms of] idle nonsense?" Cf. Helmuth Exner, *Der Einfluss des Erasmus auf die englische Bildungsidee* (Berlin, 1939), p. 119; on Erasmus' cosmopolitanism, see C. R. Thompson, "Erasmus as Internationalist and Cosmopolitan," *Archiv für Reformationsgeschichte*, XLVI (1955), 167–195.

author of *The Governour* had taken Patrizi's *De regno et regis institutione* for his model. . . . There is a very remarkable similarity in the plan of the respective works. . . . The identity of some particular passages is now . . . clearly established."[15] Croft printed at full length passages from Patrizi's book which closely paralleled parts of the *Governor*; he gave twenty such passages for Book I, twenty-one for Book II, and nineteen for Book III.[16] Many of them, however, are so short, and the resemblances so superficial, that the attempt to prove that Elyot was largely dependent upon Patrizi is unconvincing. And the resemblance in over-all plan is, as we shall see, not so close as Croft suggested.

That there is no close resemblance was noted by Josef Schlotter in a dissertation published in 1938. Schlotter took a position at the opposite extreme, though one more nearly correct than Croft's; he contradicted Croft's assertion that Patrizi's work had influenced the formal organization of the *Governor*, and he attributed all similarity of ideas to the fact that both Elyot and Patrizi were Platonists and Humanists.[17] The most thorough recent study of Elyot's sources, that written by Leslie C. Warren in 1937, avoids the extreme positions taken by both Croft and Schlotter.[18]

There is actually no question that Elyot was familiar with Patrizi's writings; the evidence supplied by some of Croft's parallel passages shows that clearly enough. Although Patrizi is now forgotten, his writings were popular in the sixteenth century, and it is not surprising that they came to Elyot's attention.[19] His first important work, a treatise on

[15] Croft, I, lxv.

[16] All passages from Book I appear in Croft's App. F, Vol. I, pp. 328–332. Those for Books II and III are scattered through the footnotes in Croft's second volume.

[17] Josef Schlotter, *Thomas Elyots "Governour" in seinem Verhältnis zu Francesco Patrizi* (Freiburg im Breisgau, 1938), p. 97.

[18] Leslie C. Warren, "Humanistic Doctrines of the Prince from Petrarch to Sir Thomas Elyot" (unpublished dissertation, University of Chicago, 1937). The section dealing with Patrizi appeared as "Patrizi's *De Regno et Regis Institutione* and the Plan of Elyot's *The Boke Named the Gouernour*," *Journal of English and Germanic Philology,* XLIX (1950), 67–77. Warren did not study all the sources of the *Governor* but limited his attention to the political treatises of Petrarch, Patrizi, Palmieri, and Pontano. Schlotter was concerned only with Patrizi.

[19] Patrizi, called Francesco Patrizi the Elder to distinguish him from the more

republican political theory, *De institutione rei publicae,* was completed in 1471 and dedicated to Sixtus IV. Its ideas would hardly have been attractive to Elyot; one chapter, for instance, bears the title *De aequalitate civium inter se.* Sir Thomas, who reiterated a hierarchical view of society, could scarcely have approved the equality of citizens.

Patrizi, however, knew how to sit on both sides of the fence, and his book on monarchies—*De regno et regis institutione*—proved far more popular than his study of the republic. The popularity of *De regno,* which was dedicated to Alfonso of Naples, is indeed amazing. The book was apparently not printed until 1518, in Paris, but in the next century it ran through at least six editions.[20] It was also translated into Italian, Spanish, and French.[21] Extracts from it and from the republican treatise were published in French under the title *Le livre de police humaine,*[22] and this in turn was translated into English by Richard Robinson as *A Moral Methode of Civile Policie* in 1576.

In spite of its popularity the treatise on kingdoms and the education of kings is not a work of any real significance. It is filled with quotations, and thus it served as a convenient source-book, but it contains little original thought. As the Humanist Vives complained, Patrizi "collected without exercising any wise choice and judgment."[23]

It is true that the arrangement of the *Governor* shows certain superficial similarities to the plan of *De regno.* Patrizi began his work with a defense of monarchy, proceeded to prescribe proper training for the king's mind and body, and concluded with a long discussion of virtues. The similarity does not extend to details, however: Elyot cast his work, for instance, in three books instead of Patrizi's nine, and Elyot's ar-

---

important younger philosopher of the same name, was born in Siena in 1413. After an education in law and the classics, he served his native city in various official capacities until 1457, when he was exiled. He was subsequently called to the Papal Curia by Pius II, the Humanistic pope, and from 1461 until his death in 1494 he was Bishop of Gaeta. He was also public orator to Ferdinand I, King of Naples.

[20] It was printed at Paris in 1518, 1519, 1567, 1582, and 1608, and at Strassburg in 1594.

[21] Italian: Venice, 1547, 1555, 1569; Spanish: Madrid, 1591; French: Paris, 1577.

[22] Comp. Gilles d'Aurigny and trans. Jehan le Blond, Paris, 1544, 1549, 1554.

[23] Foster Watson (ed.), *Vives: On Education* (Cambridge, England, 1913), p. 260.

rangement of individual topics seldom follows Patrizi's. If Elyot originally intended, as we have suggested, to write only about the education of gentlemen and later grafted on a statement of monarchical political theory, he may have calmed his fears about the book's lack of unity by noting that Patrizi had followed a roughly similar plan. It is unlikely that he consciously set out to imitate Patrizi's book. In any case Patrizi was more consistent than Elyot; he followed his praise of monarchy with a description of the education and virtues which a king—but not necessarily all members of the governing class—should possess. His tone throughout was strongly monarchical.

So far as ideas are concerned, Elyot owes nothing to Patrizi, since Patrizi can scarcely be credited with an original idea. It is possible that Patrizi's book served as an intermediary to bring Elyot some of the ideas of Plato and Quintilian as well as a number of quotations and historical examples. But in probably every instance Elyot knew the work Patrizi was following and would have consulted it directly had not the *De regno* served as a convenient source-book.

Sir Thomas accepted one of Patrizi's less common views in his chapter commending painting and sculpture; a number of Humanists were unwilling to have gentlemen study the fine arts, which they thought effeminate or degrading. Castiglione's *Courtier* is, however, obviously the direct source for Elyot's assertion that "it is commendable in a gentilman to paynte or karve exactly, if nature do therto induce him."[24] In the *Courtier*, Count Ludovico of Canossa maintains that "our Courtier ought in no wise" to omit "cunning in drawing, and the knowledge in the verie arte of painting." Even if

hee never get other profit or delite in it (beside it is a helpe to him to judge of the excellencie of Images both olde and new, of vessels, buildings, old coines, cameses, gravings, and such other matters) it maketh him also understand the beautie of lively bodies, and not onely in the sweetnesse of the Phisiognomie, but in the proportion of all the rest, as well in men as other living creatures.[25]

As for sculpture, another of Castiglione's characters argues that "carv-

[24] *Governor*, I, Chap. 8.
[25] Hoby, *The Courtier*, Everyman ed., pp. 77, 81 f.

ing is of more travaile, of more arte, and of more dignitie than painting."[26]

Elyot's comments on music are also much like Castiglione's. In the
Courtier, Gaspar Pallavicino objects that "musick . . . together with
many other vanities is meet for women, and peradventure for some
also that have the likenesse of men, but not for them that be men in
deede; who ought not with such delicacies to womanish their mindes."
But Count Ludovico supports music staunchly; he is ready to "enter in
a large sea of the praise of Musicke, and call to rehearsall how much
it hath alwaies beene renowmed among them of olde time, and counted
a holy matter."[27] Elyot repeats some of the allusions with which the
Count fortified his argument, and Elyot's comment that music "serveth
only for recreation" is reminiscent of Castiglione's caution against
professionalism: "That may bee saide to be a verie arte, that appeareth
not to be arte, neither ought a man to put more diligence in any thing
than in covering it: for in case it be open, it looseth credite cleane and
maketh a man litle set by."[28]

Elyot's comments on legal studies and his laments about the decay of
learning in England appear to be entirely original with him; this makes
even clearer what is already obvious—that these were matters about
which Elyot felt deeply from personal experience.[29] His chapters on
exercises and games contain material drawn from various sources,
though a number of the observations are Elyot's own. From Galen's
works Elyot took his account of the utility of exercise and of certain
strange exercises used by the ancients. His elaborate discussion of
dancing owes much to Lucian's *De saltatione* and something to Plato's

[26] *Ibid.*, p. 78.   [27] *Ibid.*, p. 75.   [28] *Ibid.*, p. 46.

[29] Possibly Elyot took a hint from Vives, the Spanish Humanist who was
tutor to Mary Tudor between 1523 and 1529. Vives's long treatise *De disciplinis*
contained *Septem libri de corruptis artibus*, of which the first cited *superbia,
invidia magistrorum, ambitio, avaricia,* and *pecuniae aviditas* as reasons for
the neglect of learning, while the last discussed the corruption of civil law
(*Ioannis Lodovici Vivis Valentini de disciplinis libri XX* [Antwerp, 1531],
fols. 4r–20r, 71v–76r). There is no detailed correspondence between Vives's
work and the *Governor,* however, and it is unlikely that Elyot could have seen
De disciplinis—which was published in July, 1531—before he had completed
the *Governor*. But Vives had been a member of More's circle, and it is possible
that at Chelsea Elyot discussed the decay of learning with him.

Laws, especially the passage in which Plato recommends that a committee regulate music and dancing with special regard to the differences between the sexes.[30] The third book of Patrizi's *De regno*, which praises riding, running, swimming, hunting, hawking, and ball-playing, may have suggested to Elyot that he should discuss the same forms of recreation, though his actual comments on them differ considerably from Patrizi's. Elyot's praise of shooting with the longbow, that peculiarly English exercise, is based upon nothing but English tradition and chroniclers.

THE LAST TWO BOOKS of the *Governor* are even more derivative than Book I. For Book II, Sir Thomas adapted a number of ideas which he found in the writings of Erasmus and Petrarch. He admitted that the seven things which a governor should premeditate were not devised in his own head; in fact all seven were suggested by Erasmus' *Institutio principis Christiani*. The first—that all honor proceeds from God alone —was one of Erasmus' underlying assumptions, and each of the other articles was specifically stated in the *Institutio*.[31] It was the examples with which Elyot buttressed his first and last points that were "gathered as well out of holy scripture as out of the warkes of other excellent writars," not, as he claimed, the points themselves.

A definition borrowed from the treatise *De principe* by Giovanni Pontano, a Humanist who was secretary to the king of Naples from 1486 until 1494, begins Elyot's discussion of majesty as a virtue for governors.[32] Elyot also repeats Pontano's view that majesty may be discerned in the eyes, the language, and the apparel of a nobleman.[33] Sir Thomas's recommendations about the governor's clothes agree with those of Castiglione, who wanted his courtier "to be handsome and cleanly in his apparel; to make his garments after the fashion of most, and those to be black, or of some darkish and sad colour, not garish."[34]

[30] *Laws*, VII, 10, 802*e*. See John M. Major, "The Moralization of the Dance in Elyot's *Governour*," *Studies in the Renaissance*, V (1958), 27–36.

[31] For the parallel passages, see Croft, II, 1–6.

[32] *Ioannis Ioviani Pontani Opera omnia soluta oratione composita* (Venice, 1518), I, fol. 94r.

[33] *Ibid.*, fols. 93r, 94r, 95r–v.

[34] *The Courtier*, edition in *The Tudor Translations*, XXIII (London, 1900), p. 369. Not in Everyman ed.

Petrarch, too, had urged rulers not to be over lavish in their dress or in furnishing their homes—a view expressed in his short treatise *De re-publica optime administranda*, written for Francesco di Carrara in 1373.[35]

Elyot's chapter on "very nobility" owes a great deal to the *Libro della vita civile* of Matteo Palmieri, a fifteenth-century Florentine Humanist; the stories about Numa Pompilius and the Decii have been translated almost word for word from Palmieri.[36] The idea that true nobility requires virtue as well as noble ancestry was held by most of the Humanists. Castiglione had hesitated to make noble birth a pre-requisite for his ideal courtier, and before he admitted its desirability he made Gaspar Pallavicino say that "seeing this noblenes is gotten neither with wit, force, nor art, but is rather a praise of our ancestors than our owne, me thinke it a strange opinion that the parents of our Courtier being unnoble, his good qualities should be defaced."[37] Sir Thomas More expressed a similar view in his translation, made in 1504, of a biography of Pico della Mirandola. He inserted in his ver-sion an original passage of some length showing that learning and virtue "be the thinges, whiche we may accompt for our owne: of which every man is more properly to be commended, then of the noblenes of his auncesters: whose honour maketh us not honorable. . . . The more worshipfull that our ancesters wer, the more vyle and shamefull be we, if we declyne from the steppes of theyr woorshipfull living."[38] Eras-mus agreed. "Teach the young prince," he wrote, "that nobility, stat-

---

[35] Petrarch, *Francisci Petrarchae Florentini Opera quae extant omnia* (Basel, 1554), pp. 419–534. Leslie C. Warren has suggested that Elyot modeled most of his second book on this treatise by Petrarch, but he overestimates its influence ("Humanistic Doctrines of the Prince," p. 117). Elyot does not actually follow Petrarch's form, and although he repeats most of Petrarch's ideas, several of which were commonplaces, he supports them with different examples. Certain parallels are close enough for us to be reasonably certain that Elyot knew Petrarch's work, but his debt to it is not great.

[36] Matteo Palmieri, *Libro della vita civile* (Florence, 1529), fols. 74v–76r. Croft failed to notice this parallel. His quotations from Patrizi do not succeed in proving that Elyot was indebted to the *De regno* for anything in Book II.

[37] Hoby, *The Courtier*, Everyman ed., p. 34.

[38] *The Workes of Sir Thomas More knyght . . . in the Englysh Tonge* (London, 1557), fol. a ir–v. For a study of More's additions and omissions in the biography, see S. E. Lehmberg, "Sir Thomas More's Life of Pico della Miran-dola," *Studies in the Renaissance*, III (1956), 62–74.

ues, wax masks, family trees, all the pomp of heralds, over which the great mass of people stupidly swell with pride, are only empty terms unless supported by deeds worth while."[39] Elyot was almost certainly familiar with all these works; his phrasing was not directly borrowed from any one of them.

Elyot's definition of affability as "a wonderfull efficacie or power in procuryng love" is similar to Petrarch's,[40] while his conviction that the prince must have the love of his subjects agrees with Erasmus' view.[41] On the whole, however, Sir Thomas's remarks on affability, placability, and mercy owe little to other Renaissance writers. His praise of placability was suggested, as he admitted, by Cicero's De officiis; his chapter on mercy incorporates some of Petrarch's ideas but expands them greatly.[42] Aristotle's Nicomachaean Ethics supplies much of Elyot's material on beneficence and liberality,[43] and the Governor also borrows Petrarch's statement that princes should be liberal in building temples, walls, and roads.[44] Elyot's comment that it is not true liberality to give to all men "if it be nat for a good end or purpose" no doubt stems from Erasmus' caution that the prince's liberality should not be promiscuous: "There are some who heartlessly extort from the good citizen what they squander on fools, court informers, and panderers. . . . Let merit, not fancy, be the basis of reward."[45]

Cicero's De officiis and De amicitia gave Elyot the basis of his "true description of amitie," and the tale of Titus and Gisippus with which he illustrated true friendship was, as we have seen, translated out of the Decameron. Petrarch was probably Elyot's immediate source for the common opinion that nothing is less becoming to a man or a prince than ingratitude.[46] In his final chapter, on flatterers, Elyot follows a chapter of Erasmus' Institutio very closely; three paragraphs are nearly literal translations. Erasmus stated emphatically that "every means

---

[39] Born, Education of a Christian Prince, pp. 148 f.; see also pp. 151 and 226.
[40] Petrarch, op. cit., p. 428.
[41] Born, Education of a Christian Prince, pp. 206–210.
[42] Petrarch, op. cit., pp. 242 (on mercy) and 428 f. (on cruelty and avarice).
[43] See Croft, II, 112, 118.
[44] Petrarch, op. cit., p. 425.
[45] Born, Education of a Christian Prince, p. 218.
[46] Petrarch, op. cit., p. 430.

[must be] used to stave off abject flatterers," and he was even willing to invoke the death penalty should the crime call for it.[47] Erasmus acknowledged his indebtedness to Plutarch's essay *Quomodo possit adulator ab amico internosci,* a work which Erasmus himself turned into Latin and which Elyot probably knew. Elyot may also have had in mind Castiglione's warning that friends may "become flatterers, and to make a hand [profit] by that straight familiaritie, they speake and work alwaies to please, and for the most part open the way with lyes, which in the Princes minde engender ignorance, not of outwarde matters onely, but also of his owne selfe."[48]

THE THIRD BOOK of the *Governor,* in its treatment of the four cardinal virtues, obviously rests upon a medieval commonplace derived ultimately from Plato's *Republic.* This accounts, however, for only the general outline. Much of Elyot's material comes directly from the manual *De officiis* which Cicero wrote in his old age for his son's instruction. Sir Thomas also borrows heavily from treatises by Pontano and Patrizi.

Elyot was not the first Humanist to utilize "Tullyes offyces." It was exceedingly popular during the fifteenth and sixteenth centuries and was, indeed, probably the first classical work to be printed—in 1465 editions were issued both at Subiaco, by Sweynheim and Pannartz, and at Mainz by Fust and Schöffer. Erasmus had published some notes on *De officiis* in 1501, while he was closely associated with More.[49] The first English translation was made by Robert Whittinton of Magdalen School, Oxford, and was printed three years after Elyot's *Governor.*

The first of Cicero's three books was devoted to a discussion of the cardinal virtues. It was not, however, the only work which suggested the form to Elyot, for Patrizi's *De regno* treated the four virtues, though in a less orderly manner, and Castiglione discussed them in the last book of the *Courtier.*

Elyot's chapters on justice owe most to Cicero, though they include

[47] Born, *Education of a Christian Prince,* p. 193.
[48] Hoby, *The Courtier,* Everyman ed., p. 262.
[49] See C. R. Thompson, *The Translations of Lucian by Erasmus and St. Thomas More* (Ithaca, N.Y., 1940), p. 11.

a distinction between distributive and commutative justice taken from Aristotle's *Politics* and *Ethics*.[50] Elyot's specific assertions that "fraude and deceyte . . . be agayne justyce," that "justice ought to be betwene ennemyes," and that justice includes good faith and the keeping of promises[51] are, as we have already suggested, of considerable interest. The ideas can all be traced to Cicero, who wrote that "the foundation of justice . . . is good faith—that is, truth and fidelity to promises and agreements."[52] Justice must operate even between enemies: "If under stress of circumstances individuals have made any promise to the enemy," Cicero wrote, "they are bound to keep their word even then."[53] Good faith is necessary if contracts, the very foundation of corporate life, are to be honored. "Away, then, with sharp practice and trickery, which desires, of course, to pass for wisdom, but is far from it and totally unlike it. . . . No greater curse in life can be found than the knavery that wears the mask of wisdom."[54] Cicero's entire third book treats the conflict between the right and the expedient, which is no more than a larger view of the conflict between justice and fraud.

A more important matter than Elyot's dependence upon Cicero is involved here, however. When the Elizabethans thought of fraud, deceit, bad faith, and failure to keep promises, they thought of Machiavelli. Were Elyot's assertions really an early reaction against the wiles of "Old Nick"?

Unfortunately no evidence which might enable us to determine whether Elyot was consciously attacking the *Prince* survives, if indeed it ever existed. It would be helpful to know whether Thomas Cromwell possessed a copy of the *Prince* before 1531, for if he did, Elyot might well have seen it. And there is some evidence that Cromwell knew the *Prince* then; it comes from Cardinal Pole's *Apologia ad Carolum Quintum*.[55] Here Pole described an interview with Cromwell which had taken place in 1527 at Wolsey's house in Westminster. Cromwell had asked what the duty of a councilor to his prince was; Pole replied that he should consider the prince's honor above all. Crom-

---

[50] See *Nicomachaean Ethics*, V, 2 (5).

[51] *Governor*, III, Chaps. 4–7.

[52] *De officiis*, I, vii.

[53] *Ibid.*, xiii. [54] *Ibid.*, III, xvii.

[55] In *Epistolarum Reginaldi Poli . . . Pars I*, ed. A. M. Cardinal Quirinus (Brescia, 1744), pp. 133–137.

well scoffed. Such a statement, he said, might be applauded in the universities, but the thing which mattered to a practical statesman was the inclination of his sovereign. He advised Pole to leave his studies (he had just returned from Padua) and to learn something of the actual art of government. If he would do this, Cromwell would send him the work of a modern writer, *ingeniosissimi et acutissimi,* who "did not pursue a dream like that about which Plato wrote his *Republic.*"[56] Cromwell did not send the book, and Pole thought that he later regretted the promise; but Pole found out that the work was the *Prince.*

The reliability of Pole's testimony has been questioned, and rightly. Certainly Pole disliked Cromwell, and since he wrote ten years after the interview we may doubt the accuracy of his memory even if, as his latest biographer asserts, we cannot question his honesty.[57] It has been suggested that Pole identified the book incorrectly and that Cromwell had really referred to the *Courtier,*[58] but since Castiglione's courtier is as much an unrealizable ideal as Plato's state, arguments for this identification are unconvincing. Even if Pole had hoped to discredit Cromwell, he had no reason to distort his account of the interview, for there would have been nothing strange or damaging in Cromwell's knowing Machiavelli, who became a stock villain of the Elizabethan stage only after the translation of Gentillet's *Contre-Machiavel* by Patericke in 1557.[59] Certainly Machiavelli had not assumed the role of anti-Christ by 1537, when Lord Moreley wrote to Cromwell that the *Prince* was

[56] *Ibid.,* p. 135. Original in Latin.

[57] Wilhelm Schenk, *Reginald Pole, Cardinal of England* (London, 1950), p. viii. Schenk accepts Pole's account of the interview (pp. 37 ff.).

[58] Paul van Dyke, "Reginald Pole and Thomas Cromwell," *American Historical Review,* IX (1904), 696–724. Reprinted as an appendix to van Dyke, *Renascence Portraits* (London, 1906), pp. 377–418. Miss Hogrefe's article, cited in note 4 above, accepts van Dyke's view, as does L. A. Weissberger ("Machiavelli and Tudor England," *Political Science Quarterly,* XLII [1927], 589–607). But R. B. Merriman (*Life and Letters of Thomas Cromwell* [Oxford, 1902], I, 85) thinks that Pole's statement is valid. So do Franklin le Van Baumer (*The Early Tudor Theory of Kingship,* pp. 168–170) and Pierre Janelle (*L'Angleterre catholique à la veille du schisme*). W. Gordon Zeeveld (*Foundations of Tudor Policy*) says that Cromwell knew the *Prince* and shows that his propagandist Richard Morison, another Humanist, was acquainted with it by 1536 (pp. 184–189).

[59] Cf. Weissberger, *loc. cit.,* and Mario Praz, "Machiavelli and the Elizabethans," *Proceedings* of the British Academy, XIV (1928), 49–97.

"surely a very speciall good thing for youre Lordschip, whiche are so ny abought oure Soveraigne Lorde in Counsell."[60]

Cromwell could not have had a printed copy of the *Prince* at the time of the interview, for the book was not published until 1532. Nor could he have brought a manuscript home when he returned from Italy in 1512, since Machiavelli did not finish writing until 1513. But it is known that the work gained popularity rapidly and that numerous manuscripts of it did circulate, and we cannot rule out the possibility that Cromwell obtained a manuscript copy.[61] The *Prince* was not translated into English until 1636, but since both Cromwell and Elyot knew Italian this would have raised no obstacle.

If we accept the hypothesis that Cromwell and Elyot were both familiar with the *Prince*, we must still account for the fact that Cromwell has usually been credited with accepting its views, whereas Elyot, who was under Cromwell's patronage and in no position to disagree with him in print, opposed many of its ideas.[62] Perhaps the answer is that Cromwell did not actually agree that a ruler is justified in playing the fox, even if he did think that Machiavelli's more realistic approach to government might be a valuable corrective to the idealistic dreams of philosophers. Perhaps, that is, Pole was correct in attributing to Cromwell knowledge of the *Prince*, but was biased in his interpretation of Cromwell's beliefs. All of this is speculation, but it is interesting speculation.

We are on firmer ground in discussing Elyot's chapters on fortitude, which clearly are based ultimately upon Aristotle's *Ethics* and directly upon Giovanni Pontano's treatise *De fortitudine*.[63] Elyot's definition of fortitude as a "mediocritie or meane" between timidity and audacity merely translates Pontano's chapter heading *Fortem iure medium*

[60] Ellis, *Original Letters*, 3d ser., III, 66 f. Ellis's date is 1537, but the year is uncertain and may be as late as 1539. For our purpose this is insignificant. Van Dyke (*Renascence Portraits*, pp. 413 f.) thinks this letter shows that Cromwell had not seen the *Prince* until Moreley sent it to him; but it is unlikely that Moreley would have known just what books Cromwell had already read.

[61] Cf. Garrett Mattingly, "Machiavelli's *Prince*: Political Science or Political Satire?" *American Scholar*, XXVII (1958), 482–491.

[62] See G. R. Elton, "The Political Creed of Thomas Cromwell," *Transactions* of the Royal Historical Society, 5th ser., Vol. 6, 69–92.

[63] Pontano, I, fols. 49r–86r.

tenere inter timidum et audacem.[64] Elyot adopts Pontano's definitions of timorousness and audacity,[65] and he agrees with Pontano's chapter heading, *Qui nihil temeant, eos aut insanos, aut torpidos esse.*[66] Both writers cite earthquakes as things properly to be feared—Pontano tells of a recent Italian disaster[67]—and both writers commend the fortitude of Horatius Cocles.[68] Elyot agrees with Pontano that the desire to win honor can be a spur to fortitude.[69]

Sir Thomas's discussion of patience is based upon the second book of *De fortitudine,* in which Pontano shows how fortitude means controlling the "affects" or passions and calmly accepting such misfortunes as poverty, servitude, blindness, or exile. Chapter 12 of the third book of the *Governor* is no more than a free translation of Pontano's *De tolerandis iniuriis et contumeliis;*[70] the idea is the same, and it is supported by the same historical examples. When Elyot writes of "patience deserved in repulse" he is following Pontano, *De toleranda repulsa,*[71] and he acknowledges his indebtedness by writing, "I omitte at this tyme to write any more this vertue Pacience, sens to the institution of a governor this semeth to be sufficient, to the residue he shall be better persuaded by the warkes of Plutarch, Seneca, and Pontane."[72]

Elyot regarded magnanimity as a "companyon of fortitude." He took his definition of magnanimity as "doynge all thynge that is vertuous for the achievynge of honour" from Pontano's treatise *De magnanimitate,*[73] but with it his indebtedness to Pontano ended. From Aristotle's *Ethics* he added a "more large description of the sayd vertue,"[74] and then he turned again to "the offices of Tully." After commending indifference to outward fortunes and freedom from inward passions, as Cicero had done,[75] Elyot repeated Cicero's warnings

---

[64] *Ibid.,* fol. 59ʳ.   [65] *Ibid.,* fols. 60ʳ, 62ʳ.
[66] *Ibid.,* fol. 59ʳ.   [67] *Ibid.,* fol. 56ʳ.
[68] Pontano tells of Cocles' exploits at length.—*Ibid.,* fol. 71ʳ⁻ᵛ.
[69] *Ibid.,* fol. 69ʳ, *De fortitudine civili, et iis, qui ob honorem pugnent.*
[70] *Ibid.,* fols. 84ᵛ–85ᵛ.   [71] *Ibid.,* fols. 75ᵛ–76ʳ.
[72] *Governor,* III, Chap. 13. Erasmus and Pontano are the only contemporaries whose works Elyot recommends. L. C. Warren ("Humanistic Doctrines of the Prince," p. 121) surprisingly says that "Elyot is nowhere specifically indebted" to Pontano; apparently he examined only Pontano's *De principe.*
[73] Pontano, I, fol. 233ʳ.
[74] *Nicomachaean Ethics,* IV, 3 (7).   [75] *De officiis,* I, xx.

against obstinacy or self-will[76] and against undue ambition,[77] both of which may accompany courage or fortitude. Elyot translated from Patrizi a sentence condemning "Sylla, Marius, Carbo, Cinna, Pompei, and Caesar, by those ambicion mo Romaynes were slayne than in acquiringe the empyre of all the worlde."[78]

Having turned to Patrizi, Elyot proceeded to follow his general form for six chapters—those dealing with temperance and the accompanying virtues of abstinence, continence, and moderation. He omitted Patrizi's treatment of the "conturbations" or passions,[79] though he later discussed these in his *Castel of Helth*, but he included the ideas from Patrizi's chapters *De abstinentia et continentia*,[80] *De temperantia et eius partibus*,[81] *De moderatione*,[82] *De sobrietate*,[83] *De constantia*,[84] and *De stabilitate*.[85] To Patrizi's sentiments he added ideas taken from Cicero's *Offices*, Aristotle's *Ethics*, and Plato's *Republic*. He cited Plotinus also, but in so doing he merely repeated an error of Patrizi's, for the definition of temperance in question does not actually derive from Plotinus.[86] Elyot was not bound by the classical examples in Patrizi but ranged widely for illustrative material.

Sir Thomas's definition of sapience is borrowed from Cicero[87] and supported by a number of Biblical stories. Aristotle's psychology is the ultimate source of Elyot's ideas about understanding, but some close verbal echoes suggest, as Croft has noted, that Elyot was working from Brunetto Latini's *Livre du Trésor* instead of using the *De anima* directly.[88] Although his own governmental service lies behind Elyot's comments on "the experience or practice necessary in the person of a governour of a publike weale," his statement that governors should "personally resorte [to] and peruse all partes of the countrayes under their governaunce" is much like one in Erasmus' *Education of a Christian Prince:*

[76] *Ibid.*, xix.   [77] *Ibid.*, xxv.
[78] *De regno et regis institutione*, IV, Chap. 20.
[79] *Ibid.*, Bk. V.   [80] *Ibid.*, VI, Chap. 21.
[81] *Ibid.*, Chap. 18.   [82] *Ibid.*, Chap. 24.
[83] *Ibid.*, Chap. 26.   [84] *Ibid.*, VII, Chap. 11.
[85] *Ibid.*, Chap. 14.
[86] See Croft, II, 326.
[87] *Tusculanae Disputationes*, IV, 26.
[88] Croft, II, 371, 374, 376.

It seems that the prince should first know his own kingdom. This knowledge is best gained from geography and history and from frequent visits through his provinces and cities. Let him first be eager to learn the location of his districts and cities, with their beginnings, their nature, institutions, customs, laws, annals, and privileges. No one can heal the body until he is thoroughly coversant with it.[89]

Elyot's chapter lamenting the prevalence of that "vice very ugly and monstruouse," detraction or calumny, is illustrated by an account of Apelles's "ymage of detraction" drawn from Lucian's *De calumnia*. Several painters of the Renaissance also seized upon Lucian's description; it is the basis of an allegorical painting of the calumny of Apelles by Botticelli in Uffizi Gallery and another at Hampton Court, attributed (probably incorrectly) to Federigo Zuccaro.

The *Governor* closes, as it began, on a more original note. Elyot's chapters on counsel and consultation are very largely products of his own experience and reflection. The idea that the ruler must be surrounded by capable advisers was, of course, a commonplace, and Castiglione had included it in the *Courtier*. The *Boke named the Gouernour*, however, is not directly dependent on any single discussion of the problem of counsel.

To sum up, our analysis of the sources for the *Governor* reveals that Elyot drew most of his ideas from Plato and Aristotle, from Quintilian, Plutarch, and Cicero among the ancients, and from Petrarch, Erasmus, Castiglione, Pontano, and Patrizi among the writers of the Renaissance. More space in the *Governor* is actually given, however, to the historical tales which illustrate Elyot's points and "recreate the reders" than to the ideas themselves. Plutarch's *Lives* was by far the most important source for these examples, though Sir Thomas frequently utilized Biblical stories and borrowed also from Pliny, Xenophon, Tacitus, Suetonius, and Valerius Maximus. One gets the feeling, indeed, that Elyot's primary aim in Books II and III was to recount as many episodes from ancient history as possible; his definitions of virtues supply only a unifying framework, and a not very satisfactory one at that. Elyot succeeded mainly in retailing to his fellow Englishmen popular versions of ancient and Renaissance philosophy and history.

[89] Born, *Education of a Christian Prince*, p. 205.

THERE ARE two other matters toward which we should direct a fleeting glance before we leave the *Governor*. One is Elyot's use of the English language. Sir Thomas consciously set out to enrich his native tongue; he wrote in 1533 that Henry VIII had benignly received the *Governor* and

in the redynge therof sone perceyved that I intended to augment our Englyshe tongue, wherby men shulde as well expresse most abundantly the thynge that they conceyve in theyr hartis (wherfore language was ordeyned) havynge wordes apte for the purpose: as also interprete out of Greke, Latyn, or any other tonge into Englysche, as sufficiently, as out of any one of the said tongues into an other.[90]

Some Englishmen objected to Elyot's use of "inkhorn" terms. Roger Ascham, who did a good deal to enrich the language in his own way, was probably referring to Elyot when he wrote:

Many Englishe writers, . . . usinge straunge wordes, as Lattine, Frenche, and Italian, do make all thinges darke and harde. Ones I communed with a man which reasoned the Englishe tongue to be enriched and encreased thereby, sayinge: Who will not prayse that feast, where a man shall drincke at dinner both wyne, ale and beere? Truly (quoth I) they be al good, every one taken by himselfe alone, but if you put Malmesye and sache, redde wyne and white, ale and beere, and al in one pot, you shall make a drinke neither easye to be knowen, nor yet holesome for the bodye.[91]

Elyot tried to keep his writing from being "darke and harde" by explaining each new word he used. For example, he wrote:

But nowe I remember me, this worde Magnanimitie beinge yet straunge, as late borowed out of the Latyne, shall nat content all men, and specially them whome nothing contenteth out of their accustomed Mumpsimus, I will adventure to put for Magnanimitie a worde more familiar, callynge it good courage, which, havynge respecte to the sayd definition, shall nat seme moche inconvenient.[92]

[90] "Proheme" to *Of the Knowledeg which Maketh a Wise man* (London, 1533), fol. A iii[r].
[91] Roger Ascham, *Toxophilus* (London, 1571), fol. * ii[v].
[92] *Governor*, III, Chap. 14.

Sir Thomas's writing lacks the wit characteristic of the best of More's work, but his style is less cumbersome than his mentor's. Although Elyot's style is sometimes monotonous, its clarity and precision is an achievement of considerable importance in the history of English prose.[93] Details of his own style, however, are less significant than his insistence that even the most abstruse concepts can be expressed in English. It is easy to forget that More wrote his *Utopia*, published only fifteen years before the *Governor*, in Latin.

Finally, a word on the influence of the *Governor*. Elyot's borrowings from other writers make this a complex subject: did later writers follow Elyot directly, or did they merely use the same sources? Some close verbal echoes make it virtually certain that Shakespeare was familiar with the *Governor*.[94] In particular Shakespeare borrowed Elyot's views on degree and order; in *Henry V* he gives Exeter and the Archbishop of Canterbury these lines:

> For government, though high, and low, and lower,
> Put into parts, doth keep in one consent,
> Congreeing in a full and natural close,
> Like music.
>   Therefore doth heaven divide
> The state of man in divers functions,
> Setting endeavour in continual motion;
> To which is fixed, as an aim or butt,
> Obedience: for so work the honey-bees,
> Creatures that by a rule in nature teach
> The act of order to a peopled kingdom.[95]

[93] On Elyot's style, see James Wortham, "Sir Thomas Elyot and the Translation of Prose," *Huntington Library Quarterly*, XI (1948), 219–240; Alfred Aigner, "Sir Thomas Elyot," in Henry Craik, *English Prose Selections* (London, 1893), I, 191 ff.; Cornelie Benndorf, *Die englische Pädagogik im 16. Jahrhundert*... (Vienna and Leipzig, 1905), pp. 75 ff.

[94] See Emil Grether, *Das Verhältnis von Shakespeares "Heinrich V." zu Sir Thomas Elyots "Gouernour"* (Marburg, 1938). Grether overstates his case; some of his parallel passages are worthless, but a few are very convincing. See also D. T. Starnes, "Shakespeare and Elyot's *Gouernour*," *University of Texas Studies in English*, VII (1927), 112–135, and J. E. Phillips, Jr., *The State in Shakespeare's Greek and Roman Plays* (New York, 1940), *passim*.

[95] *Henry V*, I, ii, 180–189.

Ulysses' speech on order and degree in *Troilus and Cressida* also follows the *Governor* closely in suggesting that "chaos, when degree is suffocate, follows the choking."[96]

The courtesy books so popular in Elizabethan and Jacobean England also owe a good deal to the *Governor*, since it was the first English work in their genre. It would be a difficult and fruitless study to see which of these books borrow directly from the *Governor*; most writers, however, repeat a large number of Elyot's ideas. Many of the Elizabethan and Jacobean writers on education, political theory, and courtly virtue must have fortified themselves by reading *The Boke named the Gouernour*, whether they borrowed its contents directly or not.[97]

Henry VIII, if we can believe Elyot, read the *Governor* and was pleased with it. Sir Thomas Elyot's attempt to curry royal favor succeeded so well that he was sent as Henry's ambassador to the Emperor Charles V in the autumn of 1531. The events of his embassy must now claim our attention.

[96] *Troilus and Cressida*, I, iii, 84–125.

[97] See Ruth Kelso, *The Doctrine of the English Gentleman in the Sixteenth Century* (Urbana, Ill., 1929); D. T. Starnes, "Notes on Elyot's *The Governour*," *Review of English Studies*, III (1917), 37–46; and Starnes, "Elyot's *Governour* and Peacham's *Compleat Gentleman*," *Modern Language Review*, XXII (1927), 319–322. The *Governor* was one of the books which the tutors of James I bought for him to study (D. Harris Willson, *King James VI and I* [London, 1955], p. 22), and it provided the basis for Cheke's training of Edward VI.

CHAPTER SIX

In What Opinion the Emperour Ys

I N THE SUMMER of 1531 the Emperor Charles V, ruler of the Holy Roman Empire, decided to call a solemn chapter of the Order of the Golden Fleece. It was to be the first meeting in thirteen years of the chivalric society founded by Philip the Good in 1429, for although sessions had taken place with fair regularity during Charles's youth at the Burgundian court, Charles had neglected the order in his maturity. Twenty knights had died since the Chapter of Barcelona in 1518, and it was essential to hold new elections. In July, 1531, therefore, Charles wrote asking Henry VIII to attend the proposed chapter and to suggest names of men worthy to be knighted.[1]

Eustace Chapuys, Charles's ambassador to Henry, wrote on September 4 that Henry would dispatch a new ambassador to the imperial court within ten days; the envoy would know the King's mind concerning the Order and would bring any necessary papers.[2] By September 10, Chapuys had heard that the English ambassador was to be "May-

---

[1] Karl Brandi, *The Emperor Charles V*, trans. C. V. Wedgwood (London, 1939), pp. 28 f., 320 f.; *Cal. S.P. Span.*, IV, ii, 777.
[2] *Cal. S.P. Span.*, IV, ii, 786.

stre Vullyot," whom he described as a man of 700 or 800 ducats of rent a year, once under Cardinal Wolsey's patronage.[3] Chapuys thought that Elyot had become a follower of "la dame," Anne Boleyn, but as we shall see, he was mistaken in this.

Elyot himself learned of his appointment some days earlier than Chapuys, for, recognizing the dangers of the journey, he had drawn a will[4] on August 29. It provided, among other things, that every servant who "goethe with me over the seae and abidethe have thirtene shillinges foure pence besides his wages."

The King's instructions to Elyot were written October 7. Strangely, they do not even mention the meeting of the Order of the Golden Fleece, though Elyot doubtless received supplementary oral instructions about it. Actually Henry was far too preoccupied with his "great matter"—his desired divorce from Catherine of Aragon—to bother much about Charles's chivalric society. The written instructions make it evident that Elyot was sent primarily to "fish out and know in what opinion the Emperour ys of us, and whether, dispairing of our old freindship towards him, or fearing other neewe communication with France, he seeketh wayes and meanes that might be to our detriment or noe."[5]

Well might Henry worry. It had been more than two years since Cardinal Campeggio, the papal legate, had dashed Henry's hopes by adjourning the trial of the divorce at Blackfriars, and it should have been abundantly clear that Clement VII did not intend to keep his promise, made to Wolsey in 1528, not to revoke the case to Rome. Nor could the Medici Pope have kept his word. Charles V was master of the continent after his defeat of the French at Landriano and the treaties of Barcelona (with the Pope) and of Cambrai (with France). And Charles was importuning Clement to reach a speedy decision in Catherine's favor; he told a papal legate in July, 1531, that judgment could no longer be delayed without great injury to his aunt, adding that the question could be decided nowhere but at Rome.[6]

[3] *Ibid.*, 788.
[4] P.C.C., MS. 14 Alen, printed for the first time in Appendix II below.
[5] Cotton MS. Vitellius B. XXI, fol. 60, B.M.
[6] *Cal. S.P. Span.*, IV, ii, 768.

Henry's reiteration that the case could not be tried in the Eternal City had by 1531 become tiresome and futile. As early as October 7, 1530, he had been urging Girolamo Ghinucci, one of his ambassadors to Charles, to remonstrate against revocation of the case to Rome.[7] On December 6 he wrote to William Bennet and Sir Edward Carne, who were in Italy, objecting to a trial there.[8] In February, Henry, who was threatening an appeal to a General Council, was declared Supreme Head of the Church, "so far as the law of Christ allows," by the tacit assent of Convocation. This had no tangible effect except to exacerbate his already strained relations with Charles and Clement, and diplomatic correspondence continued to follow the same wearisome line. On April 23, Henry was writing to Bennet of the great dissatisfaction in England which would accompany revocation to Rome;[9] on July 10 he again instructed Bennet to emphasize the injustice of a trial there;[10] on October 2 he threatened to recall his ambassadors to Clement and Charles if they persisted in giving sentence.[11]

It is into this pattern of sterile diplomacy that Elyot's embassy fits. His instructions contain nothing new. Sir Thomas was to remind Charles of the

words the Emperor hath heretofore spoken, concerning our great cause betweene us and the Q., how he would not medle otherwise then according to justice, and with that considering how litle cause he hath to do us wronge, or to be author or favorer of any injustice to be done to us, we having alwaies deserved favour, pleasure, and kindnes.

Henry hoped—he must have known better—that reports of Charles's hostility to his cause were false. "On our parte," he wrote, "we be induced to beleeve rather that the said Emperor is wrongfully reported by the Pope, and that they would for the extencion of their authority use the said Emperor for a visage then otherwise." Alternatively, but hardly more realistically, the King could "doubt not, if he hath so encouraged the Pope upon ignorance to do us wronge, he will himself reforme it."

The old fruitless line was still to be followed. Henry continued:

[7] *State Papers, Domestic, of the Reign of Henry VIII*, VII, 261.
[8] *Ibid.*, 269.   [9] *Ibid.*, 297.   [10] *Ibid.*, 305.   [11] *Ibid.*, 321.

And if the Emperor, desirous to have the matter more opened, shall aske what the Pope doth wherein we thinke our self wronged, ye may saye, in calling and citing us to Rome, there to appere by us or our Proctor, which is contrary to all lawes, as all lawyers affirme, and especially them in France, as friends indifferent, and answering only for the testificacion of the truth, against whome can be alleadged no cause of affection which should move them to swarve from the truth.

And if the Emperor shall reply to know what the universities affirme, and what the Chancellor and other the Presidents of the Court of Parliament of Paris doe saye, ye may answere how they saye, that we may not be cited to Rome, there to appere by us or our Proctor, and that such a citacion is not only nought, and all their process there upon following, but also manifest injurie and wronge, which [we] trust, ye may saye, themperor of his honnor will not maineteyn.

If Charles "shall say that he is not learned and understandeth not these matters," Elyot is to point out that for this reason Charles may be the more easily deceived. But the matter does not require "anie learning," and Charles needs only to follow the lead of all learned men in supporting Henry. Therefore if Charles, "intendinge only justice, . . . hath ben in this point moved to advaunce injustice, we doubt not but like a Prince of honnor he will reform himself, and rather desiste from doinge or procuringe his frend wronge, then to proceed any furder in the same." When Elyot has stated the King's case he is to ask for the Emperor's answer, to note it "to the particularities," and to report it to Henry.[12]

WE DO NOT KNOW when Elyot left for the Netherlands—probably not until October—or what messages he may have carried concerning the Order of the Golden Fleece. He was, however, in Tournai for the Emperor's festivities. None of his letters from Tournai survive, but Stephen Vaughan, the English financial agent in the Netherlands, described part of the celebration in a letter to Cromwell. The solemnities began on November 2 and lasted for three days. Vaughan saw

themperour solemply ryde from thabbey of Saynt Peter, wherin he lay, to the great churche of the towne, accompanyed with xv other of his lordes clothed in theyr long robes of [the] Order. . . . Theyr garmenttes the first

[12] Cotton MS. Vitellius B. XXI, fol. 60, B.M.

and second daye wer crymsyn velwet embrodered withe thredes of golde with themperour's recygnysance, and a hode of the same put upon theyr hedes, of the veray fasshon of the hoodes used to be worn in London by the craftes there. The thyrde day [they] ware robes and hoodes of black clothe.[13]

Commercial affairs called Vaughan back to Antwerp, so he missed the jousts in the market place. But he had seen in Tournai "one that will not fayle tadvertise you"; he must have meant Elyot.

Charles used membership in the Order as a means of strengthening friendships and alliances. Vaughan reported that one of the new knights was Henry of Nassau's son, René, Prince of Orange. He did not know who the others were.[14]

Vaughan wrote that he was sending Cromwell a letter which "Maister Ellyot the Kinges ambassadour this daye sent me . . . from Turney," and added:

As I thynke, he desireth you to be a sollycitour to the Kinges Majestie, and to his honourable Counsayle, to hym, that he maye from tyme to tyme have answer of his lettres, and be made therby more able to do the Kyng honor in these parties. It is not well done that he shulde be so long without lettres, considering his litle experyence [in] these parties, who in short tyme, in myn opinion, wolde do ryght well, [if he] wer a letle holpen.

Lack of adequate instructions was a difficulty which plagued Vaughan himself throughout his years as Henry's agent.

Some of Vaughan's general comments on the diplomatic situation must serve in place of Elyot's, which do not survive. Vaughan observed that "the Emperour entreateth us very favourably, and useth the Kynges affairs as farre as I perceyve with muche honour, reverence, and benignyte." He thought that Charles's councilors were men "of

[13] Vaughan to Cromwell, December 9, 1531, Cotton MS. Galba B. X, fols. 23–25, B.M. The edge of the MS. is charred; I have placed doubtful words in brackets. Vaughan himself later played a role comparable to Elyot's in English diplomacy; he was sent to Paris and Lyons in December, 1532, to survey French opinion and try to ensure Francis' support for Henry's proceedings.—See W. C. Richardson, *Stephen Vaughan, Financial Agent of Henry VIII* (Baton Rouge, 1953), *passim.*

[14] Actually they included the Kings of Scotland and Portugal, the Elector of Brandenburg, the Elector Palatine, the Dukes of Jülich and Saxony, and Prince Philip of Spain. Philip was only three years old.

great wisdome and experyence" who would "in no wise . . . breake withe the Kyng, ne purchase his displeasure ageinst theyr prince." Such reports were soothing but did not get to the heart of the matter; they were probably one factor contributing to Henry's unrealistic appraisal of the diplomatic situation.

Commercial difficulties played their part in the war of nerves between Charles and Henry. Vaughan wrote to Cromwell on December 30 that he had heard rumors of an embargo on the sale of English cloths in the Netherlands.[15] He had reported this to Elyot at Brussels, where the Emperor was holding court, but Elyot "neither knew ne harde of any suche thing." Even on his return to Antwerp, the commercial capital, Vaughan was unable to obtain definite information, but "the fame of the saide banyshement of clothes was commen and in the mowthe of every man." He hinted, no doubt correctly, that the embargo, whether merely threatened or actually operative, was Charles's way of trying to force Henry's hand on the divorce issue:

That it shuld be done by the Emperour's commaundement, how be it I know it not for truthe, ne for truth wold I that you shulde report it; but hereof yow maye advertise the Kynges Magestye, that it rather semythe to be true than otherwise. . . . [I] do intende . . . to knowe the truthe, and therof tadvertise you in all possible haste, for it is a matter that . . . tuchethe thentercourse made bytwene the Kynges Majestie and themperour, and soundeth to the breche therof, whiche may grow to some great inconvenyence.

The prohibition seems never to have been fully effective, though trade was certainly disturbed. Restrictions were feared in London; on January 11, 1532, Chapuys wrote to Charles of the distress of a group of London merchants who had just visited him. They spoke piteously, he said, with tears in their eyes; they blamed the divorce for threats of an embargo, which would be the worst thing that could happen to English trade.[16] No record of Elyot's role in the negotiations survives.

For some reason Henry soon became dissatisfied with Elyot's services. As early as January 22, Chapuys was writing to Charles that a new ambassador would be sent to him within a few days. It was to be

[15] Cotton MS. Galba B. X, fol. 26, B.M.
[16] *L.P.*, V, 707.

Thomas Cranmer, who already knew something of the ways of Emperor and Pope: he had been in the retinue of the Earl of Wiltshire that reached Bologna in March, 1530, just after Charles's coronation. Cranmer, though still under Wiltshire's patronage, had won the King's favor by supporting the divorce. Chapuys guessed, correctly, that while he was abroad he would be expected to obtain from German universities pronouncements favoring the divorce; the Emperor should have his movements watched. At the same time, Chapuys wrote, Edmund Bonner was to be dispatched in an effort to wring support from the Italian universities.[17]

Cranmer's instructions, dated January 24, charged him principally with presenting Henry's case to Charles in as favorable a light as possible. In addition, he was given the more hopeful task of consulting secretly with the Lutheran princes of Germany about the possibility of an Anglo-Lutheran alliance, and he was to negotiate for removal of the restrictions on trade with the Netherlands. But since Charles left the regulation of trade in the Low Countries to his sister Margaret—or at least conveniently claimed that he did—neither Elyot nor Cranmer was able to help the English merchants.

It is not entirely clear just why Henry decided to recall Elyot so soon. When Chapuys asked for the reason the King was evasive: "Le roy," Chapuys wrote, "m'a coloré la revocation de l'autre ambassadeur sur la requeste de sa femme."[18] If by "sa femme" Chapuys meant Catherine of Aragon, he can hardly have been right, for Elyot was probably more in sympathy with Catherine than anyone else whom Henry could have sent to Charles, and in any case it is unlikely in the extreme that such a request from Catherine would have moved Henry. Chapuys seems to have misunderstood Elyot's feelings about Catherine and Anne Boleyn completely.

Probably Elyot was recalled at his own request. In a letter of March 14 he thanked Norfolk "that it pleased you so benevolently to remembre me unto the King's Highness concerning my retorne into England."[19] Certainly in later years Sir Thomas frequently complained of the debts he had incurred serving the King abroad. The torrent of

[17] *Cal. S.P. Span.*, IV, ii, 888, 897.
[18] *Ibid.*, 898.
[19] Cotton MS. Vitellius B. XXI, fols. 58–59, B.M.

laments began with a letter to Cromwell dated November 18, 1532; Elyot wrote that he had acted "as it beseemyd to the King of Englondes Ambassador, that is to saye, the seconde Kinge in Christondom, bothe at my table and other entertaynement of straungers, thereby fisshing oute some knowlege that doing otherwise I sholde have lakkid." But Henry (with customary Tudor parsimony) "alowid me but xx *s.* the day and I spent xl *s.* the day, and oftentymes four marcs, and moreover I receyvyng the Kinges money in angelles, I lost in every angell xiv *d.* sterling, so that I lakkid moche of the Kinges allowance."[20] Elyot estimated his loss at 600 marks, or 400 pounds, a very large sum in the sixteenth century. Small wonder that he was anxious to end his embassy.

The King, too, had apparently grown dissatisfied. Elyot, with his lack of diplomatic experience and rather bookish nature, probably did not make a brilliant ambassador. Soon after his return to England he complained that he could "perceyve the Kinges opinyon mynisshid towarde me, . . . and I . . . had in lasse estimation than I was in whan I servid the King first in his Counsayle."[21] Elyot was a victim, no doubt, of Henry's unrealistic diplomacy; it is hard to see how anyone dispatched with instructions such as Elyot's could have sent back reports which would have pleased the King. Henry expected his ambassadors to perform miracles and was displeased when they did not. Now, instead of a new policy, he tried a new ambassador.

Although Cranmer was sent to replace Elyot, Sir Thomas did not immediately return to England. Cranmer joined him at Ratisbon, where the Emperor was holding court. By the time of his arrival the hopes for an alliance with the German princes had been dashed; it appeared that the Turks might overrun not only Hungary but Germany as well, and the need for mutual defense forced Charles to grant religious concessions at the Diet of Nuremberg and the princes to accept them.[22]

---

[20] Public Record Office, SP 1/72/36–37. The angel was an English gold coin worth 6*s.* 8*d.*; it was unpopular on the Continent because it was often debased and was frequently taken at a discount.

[21] *Ibid.*

[22] For a full discussion of Charles V's diplomacy at this time, see Stephen A. Fisher-Galati, "Ottoman Imperialism and the Religious Peace of Nürnberg," *Archiv für Reformationsgeschichte*, XLVII (1956), 160–179.

On March 14, probably soon after Cranmer's arrival in Ratisbon, Elyot wrote the only surviving dispatch of his embassy, a long letter to the Duke of Norfolk.[23] Neither of the English envoys, he complained, had been able to see Charles: "As I have written to the Kings Highness, the Emperor, being yet sore grieved with a fall from his horse, kepith himself so close that Mr. Cranmere and I can have none accesse to his majestie, which allmost grievith me as moche as the Emperor's fall grievith him." Charles was suffering from a contusion in the foot which had become inflamed with erysipelas.[24]

Sir Thomas knew little news to report. He expected that the wife of Charles's brother Ferdinand, who was King of Hungary and had just been made King of the Romans, would soon arrive: "Men do suppose [she] will somewhat doo in persuading the princes of Germany" to accept her husband's new title.[25] Elyot, always the classical scholar, noted that she was "bringing with hir all hir children, which is a high poynt of rhetorike and of much efficacie, as old writars supposid."

In lieu of other important diplomatic information, Elyot gave an account of some of the cities that had adopted the reformed religion. His comments on Worms, Spires, and Nuremberg are of considerable interest. He wrote:

I have promysid to the King to write to your grace the ordre of things in the towne of Nurenberg, specially concerning the fayth, but first I will reherse some other townes as they laye in our waye. The citie of Wormes for the more part and allmoste the hole is possessid with Lutherians and Jewes, the residue is indifferent to be shortly the one or the other. Trouthe it is that the Busshop kepith well his name of Episcopus, which is in Englissh an overseer, and is in the case that overseers of testaments be in England, for he shall have leve to looke, so that he meddle not; yet some tyme men callyth hym overseene, that is, drunke, whan he neither knowith what he doeth, nor what he owght to do.

[23] Cotton MS. Vitellius B. XXI, fols. 58–59, B.M. Nicholas Pocock prints the letter, incorrectly assigning it to Augustine de Augustinis in spite of the fact that Augustine habitually wrote in Latin (*Records of the Reformation* [Oxford, 1870], II, 228–231). It is also in Ellis (*Original Letters*, 3d ser. [London, 1846], II, 189), where it is dated 1531, either through error or because Ellis retained the reckoning of years from Lady Day.

[24] See Augustine to Cromwell, March 12, 1532, in Pocock, *op. cit.*, p. 233.

[25] Members of the Schmalkaldic League and the Bavarian dukes had refused to recognize Ferdinand.

The citie of Spire, as I here saye, kepith yet their faith well, except some saye there be many do erre in taking too largely this article Sanctorum Communionem, which hath inducid more charitie than may stond with honestie. One thing I marked: suche as were lovers, divers of them hadd theire paramors sitting with them in a draye which was drawen with a horse trapped with bells, and the lovers whipping theim caused them to trot and to draw them throughoute everi strete, making a grete noyse with their bells. The women sate with theire hedds discovered saving a chaplet or crounet wrowght with nedil wark. I hadd forgoten to tell that ther were grete hornes sett on the horsis heads. I suppose it was the tryumph of Venus, or of the Devil, or of bothe. All townes ensuing be rather wars than bettr. But I passe theim over at this tyme.

Touching Nurenberg, it is the moste proper towne and best ordred publike weale that ever I beheld. Ther is in it so moche people that I mervaylid how the towne mowght contayn them, beside them which followd the Emperor. And notwithstanding ther was of all vitaile more abundance than I could see in any place, allthowgh the countray adjoyning of his nature is very barrayn. I appointid to lodge in an Inne, but Sir Laurence Staber, the King's servaunt, came to me, desyring me to take his house, whereunto I browght with me the Frenche ambassador, where we were well entretayned, and that night the Senate sent to us xxx galons of wyne, xx^{ti} pikes, xxx carpes, a hundred dasis, with sondry confectiones. The residue of oure chier I will kepe in store untill I speke with your grace, which I pray God may be shortly. Allthowgh fissh was sent to us, yet universally and openly thrughout the towne men didd eate flessh.

Turning to a description of religion in Nuremberg, Elyot complained that he had not been permitted to have Mass celebrated privately by his own chaplain. Instead he was constrained to attend service in one of the churches, "celebrate in forme folowing":

The preest in vestments after our manner singith everything in Latine, as we use, omitting suffrages. The Epistel he readith in Latine. In the meane tyme the sub-deacon goeth into the pulpit and readeth to the people the Epistle in their vulgare. After, they peruse other thinges as our prestes do. Than the preeste redith softly the Gospell in Latine. In the mean space the deacon goeth into the pulpite and readith alowd the Gospell in the Almaigne tung. Mr. Cranmere sayth it was showid to him that in the Epistles and Gospels thei kept not the ordre that we do, but do peruse every daye one chapitre of the New Testament.

Afterwards the prest and qwere doo sing the Credo as we do. The se-

cretes and the preface they omitt, and the preest singith with a high voyce
the wordes of the consecration. And after the levacion the deacon tourneth
to the people, telling to theim in Alamaigne tung longe process how thei
shold prepare theim selfes to the communion of the flessh and blode of
Christ. And than may every man come that listeth, withoute going to any
confession. But I, leste I shold be partner of their communion, departed
than, and the Ambassadour of Fraunce followid, which causid all the people
in the churche to wonder at us, as [if] we hadd ben gretter heretikes than
thei.

The German service must have been of particular interest to Cranmer, who was already thinking of reform and use of the vernacular in
the English Church. During his stay in Nuremberg Cranmer became
a friend of Osiander, the Lutheran pastor; Cranmer convinced the German that Henry VIII's marriage was invalid, while Osiander seems
to have converted Cranmer to certain Lutheran views. At any rate
Cranmer was persuaded to break his priestly vows by marrying Osiander's niece Margaret. Elyot's disapproval was perhaps not strong,
for he wrote, "One thing liked me well (to shew your grace freely my
hart): all the priests hadd wyves, and they were the fayrist women of
the towne."[26]

Elyot's comments on Nuremberg concluded with a description of
the city's supply of ordnance and grain:

The day after our coming the Senate sent gentilmen to shew us their provision of harnes, ordnance, and corne. I suppose there was in our sight thre
thousand pieces of complete harneys for horsemen. The residue we saw not
for spending of tyme. Of gunnes grete and small it required half a daye to
numbre them. Arkbusses and crossebowes, I thowght theim innumerable.
The provision of grayn I am aferd to reherse it for jeoparding my credence.
I saw twelve houses of grete length, every house having xii floures, on every
one corne thrughoute, the thikeness of thre feete. Some of the Senate shewid
me that thei hadd sufficient to kepe fifty thousand men abundantly for one
yere. Moche of it have layen long and yet it is goode, as it shall appier by an
example that I have now sent to your grace of rye, which was layde in ther
190 yeres passid, wherof ther remaynith yit above v^e [500] quarters. I

---

[26] Cf. Sir Thomas More's *Utopia* (1516), Everyman ed., p. 125: "The priests
. . . take to their wives the chiefest women in all the country; for to no office
among the Utopians is more honour and pre-eminence given."

doubtid moche to report this to your grace but that I trustid your grace wold take it in stede of tidinges, and not suppose me to be the author, considering that moche strange report may bring me in suspicion of lying with some men which hath conceyvid wrong oppinion of me.

Had the Emperor, one wonders, ordered this display of ordnance and provisions to frighten Henry out of undertaking hostilities against the Empire?

Charles V's health must have improved soon after Elyot wrote to Norfolk, for Sir Thomas must have interviewed Charles before he left the court, and he seems to have departed early in April. Of their conversations Elyot later wrote:

How I usid me in myn accesse unto the Emperor Godd is my juge that in my replications I have seene him chaunge countenance, which, as they know that have ben with him, is no litle thinge. All be it by suche raisons as I made to serve my master, awayting oportunity and using such a prince with silken wordes, as was the counsayle of the King Darius' mother, I attayned with him suche familiaritie in communication, that he usid with me more abundance of wordes than (as some of his Counsaile confessid) any ambassador byfore me hadd founde in him.[27]

A letter written by Augustine de Augustinis, an English adventurer acting as one of the Emperor's physicians, tends to confirm Elyot's estimation of his success. Elyot "left this court to the great grief of all," Augustine wrote; "so much so that I have heard everyone say that there had been no one sent from our illustrious kingdom for many years who was more apt in doing things, more grave with princes, and also more accommodating to divers nations."[28] Elyot had promised to try to secure an English preferment for Augustine, so his words cannot be regarded as unbiased. Still they probably contain an element of truth.

AFTER ELYOT left Ratisbon he spent some time—probably about a month—in the Netherlands. As he wrote,

the King willith me by his Gracis lettres to remayne at Bruxills some space of tyme for the apperhencion of Tyndall, which somewhat minisshith my

[27] Elyot to Cromwell, November 18, [1532], P.R.O., SP 1/72/36–37.
[28] Augustine to Cromwell, April, 1532, in Pocock, *op. cit.*, pp. 247–251. Original in Latin; translation mine.

hope of soone retourning, considering that like as he is in witt moveable, semblably so in his person uncertayne to come by; and as ferre as I can perceyve, hering of the King's diligence in thapprehencion of him, he withdrawith him into suche places where he thinkith to be ferthist oute of daunger.[29]

Henry VIII, now acutely distressed by Tyndale's radical writings, had decided that the reformer should be seized and brought back to England, where he could be silenced and punished. Stephen Vaughan was thought to be too much in sympathy with Tyndale to act effectively against him, though Vaughan bitterly denied the charge with the assertion that he was "neyther Lutheran ne yet Tyndalyn."[30] Elyot was therefore charged with apprehending the reformer and bringing him to England. Sir Thomas later complained that he spent far more for bribes than Henry had allowed him, but he was still unable to smell out Tyndale's hiding place. He had to return to London empty-handed.

He must have crossed the Channel about the first of June. On the third he visited Chapuys, the Imperial ambassador. We have the Savoyard's account of their conversation in a letter to the Emperor. Elyot told Chapuys about his report to Henry; his discussion with the King had been greatly to the benefit of Charles, Catherine, and—principally —Henry, who had been eager to hear every detail of Elyot's mission. Or so Elyot thought. Chapuys himself had grave doubts that Sir Thomas's words had much effect on the King; he had disregarded remonstrances addressed to him previously, and in any case "ung ris ou une larme de la dame [Anne Boleyn] abolit tout." Elyot told Chapuys that he had sent a complete account of his conversation with Henry to Fernando de Puebla, son of the Dr. de Puebla who, as the first resident Spanish ambassador in England, had helped arrange Catherine's marriage with Henry. Elyot had written, he said, in accordance with the Emperor's wishes and in a code which De Puebla had given him. Chapuys added that, to advance Catherine's cause, he would cultivate Elyot's friendship and learn as much from him as possible.[31]

[29] Elyot to Norfolk, March 14, 1532, Cotton MS. Vitellius B. XXI, fols. 58–59, B.M.
[30] Vaughan to Cromwell, December 9, 1531, Cotton MS. Galba B. X, fol. 23, B.M.
[31] Chapuys to Charles, June 5, 1532, *Cal. S.P. Span.*, IV, ii, 453.

It looks as if Elyot was more co-operative with the Emperor's ambassadors than he should have been. It is perhaps for this reason that his embassy seems to have pleased Charles better than Henry. Elyot's call on Chapuys was a natural enough courtesy, but why did he send a detailed report to De Puebla? And why did he write it in cipher? Was it merely to protect his comments from the eyes of prying border officials, or had he said something which he did not want to get back to Henry? Although the ciphers of the time were relatively easy to break, Cromwell did not have a key to Chapuys's code before 1535,[32] and De Puebla's must have been safe enough in 1532. Unfortunately we do not know what Elyot wrote to the Spaniard; it is unlikely to have been anything very significant. But the fact that he wrote at all is important; it suggests that he tried to assume the role of mediator between Henry and Charles, assuring each of the other's good intentions. It is clear that Elyot sympathized with Catherine's cause, and he continued to give Chapuys information and support for a number of years.[33] In 1534, Chapuys went so far as to include Elyot among those who would join a Spanish-led conspiracy to rid England of her "heretic" king.[34] Elyot's policy was dangerous; had Chapuys not kept his secrets unusually well, Elyot might have been tried for treason, and another head might have rolled on Tower Green. No man could safely serve two masters if one of them was Henry VIII.

A STATEMENT about Elyot and Charles V in William Roper's biography of Thomas More has led to a good deal of confusion. Roper wrote:

Soone after [More's] deathe came intelligence thereof to the Emperour Chareles. Wheruppon he sent for Sir Thomas Elliott, our English embassadour, and said unto him: "My Lord Embassadour, we understand that the Kinge, your master, hath put his faithfull servant and grave, wise Councelour, Sir Thomas Moore, to deathe." Wherunto Sir Thomas Elliott awneswered that he understood nothing thereof. "Well," said the Emperour, "it is too true. And this will we say, that if we had bine maister of such a servante, of whose doings our selfe have had these many yeares no small

---

[32] Garrett Mattingly, *Renaissance Diplomacy* (London, 1955), p. 249.

[33] See *L.P.*, VI, 465; VII, 121; X, 601.

[34] *Ibid.*, VII, 121. See Garrett Mattingly, *Catherine of Aragon* (London, 1950), pp. 282–291.

experience, we wold rather have lost the best city of our dominions than have lost such a worthy councellour." Which matter was by the same Sir Thomas Eliott to my self, to my wife, to maister Clement and his wife, to maister John Haywood and his wife, and unto divers other his freinds accordingly reported.[35]

This passage convinced Croft that Elyot was sent as ambassador to Charles again in 1535, and he described Elyot's hypothetical travels through Spain and Italy in detail.[36] Sir Sidney Lee's article in the *Dictionary of National Biography* followed Croft in what A. F. Pollard once called "an unwonted flight of fancy."[37] We now know that Elyot was in England in 1535, busy visiting monasteries in Oxfordshire,[38] and that the ambassador to Charles at the time of More's death was Richard Pate, Archdeacon of Lincoln and later Bishop of Worcester. Pollard suggested that Charles made the remark about More to Pate and that Pate repeated it to Roper while both were in exile at Louvain. This is unlikely, however, for Roper said that the report was made to him and his wife: as E. V. Hitchcock has pointed out, Margaret Roper died in 1544 and was never an exile at Louvain.[39]

The most reasonable explanation seems to be that Charles did indeed make the comment to Elyot, but in 1532 rather than 1535. More had not died, of course, or even resigned, then; but his resignation was known to be imminent. As early as February, 1531, Chapuys had written to Charles that More was distressed by the clergy's acknowledgment of Henry as Supreme Head of the Church and was anxious to resign the chancellorship. Charles naturally sympathized with More, since More's troubles were connected with his championship of Catherine and Catholicism, but he regretted that Henry was to lose his services as a councilor. When Elyot returned to England about the first of June he must have found everyone talking of More's resignation,

---

[35] William Roper, *The Lyfe of Sir Thomas Moore*, ed. E. V. Hitchcock (London, 1935), pp. 103 f. The account by Nicholas Harpsfield in *The Life and Death of Sir Thomas More*, ed. E. V. Hitchcock ([London, 1932], pp. 205 f.), is taken almost verbatim from Roper and does not constitute an additional independent source.

[36] Croft, I, cxvii–cxxiv.

[37] *Times Literary Supplement* (London), XXIX, 592. July 17, 1930.

[38] *L.P.*, X, 1233. See below, Chap. Eight.

[39] Note to Harspfield, *op. cit.*, pp. 353 f.

which had taken effect on May 16, and it would have been natural for him to visit the members of More's circle and tell them of the Emperor's high regard for More. Roper's list of witnesses fits in well with this view. Years later, when Roper composed the biography of his father-in-law, his memory must have failed him, and he probably confused a meeting of More's friends just after his resignation with a similar gathering after his execution. The story of Charles's comment to Elyot itself is credible enough; John Clement and his wife and John Heywood were alive when Roper wrote, and they would probably have called his attention to a really serious error.[40]

LATE IN 1532 Elyot wrote two long letters to Cromwell, which complete the story of his embassy. The first was dated November 18. "Heering of the honorable and saulfe retorne of the Kinges Highness," Elyot began, "I am more joyfull than for any thing that ever hapned to me." His words were well chosen and revealing. He was referring to Henry's conference with Francis I at Calais and Boulogne in October. Charles V had given up tentative plans to attack Henry in Flanders—hence the reference to the King's "saulfe" return—and Henry had thought better of his original intention to marry Anne Boleyn while he was in France—hence Elyot's rejoicing at his "honorable" return.[41] "Feare of the greate aventure of his most royall person so attachid my harte," Elyot went on, "that . . . it hath bireft me of the more parte of my slepe, which I pray Godd may be redubbed [restored] with theise comfortable tidings of his Graces saulfe retorne." Elyot rejoiced also, he told Cromwell, that "in well using your excellent witt ye dayly augment the Kinges good opinion and favor toward you, to the comfort of your frendes."

After these preliminaries Elyot proceeded to describe his embassy:

For my part Godd and my conscience knowith that whan the Kinges Highness commaundid me to serve him as his Graces Ambassadour, knowing my disshabilitie bothe in inward and exterior substaunce, I was lothe to go, the King not offendid. But whan I perceyvid his Graces determinacion, I, con-

[40] This is in general the view advanced by Miss Hitchcock in *ibid.*
[41] See the contemporary letters printed in the appendix to J. A. Froude's edition of William Thomas, *The Pilgrim* (London, 1861), pp. 88 f.

formyng me unto his Graces pleasure, didd deliberate with my self to extend not onely my poure witt, but allso my powar above my powar in his Graces service, intending to serve his Grace no lasse to his honor than any bachelar Knight his ambassador hadd doone of late dayes. Wherfor besydes the furniture of my selfe and my servauntes, at my commyng to Bruxelles I shewid myself according as it beseemyd to the King of Englondes Ambassador, that is to saye, the seconde Kinge in Christondom, bothe at my table and other entertaynement of straungers.

Such lavish entertainment had cost Elyot a great deal of money; he wrote that the embassy was

nowe moche grievouse unto me, as well for that I have browght my self thereby in grete dett, spending therein allmoste six hundred marcs above the Kinges alowance, and thereby am constrayned to putt away many of my servauntes whome I loved well. As allso that I perceyve the Kinges opynion mynisshid towarde me by that, that I perceyve other men avauncid openly to the place of counsaylors which neither in the importaunce of service neither in chargis have servyd the King as I have doone, and I being ommittid had in lasse estimation than I was in whan I servid the King first in his Counsayle. Which I speke not for any ambition, but that onely I desyre that my true hart should not cause me to lyve bothe in poverite and oute of estimation, for God juge my soule as I desyre more to lyve oute of dett and in quyete study than to have as moche as a Kinge may give me.

Elyot explained that he normally had spent twice the King's daily allowance, that he had lost in the exchange of currencies, and that he had given "many rewardes, partly to the Emperors servauntes to gete knowlege, partly to suche as by whoes meanes I trustid to apprehend Tyndal." The result was that he owed the King 100 marks, while other creditors were clamoring for repayment of his debts to them. "Which thinges consyderid, may it like you, good Mr. Cromwell, to move the Kinge to be my good lorde either to forgyve to me my dett, or els to alow to me that I lost by myn exchange and my saide rewardes, and to graunt me some tyme to pay the residue."[42]

Sir Thomas was neither the first nor the last to lose heavily while in diplomatic service. When Richard Pate was preparing to go as ambassador to Charles V late in 1533, one of his friends wrote that he

[42] Elyot to Cromwell, November 18, [1532], P.R.O., SP 1/72/36–37.

should get a subsidy from the Bishop of Lincoln to help meet his expenses. Pate's correspondent marveled that Elyot had obtained sufficient plate and other articles necessary for entertaining, but he supposed that Henry had provided the silver.[43] It is not certain, however, that the King had been so generous. In one respect Elyot was better off than many of his contemporary ambassadors, for the *per diem* allowance was frequently not payable until the ambassador's return.[44] Elyot seems to have received money—and to have exchanged it at a loss—regularly enough.

Cromwell's reply to Elyot's letter must have been unsatisfactory, for on December 8 Elyot wrote again of his troubles. He was genuinely distressed:

Right worshipfull I recommend me unto you. And hartily thanke you for your gentill and wyse advertisements and counsayles gyven unto me in your lettres which I receyvyd of my lovying frende Mr. Raynsford. All be it, Sir, whan ye shall knowe all the occasions of my discomforte ye will not so moche blame me as pitie me if your olde gentill nature be not chaungid.

Mr. Cromwell, I knowe well howe moche my dutie is to serve my soveraign Lorde truely and diligently, which, Godd is my juge, I have doone to my powar with as goode a wille and as gladly as any man could ymagine to doo, neither for myne obedience onely, nor for hope of promocion, but for the very harty love that I bare, and doo bere, to the Kinges Highnesse besydes myn aleageance, therto movid by the incomparable good qualities bothe of his persone and witte, which I have longe wondrid at and lovid, as is my nature to doo in private persones: moche more in princes: moste of all in the chiefe Governor of this Roialm and my soveraigne Lorde and Master.

But whan I consyder myn infelicitie and losse of tyme in unprofitable study, will I or no, I am inforced to be cruciate in my poure mynde, which I confesse to be for lak of wisedom, but I have ben to little a tyme studious in philosophy. I suppose ye being wery of my longe bablying, tary to here the infelicitie that I complayne me of. I pray you than take some pacience to here some parte of my grief.

Elyot went on to tell Cromwell how he had lost more than 100 pounds in the litigation concerning his inheritance of the Findern

[43] William Robyns to Richard Pate, n.d., *L.P.*, XVI, 190.
[44] Mattingly, *Renaissance Diplomacy*, p. 35.

lands in Cambridgeshire.[45] After describing his "unthankfull travayle" as Clerk of the King's Council he continued:

So withoute office or any fee in the world (I refusing fees to thintent in servyng the Kyng I wold lyve out of all suspicion), withoute any ferme, withoute stokke of catell except foure hundred shepe to compasse the lands of my tenaunts: I have hitherto kept a pour house equall with any knight in the contrayes wher I dwell; and not withoute indignation of them which have moche more to lyve on.

A repetition of the complaint about the embassy followed. Elyot now claimed that he had spent 540 marks, or 360 pounds, above the King's allowance.

Now a new misfortune had come upon him; he had been appointed sheriff of Cambridgeshire. He begged Cromwell to see that he was excused from the office, which would only involve him in further losses:

Now that I trustid to lyve quietly and little and little to repay my creditors, and to reconsile myself to myn olde studies and pray for the King (for other promocion I lokid not for) I wote not by what malice of fortune I am constrayned to be in that office wherunto is as it were appendant losse of money and goode name: of the one I am certayne; the other is hard to eskape, all sharpnesse and diligence in justice now a dayes being every where odiouse. As Godd helpe me sens my comyng over I have dischargid out of my service fyve honest and tall personages, constrayned of necessitie, untill I mowght recover myself out of dett. And now am I compellid to augment my household eftsones, or ells shold I serve the Kinge sklenderly.

Sir Thomas concluded:

Ye here myn occasions, I pray you to blame me not thowgh I have my mynde somewhat inquietid. Not that I imbrayde the King with my servyce. But that I sorow that his Grace hath not ben so informed of me as my service requyrid. And moreover that I am not of powar to serve his Grace according to his expectation and as my pour hart desyrith.

And goode Mr. Cromwell I thank you that ye will lese so moche tyme to reade this longe letter, praying you to bear part of it in your remembrance:

[45] See above, Chap. Two.

that as opportunitie servith ye may truely aunswere for your frend, who hartily desyreth the encrease of your worship.[46]

Elyot was not able to escape sheriff's duties. But Cromwell did remember his plight, and—after a lapse of seven years—Sir Thomas's services as ambassador to Charles V were rewarded well enough.[47]

[46] Elyot to Cromwell, December 8, [1532], Cotton MS. Titus B. I, fols. 376–377, B.M.
[47] See below, Chap. Nine.

CHAPTER SEVEN

Nat Called to Counsayle

IN THE YEARS immediately following his embassy Sir Thomas Elyot viewed the King's proceedings and the final break from Rome with grave misgivings. Elyot was unwilling to criticize the King himself, and even critical comments about royal counselors had to be veiled discreetly; but Sir Thomas's opinions are clear enough. He thought Henry VIII was being led by passion, not reason, to press for his divorce, and he believed that flattery, not honesty, motivated the King's counselors. Had Elyot been called to counsel, he hinted, Henry would have been told the unpalatable truth.

Such are the ideas lurking only slightly beneath the surface of two dialogues which Elyot published in 1533. Both deal with the problem of counsel; in both Elyot used the dialogue form to put into the mouths of his characters comments which he could not safely have made with his own lips.

Concern about the proper relationship between a ruler and his counselors was not, of course, new with Elyot. Plato, having realized that philosophers would not soon become kings—nor kings philosophers—had attempted to give philosophical counsel to Dionysius of

Sicily, had met with disaster, and had written his Seventh Epistle to justify his conduct.[1] Sir Thomas More had also questioned just what an intellectual's obligation to his country is, and it was only after the inner debate echoed in Book I of the *Utopia* that he decided to enter the King's service. Elyot's problem, however, was somewhat different: he was thoroughly convinced that he had a duty to advise his sovereign, and he was frustrated because he was not given the opportunity.

His frustration gave rise to the book *Pasquil the Playne,* a dialogue first published in 1533 and reprinted in 1540. It is of considerable significance that the first edition was issued without bearing Elyot's name in any place;[2] Elyot was apparently fearful of the consequences of his criticisms of the government. But the book must have been recognized as his, and he acknowledged his authorship in the reprinting of 1540. There are otherwise only minor differences between the two texts.

The three characters in *Pasquil* hold three different views of the conduct appropriate for a counselor. Gnatho is a loquacious flatterer, "brought in by writers of comedies for suche a servante as alway affirmed what so ever was spoken of his maister";[3] no doubt Elyot thought that there were many Gnathos at the English court. Although Gnatho is a dandy wearing a "cappe full of aglettes and bottons" and "a longe estrige fether," he also plays the scholar by donning a long gown probably "pulled . . . from somme worshypfull doctour" at night in a dark alley.[4] He is, further, a meddling Protestant, and he carries with him a copy of the New Testament ("Som wil be in the bowels of divinite er they know what longethe to good humanitie," Elyot comments) side by side with a volume of *Troilus and Cressida.*[5]

Harpocrates, Elyot's second character, is not loquacious, but he is a flatterer all the same. "He speketh littell or nothing, but formynge his visage in to a gravitie with silence, loketh as if he affirmed all thynge

[1] Cf. also Third Epistle.
[2] Copies of the 1533 edition are in the Huntington and Bodleian libraries. A. W. Pollard and G. R. Redgrave (eds.), *A Short-Title Catalogue of English Books, 1475–1640* (London, 1946) is in error in listing an edition of 1532 and assigning the unique copy to Jesus College, Cambridge. No copy of an edition earlier than 1533 is now known to exist.
[3] *Pasquil the Playne* (London, 1533), fol. A 2ʳ.
[4] *Ibid.,* fol. A 3ᵛ.
[5] "Lord what discorde is bitwene these two bookes," Elyot wrote. (The chivalric romances were out of fashion.)—*Ibid.,* fol. A 4ʳ.

that is spoken."[6] He was "the prelate in the temple of Isis and Serapis, whiche were honorid for goddis in Aegypt, whose image is made holdynge his fynger at his mouthe, betokeninge silence."[7]

The most interesting of the three *dramatis personae,* and the one who speaks Elyot's own mind, is Pasquil. He is a statue come to life, "an image of stone sittinge in the citie of Rome openly, on whome ones in the yere it is leful to every man to set in verse or prose any taunte that he wil, agayne whome he list, howe great an astate so ever he be."[8] Pasquil is utterly frank; he gives honest advice, openly and freely.

In the dialogue, as Elyot says, "plainnes and flateri do come in trial."[9] Pasquil has been plain with his master, and like Elyot, he is out of favor at court. "Thou that art nat called to counsayle, arte full of bablynge,"[10] Harpocrates complains, reflecting what Elyot must have known to be the King's opinion of Sir Thomas himself. Gnatho urges Pasquil to "tourne the lefe. And whan thou herist any thing purposed by them, whom thou hast offendid, what so ever it be, affirme it to be well."[11] And again:

by myne advise leve nowe at the last thine undiscrete libertie in speche, wherin thou usest unprofitable tauntes and rebukes: I may well call them unprofytable, wherby nothynge that thou blamist is of one jote amended, and thou losest therby preferment, whiche thyn excellent wit doth require.[12]

But this Pasquil is unwilling to do. "A knecke on the heed, though it be to the scull, is not so dangerouse to be healed as an yvell affection thraste in to thy maistres brayne by false opinion."[13]

Pasquil says that he favors the advice of Aeschylus: If you are a

---

[6] *Ibid.,* fol. B 4ʳ. [7] *Ibid.,* fol. A 2ʳ.

[8] *Ibid.,* fol. A 1ᵛ. An ancient statue had been unearthed in Rome in 1501 and erected at the corner of the Piazza Navona opposite Cardinal Caraffa's palace. It became the custom to affix antipapal lampoons to the statue, which was dubbed "Pasquino" after a sharp-tongued schoolmaster. In time another statue was erected in the Campus Martius, and dialogues between Pasquino and Marforio became common. Some dealt with quite serious subjects, though in a light manner, and a number of them were printed. A likeness of Pasquino taken from such a volume printed in 1512 is reproduced here facing page 136. Elyot's dialogue is the first English pasquinade; the form was later made popular by Thomas Nash and the Marprelate tracts.

[9] *Ibid.,* fol. A 1ᵛ. [10] *Ibid.,* fol. D 5ʳ.

[11] *Ibid.,* fol. B 2ᵛ. [12] *Ibid.,* fol. A 4ᵛ. [13] *Ibid.,* fol. C 8ʳ.

counselor you should be honest, "holding thy tonge when it behoveth the, and spekyng in tyme that which is convenient."[14] He explains:

Where two hostes be assembled, and in poynt to fyght: if thou be among them, though thou be a great astronomer, it behoveth the to hold thy tunge and not to talke of conjunctions and of the trine or quartil aspectes, but to prepare the to battayle. Where a good felowshyp is sette at dyce or at cardes, thoughe thou be lerned in geometrie, holde thy tunge and speke not of proporcions of figures. . . . Where thou seeste thy frende in a great presence honoured of all men, though thou knowest in hym notable vices, yet there hold thy tonge and reproche hym not of them. Where thou seest thy lord or mayster in the presence of many, resolved in to fury or wantonnesse, thoughe thou hast all redy advertisementes howe he shall refrayne it, yet holde thy tonge than, for troublynge that presence.[15]

The philosopher-counselor must, in other words, descend from his ivory tower and limit his advice to what is useful. He must realize that there is a time and a place for everything and refrain from giving useless information at inopportune moments.

But he still has responsibilities; he cannot, like Harpocrates, sit by silently:

On the other parte. If before battaile joyned, thou beholdest thy side the weiker, and thyne adversaries more puissant and stronger: speke than of policie wherby thou hopest to optayne the victorie. Before that thy frende syttethe downe to dyce, if thou dost perceive that he shall be overmatched, discourage hym betyme, or he repent hym in povertie. . . . If thou knoweste a vice in thy frende which is of a fewe men suspected, er it be talked of at the taverne, or of his enemy reproched, warne him of the damage that may happen if it be not amended.

In particular—and surely with reference to Henry's love for Anne Boleyn:

When thou perceivest thy Maister to be resolved into wrath or affections dishonest, before wrathe be increased into fury, and affection into beastly enormitie, as oportunitie serveth the, reverently and with tokens of love towarde hym speke suche wordes as shalbe convenient.[16]

The counselor should try to find an opportune moment, but he can-

---

[14] *Ibid.*, fol. A 5ʳ.   [15] *Ibid.*, fols. A 6ᵛ–7ʳ.   [16] *Ibid.*, fols. A 7ᵛ–8ʳ.

not wait forever. "Oportunitie and tyme for a counsayllour to speke do not depend on the affection and appetite of hym that is counsayled; mary than counsaylle were but a vayne worde, and every man wolde do as hym lyste."[17] Harpocrates suggests that, even if the counselor hears of a plot to kill the king, he should not disturb his master until the danger is imminent. But Pasquil shows that the word *imminent,* which is "taken out of Latyne, and not commenly used," cannot be clearly defined, for "if ye wyll divide the tyme into instantes, bycause perchance ye be a good Dunse man," each instant can be subdivided an infinite number of times.[18] No, the counselor must warn his sovereign as soon as he hears of danger. "Is any deth so moche to be drad as perpetuall infamy, the subvercion of the common weale, or universall destruction of the hoole countrey?"[19] Clearly not. Then the ruler must be warned of any danger which might harm the state as soon as is conveniently possible.

Elyot, through Pasquil, adds bluntly that if all counselors were as honest as he and all princes willing to hear, many evils might have been prevented. "Germany shuld not have kicked agayne her mother [broken with the Roman Catholic Church]. Emperours and princis shuld not have ben in perpetual discorde, and often tymes laughted at as dissardes [jesters], saynctes blasphemed and miracles reproved for jougglynges, lawes and statutes contemned, and officers littell regarded. What must nedes folowe," Pasquil hates to imagine.[20] In an even gloomier tone he adds, later in the dialogue: "God helpe us, the worlde is almost at an ende: for . . . after noone is tourned to before noone, vertue into vice, vice into vertue, devocion into hypocrisie, and in some places men saye faythe is tourned to herisye."[21] These disasters have come because "Gnatho with his flateri and ye [Harpocrates], with your silence have ones rootid in your maisters hart false opinions and vicious affectis, whiche is the poyson that we so moche spake of." They will eventually see how wrong they have been, but then it will be "impossible with speche to remove those opinions and

[17] *Ibid.,* fol. A 8r-v.
[18] *Ibid.,* fol. C 3v. The reference is, of course, to the Doctor Subtilis, John Duns Scotus.
[19] *Ibid.,* fol. C 8r-v.
[20] *Ibid.,* fol. B 1v.
[21] *Ibid.,* fol. B 5r.

cure those affectis, except ye loved so well your mayster that for his helthe ye wolde confesse youre owne errours."[22] And, one imagines, even that may be unavailing.

Having made such strong comments, Elyot tried to cover himself by insisting that he had not meant to criticize any particular person. In the Preface he assured readers that Pasquil, although his tongue was sharp, "in this booke . . . usith suche a temperaunce that he notith not any particular persone or countrey."[23] He had Pasquil add, at the end of the book, "I have sayd nothynge, but by the waye of advertisement, withoute reprochynge of any one person, wherwith no good man hath cause to take displeasure. And he that doth, he is soon spied, to what parte he leaneth."[24] Who would admit that he was a dishonest adviser and thus Elyot's target? Probably Elyot meant that he blamed all the King's counselors, not alone the chief counselor—Cromwell—for governmental errors. He did not try to deny that his dialogue had relevance to the events of 1533. Straight to the point is Pasquil's further assertion, "Judge what menne lyste, my thought shal be free."[25] No matter how dangerous it was, Sir Thomas Elyot would think independently, and he would express his views as openly as he dared.

IN 1533, Elyot also published, this time under his name, another rather long dialogue, *Of the Knowledeg which Maketh a Wise Man.* Like *Pasquil the Playne* it deals with the problem of counsel, but it is more philosophical and less pointedly related to the problems of contemporary England than its predecessor.

Of the Knowledeg which Maketh a Wise Man is based on Diogenes Laërtius's account of Plato's experiences at the court of Dionysius of Sicily.[26] Elyot has Plato tell of his troubles thus:

On a tyme [Dionysius] willed me to declare in his presence the majestie of a kinge, and howe moch he excelled and was above the astate of any other person, which request I gladly herde, thinkinge to have had good oportunitie to warne hym of his blyndenes and foly. Therfore I began to commende the perfect ymage or fygure of God, which was manifest in the astate of a king, who ruled hym selfe and his people for the universal

[22] *Ibid.,* fol. D 2ʳ⁻ᵛ.   [23] *Ibid.,* fol. A 1ᵛ.
[24] *Ibid.,* fol. D 6ᵛ.   [25] *Ibid.*
[26] Diogenes Laërtius, *De vita philosophorum,* "Plato," XIV–XVI.

weale of them al. And whan I had described his auctorite and preeminence
by the excellency of his vertues, afterward I studiously dyd sette out a
tyraunte in his propre colours, who attendeth to his owne private commodite. Hereat kynge Dionise frowned and became angry. And inter-
ruptynge my wordes sayd unto me: This is a tale of old fooles, that can not
be otherwise occupied. And I aunswered agayne, that those wordes of his
savored of tyranny. . . . The kynge beinge inflamed with fury furthwith
wolde have slaine me.[27]

But instead of killing Plato, Dionysius let him be sold into slavery;
he was finally ransomed and returned to Athens, where he discusses his
experiences with Aristippus, the second character in Elyot's dialogue.
Sir Thomas, still following Diogenes Laërtius, pictures Aristippus as
the archetypal flatterer, much like Gnatho in *Pasquil the Playne.*[28]

The dialogue aims at showing that Plato acted fittingly when he
warned Dionysius about tyranny. Elyot makes Plato begin by defining
the knowledge which distinguishes man from the lower animals. It is
knowledge of one's self. Animals lack self-knowledge; man, in possess-
ing it, is like God. An elaborate discussion of the great chain of being,
only tenuously related to the main theme, follows. God has created
all sorts of creatures that lack reason and self-knowledge. They are all
here for the use of man; proper use brings order, while improper use
causes disorder. Man himself can descend to the level of beasts if he
allows his passions to overcome his reason; this also results in disorder.
But God's intention is that all should be well ordered, and even the
poisonous herbs and vipers which He has put in the world are for the
good of men, since they cause him to remember his mortality and thus
overcome his passions with reason. "Payne and adversitie be as expedient for them which be good, as labour and busynes are to them whiche
be industrious."[29]

So reason must rule in the soul of the wise man; and he must live

[27] *Of the Knowledeg which Maketh a Wise Man* (London, 1533), fol. B
3r–v.

[28] Diogenes Laërtius, "Aristippus," III: "He was always in greater favour
with Dionysius than any of the others, as he always made the best of existing
circumstances. . . . On which account Diogenes used to call him the king's dog."
(Translation by C. D. Yonge in *Lives of the Eminent Philosophers* [London,
1835].)

[29] *Of the Knowledge*, fol. M 6v.

well himself, not merely urge others to do so. The wise man cannot live well and yet tell falsehoods; this is being untrue to himself. "As truth is good, so falshod is yl."[30] Therefore Plato was bound to tell Dionysius the truth; had he not, "than shulde I have proved my selfe to have ben a foole and no wyse man."[31] "Whan [Dionysius] demed me to be a wise man, he with that opinion bounde me that I coulde not deceive hym."[32] Plato was never ruled by his passions and hence "never fell from that place in the lyne of ordre, wherin God had set" him; Dionysius, Aristippus concedes, "hath bothe lost him selfe by refusing the sayde knowlege, . . . and also he hath moste folishly lost the, Plato."[33] Plato had converted his antagonist. His conclusion was the same as Pasquil's: a counselor must give frank warnings whenever his master acts unwisely.

Elyot's Preface suggests that his earlier *Pasquil* had not been calmly received. Some men, finding in Sir Thomas's books "the thing dispreysed whiche they do commende in usynge it," thought that he wrote with "no lyttell presumption." And, he added, "some wyll maliciously divine or conject that I wryte to the intent to rebuke some particuler persone, covaytinge to brynge my warkes and afterward me into the indignation of some man in authorytie"[34]—doubtless Cromwell. Elyot again protested that he was not criticizing any particular individual:

In no boke of mi making I have intended to touche more one manne than an nother. For there be Gnathos in Spayne as wel as in Grece, Pasquilles in Englande as welle as in Rome, Dionises in Germanye as welle as in Sicilie, Harpocrates in France as wel as in Aegipt, Aristippus in Scotland as well as in Cyrena; Platos be fewe, and them I doubte where to fynde.[35]

If he thought all Henrician counselors were Gnathos, Elyot could quite truthfully claim that his shafts were aimed at no single figure in the government. Again he did not pretend that his comments had no contemporary relevance: there were Pasquils in Tudor England, though (like Elyot) they might not be properly esteemed.

Although he was clearly rebuking both Henry VIII and Thomas

[30] *Ibid.*, fol. N 7ᵛ.
[31] *Ibid.*, fol. P 2ᵛ.
[32] *Ibid.*, fol. O 6ᵛ.
[33] *Ibid.*, fols. P 4ᵛ–5ʳ.
[34] *Ibid.*, fol. A 2ᵛ.
[35] *Ibid.*, fol. A 5ᵛ.

Cromwell, Elyot made every effort to mollify them. He wrote in his Preface that his enemies were greatly unlike the King, who had benignly received *The Boke named the Gouernour:*

Ne the sharpe and quycke sentences, or the rounde and playne examples set out in the versis of Claudiane the poete in the seconde boke, or in the chapiters of affabilitie, benevolence, beneficence, and of the diversitie of flaterers, and in dyvers other places, in any parte offended his hyghnes: but (as hit was by credible persones reported unto me) his grace . . . with princely wordes ful of majestie commended my diligence, simplicitie, and courage in that I spared none astate in the rebukynge of vice.[36]

Doubtless he was hoping that Henry would receive the dialogues in the same spirit and profit from their contents.

He specifically asked Cromwell to "recommend one of theise bookes unto the Kinges highness whan ye shall fynde therunto oportunitie." The request was made in a letter accompanying a presentation copy of the dialogue *Of the Knowledeg which Maketh a Wise Man.* Sir Thomas hoped that Cromwell would find time to read the book, in which "your goode witte shall finde more frute than ye wolde have lookid for of any thinge that sholde have passid from my folissh hedd." Apparently Cromwell had advised Elyot to disregard those who spoke ill of him: Sir Thomas wrote that "according to your voise and frendly aunswere unto me I can not compelle men to esteme me as I wolde that thei sholde, that is (as I saye) benevolent unto my contraye and faithfull unto him that will trust me." He hoped that Cromwell would not join his enemies after years as his friend, and concluded: "I pray you to take [this book] in goode part, and after your olde gentill manere defend your frende in his true meaning agayne theim whoes myndes have suche a fewer [fever] contynuall that every goode counsaile is in their taste unsavery and bitter."[37]

[36] *Ibid.,* fol. A 3r-v.
[37] Harley MS. 6989, fol. 33, B.M. Croft printed the letter and surmised that it accompanied a presentation copy of *The Castel of Helth* (Croft, I, cix–cx). But in the letter Elyot wrote: "The matter contayned in this booke is of suche importance that it requireth a quyete lesson and a pregnant judgement with allso a stable remembrance, to the holp wherof I have of purpose usid often repeticions, whereby the maters seemyth the lenger; but being radd diligently and well concoct to theim in whome is any aptness to receyve good counsayle it will not seeme very tediouse." This certainly refers to *Of the Knowledge,* in

Probably neither Cromwell nor his master found time to peruse Elyot's dialogues; they would almost certainly have been displeased had they read them carefully. Elyot had spoken courageously against what he believed to be grave error by the government. He was one of the few to criticize Henry VIII in the 1530's and remain alive in the 1540's.

---

which Elyot makes Plato say: "In matter of great importaunce . . . there is required a plaine and sensible forme of raisoning, broken now and than with often repetitions: whiche all though to froward herers it semeth to make the matter tediouse, yet if they can abide it, they shal therby retain some sedes of knowlege" (fols. H 5ᵛ–6ʳ). *The Castel of Helth* contains very few repetitions.

CHAPTER EIGHT

Frutes of My Study

I F THE REDERS of my warkis, by the noble example of our mooste dere soveraygne lorde, do justly and lovyngely interprete my labours," Elyot had written in the Preface to his Platonic dialogue, "I durynge the residue of my lyfe wyll nowe and than sette forthe suche frutes of my study profitable (as I trust) unto this my countray."[1] A number of such fruits did ripen in the years between 1532 and 1536; Elyot published translations from Isocrates, Plutarch, Saint Cyprian, and Pico della Mirandola, as well as a collection of adages and the first edition of his tremendously popular *Castel of Helth*.

Sir Thomas called his translation from Isocrates *The Doctrinal of Princes*. It is a version of an oration which Isocrates had made before his pupil Nicocles when the youth became King of Salamis.[2] Elyot's

---

[1] *Of the Knowledeg which Maketh a Wise Man* (London, 1533), fols. A 6ᵛ–7ʳ.

[2] It is impossible to date the translations from Isocrates and Plutarch exactly. Probably they were first printed in 1533. One reason for assigning this date is the list of his works which Elyot gave in the Preface to *The Image of Gouer-*

translation is of considerable importance because it is probably the first to have been made directly from Greek into English.[3] He was consciously experimenting; he wrote in his Preface:

This little booke whiche (in mine opinion) is to be compared in counsaile and short sentence with any booke, holy scripture excepted, I have translated out of Greke, not presumyng to contende with theim, whiche have doone the same in Latine: but to thintent onely that I wolde assaie if our Englisshe tunge mought receive the quicke and propre sentences pronounced by the Greeks.

He thought his experiment was a success:

And in this experience I have founde (if I be not muche deceived) that the forme of speakyng, used of the Greekes, called in Greeke, and also in Latine, *Phrasis,* muche nere approcheth to that, which at this daie we use, than the order of the Latine tunge: I meane in the sentences, and not in the wordes: which I doubte not shall be affirmed by them, who sufficiently instructed in all the saide three tunges, shall with a good judgement reade this worke.[4]

"The chiefe cause of this my litle exercise," he added, "was to the intent that thei which do not understande Greeke nor Latine shoulde not lacke the commoditie and pleasure whiche maie be taken in readyng therof." Elyot was again trying to bring his countrymen, in their own vernacular, the wisdom of the ancients.

The oration itself consists of a sensible but boring series of exhortations to the king. At Nicocles' coronation others brought him "gar-

---

nance (1541); it seems to give them in chronological order, and it places the translations between the *Governor* (1531) and *Pasquil* (1533). See below, Chap. Ten. Elyot was probably too busy with the embassy and its aftermath to get any books into print in 1532. On *Ad Nicoclem*, see Werner Jaeger, *Paideia,* trans. Gilbert Highet (Oxford, 1945), III, 84–105, and Norman Baynes, "Isocrates," *Byzantine Studies and Other Essays* (London, 1955), pp. 144–167.

[3] See H. B. Lathrop, *Translations from the Classics into English* (Madison, Wis., 1933), p. 41.

[4] *The Doctrinal of Princes* (London, 1533?), fol. A ii[r-v]. In his Latin-English dictionary Elyot defined *Phrasis* as "the propre fourme, or maner of speche, whyche in one countraye is oftentymes dyverse, as Southerne, Northerne, Devenysshe, Kentyshe, Frenche, Pycarde, Gascoygne, Walon. Some do set the negative before the affyrmative, some contrarye, somme speache is quycke, some grave, some flouryshynge, some temperate" (*Bibliotheca Eliotae* [1542], fol. Cc iii[r]).

mentes, vessell, or plate, or other lyke jewells," but Isocrates thought it more profitable, as his gift, to tell the youth "by what studies desiryng, and from what workes absteinyng, thou maist best order thy roialme and citee."[5] The treatise continues with disconnected precepts, for instance: "Thinke that the beste and most sure garde of thy person be frendes vertuous and honest, lovyng and benevolent subjectes, and thine owne wyll stable and circumspect: for by those thynges authoritee is opteined and lengest preserved."[6] The oration occupies only sixteen pages, and Elyot follows it with an "addicion, to fill up vacant pages," giving Solomon's views on the duties of kings.

Elyot dedicated his translation of Plutarch's treatise on *The Education or Bringinge vp of Children* to his sister, Margery Puttenham. In the Preface he expressed regret that he and his wife had no children: "In this temporall lyfe no thing is to naturall man so desyrous as to have by lefull encrease procreacion and frute of his body." But

the lacke of children shuld nat be to me so payneful, as feare of havinge heires in whom shulde be lacke of vertue and lerning. Wherfore, good sister, endevour your selfe to adapte and forme in my lyttell nevewes inclinacion to vertue and doctrine, acording to min expectation: which ye shall with more facilitie performe if ye beare the contentes of this lyttell boke in remembrance.[7]

He added that he had not translated all of Plutarch's treatise literally but had "declared at lengthe dyvers histories, onely touched by Plutarch" and had omitted "some parte of the matter" because it was "strange frome the experience or usage of this present time" and because it reproved certain vices which "ought rather to be unknowen, than in a vulgare tonge to be expressed."[8]

Sir Thomas had drawn on Plutarch for his discussion of education

---

[5] *Doctrinal*, fol. A iii[r].   [6] *Ibid.*, fols. A viii[v]–B i[r].

[7] *The Education or Bringinge vp of Children* (London, 1533?), fol. A ii[r] (misprinted as A i[r]). One of the nephews was the George Puttenham who was probably the author of *The Arte of English Poesie*. Croft thought that the *Art* was written by George Puttenham's brother Richard (Croft, I, clxxxii–clxxxix), and Sir Sidney Lee followed him in his article in the *D.N.B.* But Gladys D. Willcock and Alice Walker have made a very good case, partly on stylistic grounds, for George Puttenham in their edition of *The Arte of English Poesie* (Cambridge, England, 1936), pp. xi–xliv.

[8] *The Education*, fol. A iii[r].

in the *Governor*, and the translation adds little to what he said there. It begins with a chapter on procreation (and an admonition to parents not to drink, except a "litle wine only for that it is nourishing to nature," before "the acte veneriall"), continues to discuss the duties of parents and teachers, and ends with an examination of "the meanes to diswade yonge men from vice." "To do all that hath ben rehersed," Elyot concluded, "peradventure I may soner wysshe it than persuade it: but to folowe it as nere as we can, it requireth the goodnes of nature, and also diligence; I am sure, that by mannes witte it may be performed and brought to passe."[9]

A Swete and Devoute Sermon of Sayngt Ciprian of the Mortalitie of Man and *The Rules of a Christen Life made by Picus Erle of Mirandula*, "translated into Englyshe by Syr Thomas Elyot, Knyght," were joined in a small volume printed in 1534. Elyot dedicated the book to his stepsister Susan Fetiplace, who had become a nun after the untimely death of her husband, John Kingstone, in 1514.[10] Since death may overtake us at any time, Elyot writes, we must have "a pure and constante faythe, havynge therto joyned wysedome and pacience." All this was

excellently declared and taughte by the holy doctour and martyr sayncte Cyprian, in a sermon which he made to the people of Affrica, where he was Bushop, in the time when there was continuall persecution of paynyms, and

---

[9] A translation of Plutarch's *Howe one may take Profit of his Enemyes* appeared about the same time as Elyot's version of the educational treatise. This book does not name the translator, but there are several reasons for thinking that it was Elyot: The volume was printed by Thomas Berthelet, who published all of Elyot's works; the style is like Elyot's; Elyot was familiar with other parts of Plutarch's *Moralia*. The book, like Elyot's translation of Isocrates, ends with an addition "to fylle up the pages, that els wold have ben voide"; the translator thought that "it shuld nother hurt nor displease, to add hereunto a few sayenges, howe a man shulde chose and cherysshe a frende"— one of Elyot's favorite topics. These indications amount to less than proof, of course, that the translator was Elyot; but there is no evidence which points to anyone else, and there is at least a good chance that it was he. The central idea expressed in the treatise is that one ought to learn from the rebukes of an enemy: "If he cal the unlerned, aplye thou thy selfe to study, and quicken thy endevour; if he call the cowarde, styrre thy corage and the redynes of thy mynde; if he calle the unchast and vicious, chace out of thy mynde the desyre of luste, if any suche printe, unware to the, stycke in the" (fol. A vi[r]).

[10] See the genealogical table in Appendix I.

also mortalitie by general pestilence. Whiche sermone whan I had ones perused in redynge, I liked it so well, that I desired that all other persones
mought understand it. . . . Wherfore as well for theyr instruction as myne,
howe we may be alway prepared agaynst those naturall and worldly affections, I have traunslated this lyttell boke.

Elyot has translated freely, "not supersticiouselye folowynge the letter,
whiche is verely elegante, and therfore the harder to translate into
our language." He dedicated the work to Susan to show her that he
loved her "not onely for our allyaunce, but also moche more for your
perseverance in vertue and warkes of true faith."[11] The otherworldli-
ness of the sermon is strongly reminiscent of the *Dialogue of Comfort
against Tribulation*, which More wrote in 1534 while a prisoner in the
Tower, and it is possible that the misfortunes of his old friend caused
Elyot to turn to meditations filled with *contemptus mundi*.

To the sermon Elyot added "a litel tretise, but wonderfyl fruitful,
made by the vertuouse and noble prince John Picus Erle of Mirandola,
who in abundance of lerning and grace incomparable excelled all other
in his tyme and sens, whose picture I wolde to God were in all noble
mens chambers, and his grace and vertues in theyr soules and maners."[12] Elyot probably owed his interest in these sayings of Pico to
More, who appended a poetic version of them to the biography of
Pico which he had translated in 1504.[13] More's translation had been
published in 1510—about the beginning of Elyot's association with
his circle—and Elyot must have been familiar with it. It is an interesting coincidence that More's translation was also made for a nun, Joyce
Leigh, sister of the Edward Leigh or Lee who became Archbishop of
York.

ABOUT 1534 Elyot also published his *Bankette of Sapience*. The *Banquet* is a collection of adages set forth by Sapience as if they were
dishes at a feast:

[11] *A Swete and Devoute Sermon of Sayngt Ciprian* (London, 1539), fols.
A ii^v–iii^v.

[12] *Ibid.*, fol. A iiii^r. Cf. *Iohannis Pici Mirandulae omnia opera* (Bologna,
1496), I, fols. YY iiii^v–v^v.

[13] *The Workes of Sir Thomas More . . . wrytten in the Englysh Tonge* (London, 1557), fols. b iii^r–v^r.

Sapience hath builded a house for her selfe [runs Elyot's introduction], she hath prepared her wine and laide forth her table, she calleth out abrode in the stretes and in the chiefe assembly of the people, and at the gates of the cytie she speketh with a loude voice: Ye babies, how long wil ye delyte in childyshnes? And how longe wyl fooles covete those thynges whiche shall hurt them? And they which lacke wit, hate knowlege and lernyng? Come on and eate ye mi brede and drinke my wine that I have ordeined now for you. . . . I will make them ryche that do love me, and fil up their treasure.[14]

The book is dedicated to Henry VIII in a preface which elaborates the same theme:

After longe fasting and also moche travaylle, it hath ben thought ever, most noble prince, not onely convenient, but also to stande with good reason, to have a dyner or supper provyded with meates suffycient, as well to recreate the vytall spirites, as to restore eftesoones the strength abated by labours.

Elyot was writing in the spring, when a banquet was especially appropriate after "the longe abstinence and fastyng of this presente Lent"; he followed the example of Plato, Xenophon, and Plutarch, who had written works "whiche they named *Symposia*, called bankettes in Englisshe." The banqueting dishes are "sondry wyse councels, gathered by me out of the warkes of moste excellent persons, as well faithful as gentyles, . . . served forth to the table by them, which dyd wryte or pronounce them."

And as for me, I have no more parte in the bankette, nor deserve any more praise therfore, than one of them that beareth a torche before every course whan they come from the dresser. And yet where there is such abundance, I may perchance for my labour have the revertion or scrappes of som of the dishes.[15]

---

[14] *The Bankette of Sapience* (London, 1539), fol. A iiii^v. No copy of an earlier edition is known to survive, but the 1539 edition cannot be the first, for its title page includes the words "newely augmented." The wood-cut border used in the 1539 edition bears the date 1534; possibly this indicates that the first edition was printed in that year, though this is by no means certain. Berthelet had the irritating habit of re-using borders without correcting the date. Elyot's list places this book after Cyprian's sermon and before *The Castel of Helth*, but since we do not know the date of the first edition of the *Castle* this is not very helpful. Copies of five different sixteenth-century editions of the *Banquet* survive, so it must have been quite popular.

[15] *Ibid.*, fol. A ii^v.

Sir Thomas's banquet consists in fact of common adages, arranged according to subject. There are well over a hundred headings, running more or less alphabetically from Abstinence, Adversitie, Affection, Ambition, Authoritie, Amitie, Apparayle, and Almes deede through Kunnyng and Kynge to Voluptuousnes, Wyfe, Vaineglory, Virginitie, and, finally, Wrathe. Elyot gives marginal citations showing the source of more than half of the sayings; it is interesting to see the range of writers from whose works he borrowed. There are in all just above five hundred citations to eighty-seven different sources; the largest number (sixty-four) are to Seneca, while Cicero, Solomon, and Augustine follow closely with fifty-six, fifty, and forty-one, respectively. Plato fares very badly, with only five citations; if we add the three references to Socrates it brings Plato's total up to eight, the same as Aristotle's. Slightly more than half of the citations are to Christian writers, though the number of classical sources is surprisingly large. Table 1 lists the authors whom Elyot cited more than once.

TABLE 1

Sources* Cited More Than Once in *The Bankette of Sapience*

Source	No. of Citations	Source	No. of Citations	Source	No. of Citations
Seneca	64	St. Bernard	8	Plautus	3
Cicero	56	Gregory	8	Socrates	3
Solomon	50	Sapientia	7	Tacitus	3
St. Augustine	41	Jacob	6	Agesilaus	2
Ecclesiastes	34	Lactantius	6	Alexander	2
St. Jerome	26	Livy	6	Cato	2
St. Paul	23	Galen	5	Euripides	2
Plutarch	14	Plato	5	Gelasius	2
St. Ambrose	11	Jeremiah	4	Pontanus	2
St. Matthew's		Boethius	3	Proverbs	2
Gospel	10	Christ	3	Sextus Aurelius	2
Quintus Curtius	10	David	3	Theopompus, King	
Sallust	10	Democritus	3	of Lacedemonia	2
Chrysostom	9	Isaiah	3	Tobias	2
Aristotle	8	Isidore	3		

* Sources are cited as they appear in Elyot's marginal notes.

THE MOST POPULAR of Elyot's works in his own century was his *Castel of Helth*. Published about 1536, it was reprinted in 1539, twice in 1541, and again in 1544, 1547, and 1548.[16] In all it was printed at least fourteen times before 1610, while the *Governor* was going through only eight editions.[17]

In the *Castel of Helth* Elyot aimed at providing his fellow countrymen with the knowledge necessary for preserving health and treating common ailments. He was not alone in this endeavor; it was a Humanistic commonplace that the wise man should care for his body as carefully as for his mind, and a number of Humanists provided suitable hygienic guides. Thus the title page of Linacre's translation of Galen's *De temperamentis* into Latin, printed at Cambridge in 1521, bore the words "Opus non medicis modo, sed et philosophis oppido quam necessarium" [a work not for doctors alone, but very necessary for

---

[16] No copy of an edition printed before 1539 is now known to exist, and 1539 is frequently given as the date of the first edition. But Elyot's letter dedicating the 1539 edition to Cromwell states that there had been an earlier version, hastily printed, which required corrections. This dedication contains Elyot's only reference to his membership in the Parliament of 1539:

He giveth twice that gyveth quyckly (saith Senek). The griefe, which I had for your lordshyps disease, with the desyre that ye mought lyve longe without syckenes, caused suche spede in buyldynge the castell of helthe, that therein lacked som part of perfection, but yet the promptnes in gyvyng that thynge, whyche I thoughte necessary, to declare myn affection, I doubt not, was no lasse estemed of your good lordshyp than afore is rehersed. Not withstandynge, whan I had eftesones perused that lyttell fortresse, and founde here and there some thynge that lacked, I toke my penne in the stede of a truelle, and amended the faultes, and added somwhat more, where I thought it convenyent: And yet perchance some thynges mought happen to escape, which were as nedeful to be corrected, myne attendance on the parlyament, I being a member of the lower house, withdrawyng from me leysure convenyente to fynde in this warke all the fautes whiche moughte be amended. Maye it nowe lyke your good lordshyppe to take in good parte, not eftesones the Castelle, whiche I all redye have gyven you, but my good wyll and dylygence in amendynge or repayrynge the same, whiche is also prynted in a moche better letter (for. A iʳ⁻ᵛ).

Mr. L. M. Payne, assistant librarian to the Royal College of Physicians, writes (in a letter to the author dated June 13, 1957) of a book-seller's catalogue listing the first edition of the *Castle*. Apparently it was undated but was dedicated to Cromwell as Lord Privy Seal, an office which he did not assume until 1536. If this is correct it places the first edition between 1536 and 1539, and probably early in this period. In the 1539 edition Berthelet re-used a wood-cut border carrying the date 1534; this has led the *D.N.B.* to suggest 1534 as the date of the first edition.

[17] See Appendix III for a list of the editions of Elyot's works.

philosophers also], and Plutarch's brief treatise *De sanitate tuenda*, translated into Latin by Erasmus, claimed that one need not be a physician to write about health.[18] In addition to these translations there were a number of hygienic manuals by Italian Humanists, among them Michele Savonarola, grandfather of the Florentine reformer and himself physician to Lionello d'Este.

Although such guides were available in Latin, Elyot's *Castle* is the earliest important manual of health originally written in English.[19] It is divided into four books, of which the first, mostly tables, explains the classical theory of the humors and complexions. The second is largely given over to consideration of more than a hundred different foods, from gourds to whey, although there is also a section on forms of exercise. Means of purging an excess of any humor and a philosophical discussion of the "affectes" of the mind—"ire, dolour, and joye"—fill Book III. The last book considers "cruditie"—which turns out to be poor digestion—and the symptoms, particularly those appearing in urinalysis, of disease. It concludes by recommending a diet which will supposedly preserve health in time of pestilence.

Basic to the *Castle* is the theory that man's body is governed by four humors, a system borrowed from the ancients and popularized in Tudor England by Elyot. "In the bodye of man be foure pryncipall humours," Elyot explains, "whiche contynewyng in the proporcion that nature hath lymytted, the bodye is free frome all syckenesse. Contrarye wyse, by the increase or dyminution of anye of theym in quantitie or qualitie . . . inequal temperature commeth into the body, which syckenesse foloweth."[20] Table 2 (see page 134), a summary of the first three chapters of the *Castle,* explains the system.

Earth and water are at the bottom because they are, as Elyot says, more "groose and ponderouse" than air and fire. Thus Shakespeare

---

[18] Erasmus' version was printed in 1513, and a complete English translation of it almost certainly followed, although only an imperfect English text survives, printed (probably pirated) by Robert Wyer. A respectable translation by John Hales was printed in 1543. See Lathrop, *op. cit.,* p. 50.

[19] Thomas Paynell had published an English translation of the *Schola Salernitana: Regimen sanitatis Salerni* in 1528.—See H. S. Bennett, *English Books and Readers, 1475 to 1557* (Cambridge, England, 1952), p. 103.

[20] *The Castel of Helth* (London, 1541), fol. 8ʳ. (All page references are to the octavo edition of 1541; a quarto edition was printed in the same year.)

TABLE 2

The Complexions and Humors

Element of the Earth	Its Qualities	Corresponding Complexion in Man	Dominant Humor
Air	Hot and moist	Sanguine	Blood
Fire	Hot and dry	Choleric	(Red) choler
Earth	Cold and dry	Melancholic	Melancholy (or black choler)
Water	Cold and moist	Phlegmatic	Phlegm (or fleume)

has the Dauphin in *Henry V* praise his horse as being "pure air and fire, and the base elements of earth and water never appear in him"; and Cleopatra, preparing to kill herself, says, "I am fire and air; my other elements I give to baser life."[21]

Elyot gives tables to show the characteristics of the brain too hot, cold, moist, or dry, or too hot and moist, cold and moist, hot and dry, or cold and dry. For example:

Brayn cold
and dry
dystempered
hath

{
The head colde in felyng and without colour,
The veins not appering,
Sone hurte with colde,
Often diseased,
Wytte perfect in chyldehode, but in age dull,
Aged shortly, and balde.[22]
}

There are similar tables for the heart, stomach, and "genitories."

Recommendations for a diet which will keep the humors in balance form the main body of the *Castle*. Six things are considered with regard to food: the substance, quality, quantity, custom, time, and order. He lists the meats whose substances engender each of the humors and

[21] *Henry V*, III, vii; *Anthony and Cleopatra*, V, ii. A diagram from Thomas Walkington's *Optick Glass of Humors* (1639), which faces page 137, sets out the same system. The innermost ring names the complexions; the next gives the period in man's life during which they tend to be dominant; then comes the season in which they are preponderant; next follows the dominant wind; then the corresponding element; and finally the ascendant planet. Outside the circle are the associated zodiacal seasons.

[22] *Castle*, fol. 4ᵛ.

those which are good for the teeth, eyes, head, heart, liver, lungs, and stomach. Quantity, he thinks, should be proportioned to the substance of the meat and to the complexion of its eater; working men in England are allowed to eat "grosse meates . . . in a great quantitie," providing that they "eate withoute gourmandyse, or leave with some appetite."[23] But Elyot deplores overindulgence in either meat or drink; "in moche meate shal be sycknes."[24]

The quality of a meat depends upon whether it is hot or cold, moist or dry; the quality should suit the dominant humor of the eater. This is the theory behind the lines with which Shakespeare has Petruchio justify the taming of his shrew by starvation:

> I tell thee, Kate, 'twas burnt and dried away,
> And I expressly am forbid to touch it,
> For it engenders choler, planteth anger;
> And better 'twere that both of us did fast,
> Since of ourselves, ourselves are choleric,
> Than feed it with such over-roasted flesh.[25]

Meat that was burnt—hot and dry—would be of the wrong quality for choleric people, whose dominant humor makes them already too hot and dry. Kate needed something cold and moist: a melon or cucumber.

Custom also needs to be considered in prescribing a proper diet, Elyot says: "Those meates, to the which a man hath ben of long time accustomed, thoughe they be not of substaunce commendable, yet do they sometyme lesse harme than better meatis, wherunto a man is not used."[26] Turning to the question of time, Elyot notes that a proper diet must fit both the season, since each time of the year tends to engender one of the humors, and the age of the eater, for different humors tend to dominate at different ages. He urges Englishmen to eat hearty breakfasts, though Continental writers thought this neither necessary nor desirable. The order in which foods are eaten at a meal is to be regulated according to the temperatures required in the stomach to di-

---

[23] *Ibid.*, fol. 16^{r-v}. A number of Tudor writers were proud that even the lowest classes in England were able to eat meat, and they expressed mixed sympathy and scorn for French peasants, who had only salads.

[24] *Ibid.*, fol. 17^r.

[25] *Taming of the Shrew*, IV, i.   [26] *Castle*, fol. 17^v.

gest each dish; since different meats call for different digestive temperatures, they should not be eaten at the same meal. Digestion is accomplished by the action of the liver, "whyche is to the stomake as fyre under the potte."[27]

Elyot inserts a long discussion of specific foods between his chapters on custom and time. On the whole he is skeptical of the virtues of fruits. He admits that they were probably the only food of primitive man, "but by change of the diete of our progenytours, there is caused to be in our bodies suche alteration from the nature whiche was in men at the begynnyng, that nowe all fruites generally are noyfull to manne, and do ingender yll humours, and be oftentymes the cause of putrifyed fevers, yf they be moche and contynuelly eaten."[28] Elyot shows how each of twenty-one fruits (for him the term includes nuts and olives) should be prepared, who should eat it and when, and what its medicinal qualities are. This passage is typical:

CUCUMBERS

do not exceede so moch in moisture as melons, and therfore they be not so soone corrupted in the stomake: but in some stomakes, beynge moderately used, they do dygeste well, but yf they be aboundantly eaten, or moche used, they ingender a colde and thycke humour in the vaynes, whiche never or seldome is tourned into good bloude, and sometyme bryngeth in fevers. Also they abate carnall luste. The seedes as well therof, as of melons and gourdes, beyng dryed, and made clene from the huskes, are very medicinable agaynst syckenesses procedyng of heate, also the dyfficultie or let in pyssyng. They be colde and moyst in the seconde degree.[29]

Sir Thomas shows only moderate enthusiasm for vegetables: "Generally al herbes rawe, and not sodden, do ingender colde and watry juyce, if they be eaten customably, or in abundance: all be it some herbes are more comestyble, and do lasse harme unto nature, and moderately used, maketh metely good bloudde."[30] He sets out the virtues and vices of thirty vegetables, commending lettuce most highly.

He mentions twenty kinds of "flesshe," mostly of fowls. Sir Thomas hints at his objection to the enclosure of parks when he writes that deer "consume a good parte of the best pasture in the realme, and are in

27 *Ibid.*, fols. 47v–48r. 28 *Ibid.*, fol. 19r.
29 *Ibid.*, fols. 19v–20r. 30 *Ibid.*, fol. 23v.

Carmina ad ſtatuam Paſquini in figuram
Martis præſenti Anno.M.d.xii.conuerſi.

Woodcut of the Pasquino statue, from an anonymous collection of verses affixed
to the statue, 1512.
(University Library, Cambridge, class mark F.151.2.24)

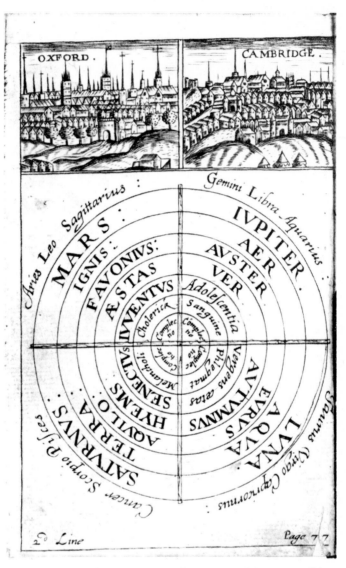

The complexions and their correspondences, from Thomas Walkington,
An Optike Glass of the Humors, 1639.
(University Library, Cambridge, class mark Syn.8.63.183)

nothynge profytable" except for leather.[31] He gives the qualities of fish, butter, eggs, and cheese; cheese he considers an "enemye unto the stomache."

Elyot's ideas about drink do not seem entirely consistent; at least, they are very catholic. He begins with lavish praises of water, noting the good health of those who have drunk nothing else. This is not a view with which all of Elyot's contemporaries agreed; Andrew Boorde (1490?–1549), for instance, wrote that "water is not holsome, sole by it selfe, for an Englysshe man," while "ale for an Englysshe man is a naturall drink [and] maketh a man stronge."[32] Elyot himself calls ale "a necessary and convenient drynke, as well in syckenesse as in helth," but he thinks that it is "not to be compared to wyne, consyderynge, that in [ale and beer] doo lacke the heate and mosyture, whyche is in wyne."[33] He waxes ecstatic in praise of wine; it is especially good for aged people, that "thereby they should seeme to retourne unto youth, and forgette heavynesse."[34]

The comments on exercise in the *Castel of Helth* are of considerable interest, since Elyot had already said in the *Governor* that he thought exercise a necessary part of the training of the man who would become a governor. In the *Castle* he praises exercise because it produces

two commodyties, evacuation of excrementes, and also good habyte of the body; for exercise beynge a vehement motion, thereof nedes muste ensue hardenesse of the members, wherby labour shal the lesse greve, and the body be the more stronge to labour. . . . This thynge is soo necessary to the preservation of helth, that without it noo man may be longe without sickenesse.[35]

Elyot quotes approvingly Galen's opinion that exercise should be taken when digestion is complete and it is nearly time to eat again. He recommends three unusual types of exercise: fricasies, gestation, and vociferation. Englishmen may use fricasies

in this forme. In the mornyng, after that thei have ben at the stoole, with their shirte sleves or bare hande, if theyr fleshe be tender, they do fryste

[31] *Ibid.*, fol. 30r.

[32] *A Compendious Regyment or a Dyetary of Helth*, ed. F. J. Furnivall (London, 1870), pp. 252, 256.

[33] *Castle*, fols. 36v–37r.

[34] *Ibid.*, fol. 34v. [35] *Ibid.*, fol. 48r.

softely, and afterwarde faster, rubbe theyr breaste, and sydes downwarde, and overthwart, not touchinge their stomacke or bealy, and after cause their servaunt semblablye to rubbe overthwarte theyr shoulders and backe, and beginninge at the neckbone, and not touchyng the raynes of their backe, excepte they doo feele there moche colde and wynde, and afterwarde theyr legges from the knee to the ancle: laste theyr armes, from the elbowe to the handwreste. And in this forme of fricasye I my selfe have founden an excellent commoditie.[36]

For further information on the efficacy of rubbings Elyot refers his readers to Galen's *De sanitate tuenda,* "translated moste truely and eloquently out of Greke into Latyne by Doctour Lynacre, late physytion of mooste worthye memorye to our soveraygne lorde Kynge Henry the VIII."[37]

Gestation—"that is to say, where one is caried, and is of an other thynge moved, and not of him self," as in a chariot or a boat—is recommended for sufferers from palsy, gallstones, or gout.[38] Vocifera-tion consists of "syngynge, redynge, or criegne" and is "the chiefe ex-ercyse of the breste and instrumentes of the voyce. . . . He that intend-eth to attempte this exercyse, . . . lette hym speake with as base a voyce as he can, and walkynge, begynne to synge lowder and lowder, but stylle in a base voyce, and to take no hede of swete tunes or armony."[39] Surely such exercise is best taken in private!

Book III of the *Castle* falls into three sections. The first nine chap-ters deal with evacuation, which may be accomplished by nine methods: abstinence, vomiting, purgation by siege (laxatives or enemas), blood-letting, scarifying or cupping, sweating, provocation of urine, spitting, and bleeding at the nose or hemorrhoids. The "affectes" of the mind—ire, sorrow, and joy—are next treated in two ways. Elyot, following the Stoics, first gives philosophical reasons for disregarding these pertur-bations; he then tells how their effects on the body may be remedied by physic. The book concludes with six chapters on "the dominion of sundry complections," together with appropriate diets for sanguine, choleric, phlegmatic, and melancholic men.

Crudity ("a vicious concoction of thynges receyved," or bad diges-tion) and lassitude ("a disposition towarde sycknes") are the subjects

---

[36] *Ibid.,* fol. 49[r-v].   [37] *Ibid.,* fol. 49[v].
[38] *Ibid.,* fol. 51[v].   [39] *Ibid.,* fol. 52[v].

of Book IV. Elyot's comments on crudity are of particular interest because here he does not rely upon the authority of ancient writers but rather tells of his own experience:

And for my parte, beynge of a cholerike humour myxte with fleume, many yeres continually in cruditie, I never founde any thyng better than fyne Reubarbe chewed with raysons of corens [currants], which I toke by the counsayle of the worshypfull and well lerned phisition, mayster Doctour Augustyne, who in his maners declareth the gentilnesse of his ancient bloudde, whiche medicyne I doo not leave to use dayly, fastynge, when I fele suche cruditie to begynne. . . . If the humours in the stomake be not putrified, but that it is greved with aboundaunce of salte fleume, I have founde that mylke, newe mylked, wherin is put a quantitie of good hony or sugar and three leaves of good speare myntes, and a lyttle boyled, so beynge drunke warme fastynge, the quantitie of a pynte, and restynge on it, without eatynge or drynkynge any other thynge the space of thre houres after, have abundantly purged and comforted the stomake, but where there is no fleume, but only choler, is not so holsome.[40]

Distillations and rheumes, Elyot thinks, are the forms of crudity most common in England. The most intimate glimpse of his private life that Elyot left us he records in his own treatment for what amounts to the common cold:

I doo moche mervayle that our phisytions do not more studyousely provyde therfore remedyes. I my selfe was by the space of foure yeres continually in this dyscrasy, and was counsailed by divers phisitions to kepe my head warme, and to use *Diatrion piperion,* and suche other hotte thinges as I have rehersed. At the last felyng my selfe very feeble, and lackynge appetite and slepe, as I hapned to reade the boke of Galene *De temperamentis,* which treateth *De inaequale temperature,* and afterwarde the vi boke, *De tuenda sanitate,* I perceyved that I had ben longe in an errour. Wherfore fyrste I dyd throwe away my quylted cappe, and my other close bonettes, and onely dyd lye in a thynne coyfe, which I have ever sens used bothe wynter and sommer, and ware a lyghte bonette of velvette onely; than made I oximelle [a concoction with a base of honey] after the doctrine of Galene, savynge that I boyled in the vyneger rootes of betayne [betony], and after that I hadde taken it thre dayes continually, every day thre sponesful in the

---

[40] *Ibid.,* fol. L vi^r–v, incorrectly paginated fol. 60, *recte* fol. 78. Augustine had been physician to Wolsey and was in the service of Charles V at the time of Elyot's embassy. See above, Chap. Six.

mornynge warme, than toke I of the same oxymell, wherin I had infused or stieped one dramme of Agarike, and halfe a dramme of fyne Reubarbe, the space of iii dayes and iii nyghtes, whiche I recyved in the mornynge, eatynge no meate vi houres after, and that but a lyttell brothe of a boyled henne, wherof ensuyed viii stoles abundaunt of choler and fleume: soone after I slepte soundly, and had good appetite to eate; after supper I wolde eyther eate a few colyander sedes prepared or swalow downe a lyttell fyne mastix [mastic], and forbeare wyne, and dranke only ale, and that but lyttell and stale, and also warmed. . . . And by this diet I thanke almighty God, unto whome onely be gyven all glory, I was reduced into a better state in my stomake and head, than I was xvi yeres before, as it may appere unto them, whiche have longe knowen me.

And this have I not written for vaynglorye or of presumption, but to the intent that they whiche have their bodyes in like temperature as myne was, that is to say, being colerike of complexion, and havyng reumes fallyng out of a hotte head, may if they lyst assaye myne experience. . . .

Fynally this dare I affirme, that the reumes, whyche of late time have ben more frequent in this realme than they were wont to be xl yeres passed, have hapned of none occasion more than of bankettynges after souper, and drynkyng moch, specially wine a lyttell afore slepe. An other thyng is the kepyng the head to hotte or to longe covered, wherby the brayne, which is naturally colde, is distempered with hotte vapours ascendyng from the stomak.[41]

He follows with a censure of clergymen for using elaborate velvet caps.

Lists of symptoms and suggested diagnoses fill the chapters on lassitude. Illnesses most common to each season of the year are noted, as are diseases of youth and age; symptoms of disorders in the brain, heart, liver, stomach, and breast are listed. For Elyot, however, the best means of diagnosis is urinalysis. In this he follows a characteristic interest of the late Middle Ages and the Renaissance, for many manuscripts from the eleventh to the sixteenth centuries describe the "tokens of urines."[42]

[41] *Ibid.*, fols. L v^v–M i^r, paginated 71^v–73^r, *recte* 79^v–81^r.

[42] A complete discussion of urines was given by John de Ketcham in the *Fasciculus medicinae*, printed at Venice in 1491. Early studies by Englishmen were Henry Daniel's *Urocrisiae* (1379) and Hare's *Speculation of urynns* (MSS. Ashmole 1404, 1405). Dr. Robert Recorde, of All Souls, Oxford, continued the study well into Elyot's time. An anonymous compilation called *The*

Elyot's specific comments on urines are not original observations and are less significant than the mere fact that he deals with the subject at length. He holds that it is necessary for every man to understand the meaning of varying colors and substances of urines, since they will be altered if the urine stands or is carried to a physician for analysis. But the layman should not make his own diagnosis: "All this must be dylygently marked," Elyot concludes, "and therof separately to advertise the phisition, unto whom I referre the judgement of the sickenes, . . . for as moche as the judgement of theym is very subtylle."[43]

This is not the only manifestation of Elyot's concern that the layman should not take too much into his own hands; in his discussion of purgatives he writes, "They whyche wyll take sharper purgations, . . . lette theym take the counsayle of an honest and perfyte physytion, and not adventure to myxe thynges together, withoute knowynge the temperaunce of theym in degrees."[44] This suggests that Sir Thomas was trying from the first to mollify the physicians, who he feared would not take his work kindly. The last words in the edition of 1539 confirm this view:

Thus make I an ende of this treatyse, desyrynge them that shall take profyte therby to defende it agaynste envyouse disdayne, on whom I have set the adventure for the love that I bare to my countrey: requyrynge all honest phisitions to remember that the intent of my labour was that men and women readynge this warke, and observynge the counsayles therin, shulde adapte therby their bodyes to receyve more sure remedye by the medicines prepared by good phisitions in dangerous sycknesses, they kepyng good diet, and infourmynge diligently the same phisytions of the manner of their affectes, passions, and sensyble tokens. And so shall the noble and moste necessarye science of phisycke, with the ministers therof, escape the sclander whyche they have of longe tyme susteyned, and accordynge to the precept of the wyse man, be worthily honoured, forasmoche as the hyghest God dyd create the phisition for mans necessitie, and of the earth created medicine, and the wyse man shall not abhorre it.[45]

---

seynge of uryns was first printed in 1525 and proved so popular that it had reached its tenth edition by about 1555. *The grete herball* (1526) also contained a treatise on urines. See Bennett, *op. cit.*, pp. 105, 109.

[43] *Castle*, fol. N i^r, paginated 81^r, *recte* 90^r.

[44] *Ibid.*, fol. 60^v.

[45] Reprinted in the 1541 ed., fol. L viii^{r–v}, paginated 86, *recte* 97.

Such declarations proved insufficient to win the approval of medical men. In the third edition of the *Castle* (1541) Elyot had to defend his knowledge of physic, and incidentally his use of the vernacular, in stronger terms. It is an interesting passage:

But yet one thynge moche greveth me, that not withstandynge I have ever honoured, and specially favored the reverende colledge of approved phisitions, yet some of them hearynge me spoken of, have sayd in derysion, that all though I were pretyly sene in hystoryes, yet being not lerned in phisycke, I have put in my boke dyvers errours, in presumyng to wryte of herbes and medycines. Fyrste as concernyng hystoryes, they be not so lyght of importaunce as they done esteme theym, but may more surely cure mennes affections than dyverse phisitions doo cure maladyes.

Nor whan I wrate fyrste this boke, I was not all ignorante in phisycke. For before that I was twenty yeres olde, a worshypfull phisition, and one of the most renoumed at that tyme in England, perceyving me by nature inclyned to knowledge, radde unto me the workes of Galene of temperamentes, naturall faculties, the Introduction of Johannicius, with some of the Aphorismes of Hippocrates. And afterward by myn owne study, I radde over in order the more part of the warkes of Hippocrates, Galenus, Oribasius, Paulus Celius, Alexander Trallianus, Celsus, Plinius the one and the other, with Dioscorides. Nor I dyd omytte to reade the longe Canones of Avicena, the commentaries of Averroys, the practyses of Isake, Halyabbas, Rasis, Mesue, and also of the more part of them whiche were their aggregatours and folowers. And although I have never bene at Mountpellier, Padua, nor Salerne, yet have I founde some thynge in physyke, whereby I have taken no lyttell profyte concernynge myne owne helthe.

Moreover I wote not why phisitions shulde be angry with me, sens I wrate and dyd set forthe the Castell of helthe for theyr commoditie, that the uncertayne tokens of urines and other excrementes shuld not decyve them, but that by the true information of the sycke man, by me instructed, they mought be the more sure to prepare medicines convenient for the dyseases. Also to the intent that men observyng a good order in diete, and preventyng the greate causes of syckenesse, they shuld of those maladies the sooner be cured.

But yf phisitions be angry that I have written physyke in Englyshe, let theym remembre that the Grekes wrate in Greke, the Romayns in Latyne, Avicena and the other in Arabike, which were their owne propre and maternal tonges. And yf they had bene as moche attached with envy and covetyse as some nowe seeme to be, they wolde have devysed some partycular language, with a straunge syphre or fourme of letters, wherein they wolde have writen theyr scyence, whyche language or letters noo man shoulde have knowen that hadde not professed and practysed physyke: But those, although they were paynymes and Jewes, in this part of charytie they farre surmounted us Chrystyanes, thath they wolde not have so necessarye a knowledge as physike is, to be hydde from theym whyche wolde be studyouse about it.[46]

ELYOT'S DESCRIPTION of his study of physic raises the question of his sources for the *Castel of Helth*.[47] It would have been natural for him to draw material from the writers whose works he had read either under the "worshypfull phisition" or later in his own study, and as a matter of fact the *Castle* is heavily indebted to them. Elyot suggests the debt when he writes, at the end of his chapter on urines, "This I truste shall be sufficient to instruct a physicion: he that desireth to knowe more particulerly hereof, let hym reade the bookes of Hippocrates, Galene, Cornelius Celsus, Actuarius, Paulus, and divers other late writers, for this littell treatise maie not receive it."[48] The list of "suche thynges, whiche of their propertee dooe digest or pourge superfluous humors" is, Elyot states, "gathered out of the bookes of Dioscorides, Galene, Paulus Aegineta, Oribasius, and Aetius, and other late writers."[49] In another passage he writes, "All the residue concernyng thynges natural conteined in the Introduction of Joannitius, and in the littell craft of Galene, I pourposely passe over for this tyme, for as muche as it doeth require a reader havyng some knowlage in philosophie naturall, or els it is hard and tedious to be understand."[50]

A clearer key to Elyot's borrowings, however, lies in his marginal citations—those predecessors of footnotes. They reveal that by far his

[46] *Ibid.*, fols. A iiiv–ivv. William Turner, the great naturalist, was also accused of spreading what some believed should have remained professional secrets. In his *New Herball* (1551) he reminded critics that the works of Galen and Dioscorides were in the vernacular of their original readers: "If they gave no occasion unto every olde wyfe to practise Physick, then give I none. If they gave no occasyon of murther, then gyve I none" (quoted in Bennett, *op. cit.*, p. 102).

[47] I am deeply indebted to Professor D. T. Starnes, of the University of Texas, for his kindness in allowing me to use the books, photostats, and notes which he collected for his own study of the sources of the *Castel of Helth*.

[48] *Castle*, fol. 84v.   [49] *Ibid.*, fol. 59v.   [50] *Ibid.*, fol. 11v.

greatest debt is to Hippocrates, the great contemporary of Socrates and Plato, and to his follower Galen of Pergamum (A.D. 134–201): Hippocrates is cited in eleven notes, Galen in twenty-seven. Most of Hippocrates's ideas were readily available in Galen's writings, particularly in Galen's *Commentaries* on *Hippocrates's Aphorisms*. Elyot may have read Galen in the original Greek, for Aldus had printed a five-volume Greek text in 1525, but he most likely worked directly from a Latin translation. Diomedes Bonardo, a Brescian physician, was the translator of the first published translation of Galen's works, which appeared in 1490; Elyot probably used the better versions by Linacre of Galen's *Commentaries* (1516), *De sanitate tuenda* (1517), *Methodus medendi* (1519), and *De temperamentis* (1521).[51]

Despite the overwhelming influence of Galen and Hippocrates on Elyot, as indeed on all Renaissance medical scholars, Sir Thomas was not content merely to summarize their views. He had studied the other principal writers of antiquity and of the Middle Ages, and much information from their works found its way into the *Castel of Helth*. Of those who wrote during the ages separating Hippocrates and Galen, one of the chief was Cornelius Celsus. Sometimes called "the Latin Hippocrates," Celsus was a member of a patrician Roman family and worked in the Eternal City during the reigns of Augustus, Tiberius, and Caligula. His works, first published at Florence in 1478, became very popular during the Renaissance; at least thirty-five different editions appeared between 1478 and 1667.[52] From Celsus, Elyot takes material about such varied topics as food and drink, sluggishness, exercises (especially gestation), abstinence, vomit, purgations, and urines.[53] Celsus' contemporary Dioscorides, a Greek writer remembered for his highly respected medical herbal, furnished Elyot with comments on the properties of sorrel and radishes,[54] while from So-

[51] *De temperamentis* was printed at Cambridge by Siberch and is probably the first instance of the use of Greek type in England.

[52] These editions are listed in *Aur. Corn. Celsi de Medicina libri octo* (Amsterdam, 1713), fols. * * * * 5ᵛ–6ʳ.

[53] See *Castle*, fols. 46ᵛ, 48ᵛ, 51ʳ, 52ʳ, 54ᵛ, 56ᵛ, 57ᵛ, and 84ᵛ.

[54] *Ibid.*, fols. 25ʳ, 26ᵛ. The Greek text of Dioscorides's works was published by Aldus in 1499; a number of other editions appeared early in the sixteenth century.

ranus of Ephesus, a Greek physician practicing in Rome about the time
of the Emperors Trajan and Hadrian, Elyot translated passages explaining "the tymes appropried to every naturall humour" and "peculiar remedies against the distemperaunce of every humour."[55]

The writings of Galen's later followers were also useful to Elyot;
he borrowed heavily from Oribasius, Aëtius, and Paulus Aegineta.
Oribasius, born in Pergamum about two centuries after Galen, was a
friend of Julian the Apostate and traveled with him on many of his
military campaigns; his *Euphoriston* was printed at Basel in 1529 and
was thus readily accessible to Elyot. From the *Euphoriston* Elyot took
material concerning repletion, blood-letting, the power of milk to
purge melancholy, and the diet of children and old men.[56] It is interesting to note that the passage about blood-letting was borrowed by
Oribasius himself from Galen; here, as in so many other places, Elyot
worked from a convenient secondary source even though he knew the
original.

Aëtius, who lived about a century and a half after Oribasius, was
another follower of Galen whose writings Elyot utilized; the chapters
in the *Castle* on "lassitude extensive" and "lassitude with the felyng of
inflammacion" are close translations of Aëtius's sections "de spontanea
lassitudine extensiva" and "de spontanea lassitudine inflammationis
sensum inferente."[57] Elyot's treatment of "distillacions called commonly reumes" depends in part on Aëtius,[58] as do his descriptions of
the medical properties of almonds, olives, prunes, figs, and lettuce;[59]
Elyot's chapters "of vociferation" and "of gestacion" are clear translations of Aëtius's "de vociferatione," "de gestatione," and "de equita-
tione," though the material derives ultimately from Galen.[60] Paulus
Aegineta, a seventh-century follower of Galen, gave Elyot much the
same material about gestation as did Aëtius, and it is difficult to

[55] *Castle*, fols. 71ᵛ–72ʳ. See Soranus, *In artem medendi*, Chap. V.
[56] *Castle*, fols. 54ᵛ, 61ʳ⁻ᵛ, 36ʳ, 40ᵛ–41ᵛ. See *Oribasii Sardi Iuliani Caesaris
Archiatri Euphoriston* (Basel, 1529), pp. 248, 286–287, 244–245, 249.
[57] *Castle*, fols. 78ᵛ–79ʳ. See *Aetius Amideni quem alii Antiochenum vocant
medici clarrismi libri XVI* (Basel, 1535), Bk. IV, Chaps. XLIIII, XLV.
[58] *Castle*, fols. 72ᵛ–75ᵛ; Aëtius, *Sermo octavus*, Chap. LIII.
[59] *Castle*, fols. 20ʳ–23ᵛ.
[60] *Ibid.*, fols. 51v–53ʳ; Aëtius, Bk. III, Chaps. V, VI, VII.

determine exactly what he took from each source. Paulus also yielded information, again based on Galen, concerning urines, the diet of old men, "fricasies," and the utility of rubbings to prevent crudity.[61]

It was Arabian physicians who kept medical studies alive during the darkest days of the Middle Ages in Western Europe; Elyot knew their chief works and utilized them in preparing his *Castle*. He must have recognized that their ideas were less advanced than Galen's, for he relied on them much less heavily; but he did take material from Rhazes and Damascenus. Rhazes, a celebrated Arabian physician who worked at the beginning of the tenth century and whose works were published in Brescia as early as 1486, supplied information about plagues; Elyot mentions the virtues of the "very excellent . . . pylles called commonly Pillule Rasis" in warding off pestilence, adding that in fact Rhazes himself was not their inventor.[62] The *Aphorisms* of Damascenus, probably a contemporary of Rhazes, had been published in two separate editions before 1500; Elyot took from them the view that abstinence from food in summer is dangerous, for "Damascene saith, it drieth the bodie, it maketh the colour sallow, it ingendreth melancholy, and hurteth the sight." Damascenus also supplied cautionary comments on the deleterious effects of overfrequent blood-letting.[63]

Two other late medieval writers complete the list of physicians from whom Elyot borrowed. Actuarius, a Greek practicing medicine at the court of Constantinople sometime between the eleventh and fourteenth centuries, supplied some of Elyot's comments on urines,[64] and Arnoldus of Villanova, a French physician, alchemist, and theologian of the late thirteenth century, provided information about the merits of blood-letting and the best times of the year for its practice.[65]

Although he does not mention Francesco Patrizi in the *Castel of Helth*, Elyot's discussion of the "affectes of the mynde" probably stems from Patrizi's *De regno et regis institutione*.[66] As we have seen, this

---

[61] *Castle*, fols. 51ᵛ, 84ᵛ, 41ʳ, 49ʳ, 71ᵛ. See *The Seven Books of Paulus Aegineta*, trans. Francis Adams (London, 1844), I, 19, 20–23, 36, 224–228.

[62] *Castle*, fol. 89ʳ. See *Razae de pestilentia libellus* (Venice, 1552), published in a volume dedicated to Archbishop Cranmer and containing also the medical treatise of Alexander Trallianus.

[63] *Castle*, fols. 56ʳ, 62ʳ. [64] *Ibid.*, fols. 82ᵛ, 84ᵛ.

[65] *Ibid.*, fols. 61ʳ, 62ʳ.

[66] *Ibid.*, fols. 64ʳ–70ʳ. See *De regno et regis institutione* (Paris, 1519), Bk. V.

was one of the principal sources for the *Governor*, though Elyot did not incorporate Patrizi's study of the emotions into his own earlier book. The *Castle* does not follow Patrizi literally, and Elyot ranges through the Bible and the writings of Seneca, Appian, and Livy for illustrative material. Still it is likely that the whole subject was suggested to him by Patrizi's book.

His lack of formal medical training and his desire to popularize basic medical knowledge might suggest that Elyot was far behind the best medical opinion of his time. This is not, however, true. Modern medical science did not really begin before Harvey's discovery of the circulation of the blood in the seventeenth century; by the 1530's the best Western physicians had barely regained the level of Hippocrates and Galen. Even the most advanced student of anatomy in Elyot's time, Vesalius, admitted that it was difficult for him to believe the results of dissections when these differed from Galen's descriptions; Cambridge dons still delight in telling how the celebrated Dr. Caius once incarcerated a student until he was ready to accept Galen's views. Sir Thomas was far from being alone in his veneration for the physician of Pergamum. Medical treatment in Elyot's time was universally based upon the theory of the humors; blood-letting was the panacea, uroscopy the fashion. It is to Elyot's credit that he did not always blindly accept traditional views; we have noted two cases in which he suggested treatments which had preserved or restored his own health, and such instances could easily be multiplied.[67] Of course, his was the interest of an amateur. He made no effort to advance anatomical studies, and such observations as he made were based upon his own experience, not upon clinical experimentation. Still, it is hard to escape the conclusion that he knew more than many of the physicians who criticized his book. The large numbers of Englishmen who bought copies of the *Castle* must have thought so, and even professional writers found Sir Thomas's work useful: as late as 1584 Thomas Cogan, author of the *Haven of Health*, was admitting that he had quoted whole sentences from Elyot.[68]

Well might Sir Thomas take pride in the fruits of his study.

[67] See *Castle*, fols. 25^r, 26^v, 28^r, 32^v, 39^v, 43^r, 56^v, 68^r, and 70^r.
[68] *The Haven of Health* (London, 1584), fol. ¶ iii^v.

CHAPTER NINE

Hanging over Us a Grete Kloude

WE HAVE hanging over us a grete kloude," Elyot wrote in April, 1533, to John Hackett, English ambassador in the Netherlands, "which is likely to be a grete storm whan it fallith." He referred to the English Reformation, the progress of which, as we have seen, he was watching with apprehension. "I wold I had some comfortable newes to send you oute of these partes," he continued, "but the world is all other wise." He explained that Hackett would hear, "or it be longe, some straunge thinges of the spirituality, for betwene theim selfes is no perfect agreement. Some do say that thei digged the diche that thei be now fallen in, which causith many goode men the lasse to pitie them." The clergy got small sympathy from Elyot, as indeed from most Englishmen, in those anti-clerical days.

Doctrinal innovations, however, were more serious. Elyot told Hackett of his prayers that God would grant the King "comfort of spirit" and move him to let "truth . . . be freely and thankfully herd."

For my part, I am finally determined to lyve and dye therein. Neither my importable expences unrecompencid shall so moche feare me, nor the advauncement of my successor [Cranmer] the Busshop of Canterbury so moche alure me that I shall ever deklyne from trouthe or abuse my soveraigne lorde unto whome I am sworne. For I am sure that I and you allso shall ones dye, and I know that there is a Godd, and he is all trouthe, and therefore he will grievously punish all fallshode and that everlastingly.[1]

It is not easy to know precisely what Elyot thought "truth" was, but presumably it allowed no tampering with traditional beliefs. He would not "abuse" his sovereign lord: but what if the sovereign lord abused the truth? That dilemma Elyot was unwilling to face. Royal supremacy did not distress him very much, but Protestant doctrines did. He revealed his abhorrence of justification by faith and of predestination in his last published book.[2]

Elyot made his position clearer in a letter to Cromwell written in December, 1534. Sir Thomas had read the King's proclamation concerning seditious books—possibly Cromwell suspected that Elyot had a large number and specially sent him a copy of the decree. Elyot told Cromwell that he had

ben ever desyrous to reade many bookes, specially concerning humanitie and morall philosophy, and therefor of suche studies I have a competent numbre. But concerning holy scripture I have very fewe. For yn questionistes I never delighted: unsavery gloses and comentes I ever abhorred: the bostars and advauncars of the pompouse authoritie of the Busshop of Rome I never esteemyd. But after, that by moche and seriouse reading I hadd apprehendid a jugment or estimacion of thinges, I didd anon smell oute theire corrupt affections, and beheeld with scornfull eyes the sondry abusions of theire authorities, adorned with a licentiouse and dissolute forme of living. Of the which, as well in them as in the universall state of the clergy, I have oftentymes wished a necessary reform.

Elyot added that his views had brought about

no little contencion betwixt me and suche persones as ye have thowght that I have specially favored, even as ye also didd, for some laudable qualities

---

[1] Elyot to John Hackett, April 6, [1533], P.R.O., SP 1/75/81. Elyot concluded by asking Hackett to commend him to several of Charles V's lords and, quaintly, to "the gentill Mr. Adrian and his goode bedfelowe Mistres Philip, whoes honesty, pacience, and moste gentill entretaynement I cesse not to advaunt amonge oure women."

[2] *A Preservative agaynste Deth* (1545); see below, Chap. Ten.

which we supposed to be in theim. But neither they mowght persuade me to approve that which both my faith and my raison condemned, nor I mowght dissuade them from the excusing of that which all the world abhorred. Which obstinacy of bothe partes relentid the grete affection betwene us and withdrue our familiare repayr.

Who were these persons whom Cromwell thought Elyot specially favored? Was one of them More, whom Elyot now condemned for obstinacy and for excusing the inexcusable errors of the papacy and the clergy?

Coming to the point of his letter, Elyot wrote that he did indeed have some books which supported the Pope's authority, "joyned with diverse other warkes in one grete volume or twoo at the moste, which I never founde laysor to reade."³ He had none of John Fisher's works "except one litle sermone, which aboute eight or nyne yeres passid was translatid into Latine by Mr. Pace, and for that cause I bowght it more than for the author or mater." Elyot was not sure where the book was; he had read it only once.

He pleaded that he had been ill and that his books were scattered "in sondry houses of myn owne and farre asonder." But, if the King required it, he would "make diligent serche; and suche as I shall finde savering any thinge agaynst the Kinges pleasure, I will putt theim in redyness either to be browght to you, or to be cutt oute of the volume wherein they be joyned with other."

In conclusion he assured Cromwell of his sincerity and fidelity. "Perchance naturall simplicitie not discretely ordred mought cause men [to] suspect I favored hypocrasy, supersticion, and vanitie. Notwithstanding if ye mowght see my thowghts as Godd doeth, ye shold finde a reformar of those thinges and not a favorar, if I mowght that I wold."⁴

Had the path of Erasmian reform still been open Elyot would no doubt have chosen it. He would not follow More to the block over the question of the supremacy; besides wanting to preserve his neck in-

---

³ Thus the MS. John Strype, *Ecclesiastical Memorials* (Oxford, 1822), I, ii, 228–230, reverses Elyot's meaning by reading "which I have found [*sic*] leisure to read."

⁴ Elyot to Cromwell, "the Vigil of Sainct Thomas" (December 20), [1534], Cotton MS. Cleopatra E. VI, fol. 254, B.M.

tact he probably believed conscientiously that the King was more likely to reform abuses than the Pope. So far, but no farther: Elyot never suggested, even in his most servile letter, that he would willingly see the King tamper with the traditional beliefs and ceremonies. He hoped for superficial purification without fundamental change.

ONE OF THE MEN who thought that Elyot favored superstition and the papacy was a certain John Parkyns. In an incoherent and nearly illegible letter to Cromwell of January 21, 1537, he accuses Elyot of supporting the monasteries, which were out of favor after the break with Rome and were being dissolved. If we may believe Parkyns and his source of information—the "vaine glorious abbat of Ensam" (Eynsham, Oxfordshire)—Cromwell had already warned Elyot against religious conservatism. According to Parkyns,

you, my right honorabill lord, Lord Privye Seall, had Sir Thomas Elyot att soupper with your good lordship. And souper completid, your honorabill lordshipp callid Sir Thomas Eliot to a wyndow and than and there said to hym that he ones did to your lordshipp a good turne, and that your good lordshipp bad hym he shold not be supersticious, sayinge that your honorabill lordshipp was not marrid to abbates.

But Elyot had not profited from Cromwell's admonition. "Whan he is in these parties, thabbat of Ensam and he be but lityll space a sondre." And what is worse, Elyot once rode to Hanborough, "beynge a myle distent from Ensam," only to drink with one Doctor Holyman. "This is but a faynyd matter," Parkyns insisted, "for suche a worshipfull knyght to take hys yournay only to drynke withe suche a base preste. And no doubte, my good lorde, but that same Doctor Holyman is a privy fautor to the Busshop of Rome." Parkyns did not bother to explain that Hanborough lay midway between Eynsham and Elyot's manor of Long Combe; rather he went on to accuse Sir Thomas of being "mervillous familiar withe thabbates of Redynge and of Ensam and with Doctor London, warden of the Newe College in Oxford." Dr. John London was one of the leaders in the suppression of the monasteries in 1538; he was apparently an able man, if somewhat sour. Abbot Hugh Cook of Reading was more of a papist; before his monastery could be dissolved in 1539 he had to be sent to the scaffold on trumped-up charges of treasonable correspondence with Reginald Pole, the Marian archbishop, and Pole's relatives. Anthony Dunstone or Kitchen, abbot of the Benedictine Abbey of Eynsham, was accused by his monks of permitting his sister to live in the precincts and of supporting her relatives with monastic funds, but there is no record that he had other notable vices; he lived on to achieve the dubious distinction of being the only Marian bishop to acquiesce in the Elizabethan religious settlement.[5]

For good measure Parkyns threw in another piece of information: Elyot had told the Abbot of Eynsham that "the Imperator of Allmayn did never speke of the Bisshop of Rome but he avaleid his bonett." Just what the Emperor's act was supposed to prove about Elyot's beliefs is not quite clear.[6]

Parkyns's accusations found their way to the King and his Council, and on January 18, 1537, Henry appointed a commission of eight men, including the Mayor of Oxford and Sir Simon Harcourt, to inquire "with as moche diligence as ye convenyently may" whether the Abbots of Eynsham and Osney "shulde speke certain wordes against us and our dignite contrary to the alliegaunce they ought to bear unto us."[7]

The commissioners met four days later to examine Parkyns, who now turned the tables and tried to discredit the Abbot of Eynsham by accusing him of associating with the superstitious Elyot.[8] The commis-

---

[5] Dom David Knowles, *The Religious Orders in England, Vol. III: The Tudor Age* (Cambridge, England, 1959), p. 354; Geoffrey Baskerville, *English Monks and the Suppression of the Monasteries* (London, 1937), pp. 85, 127 f., 171 f. The whole story of Parkyns's raving is told in "The Fool of Oxford," Chap. I of G. R. Elton, *Star Chamber Stories* (London, 1958), pp. 19–51. Elton reads *Harborough* for *Hanborough* and suggests that Warwickshire village as the site of Elyot's alleged conference with Holyman. Though the manuscript is open to either interpretation, I find the Oxfordshire setting more plausible.

[6] John Parkyns to Cromwell, January 21, [1537], P.R.O., SP 1/114/257–258. Parkyns was also busy "compassing a politakke menes to destroy the rebellious traytors in the Northe parties."

[7] P.R.O., St. Ch. 2/34/12, fol. 1. Osney was one of the most important houses of the Augustinian canons in England; at the time of its dissolution its abbot became the bishop of Oxford and its abbey church the cathedral. The abbey's income in 1535 was more than £654 (David Knowles and R. N. Hadcock, *Medieval Religious Houses: England and Wales* [London, 1953], p. 149; Baskerville, *op. cit.*, p. 248).

[8] Parkyns to Cromwell, [January 23?, 1537], P.R.O., SP 1/115/107–112.

sioners concluded that all his charges were but "lyght matters of malyce," and they ordered that Parkyns spend the rest of the week in prison. During the day he was to be exhibited in the market place at Carfax with a sign reading "For Faulse Accusacyon." And if he dared to remain in Oxford after "the iii^de daye of February, then he should be sett in the pyllory in the sayde markett place callyd Carffaxse, by the space of one hower."[9] When Parkyns was not parading in Carfax, he spent his time writing furious but futile letters to Cromwell.[10]

Parkyns was, as one of the commissioners said, a fanatic, more than half mad. Although the things he said about Elyot were no doubt basically true, they added up to nothing. But these charges, even if they are of little intrinsic significance, are of considerable interest, for clearly the belief that Elyot was a papist was fairly widespread. Had it not been, Elyot need not have used so much ink combating it. Parkyns was not content to harbor suspicions; he had to voice his charges loudly and often. His fanatical accusations have thus been preserved while the similar comments of milder men have left no traces.

It was perhaps with reference to Parkyns's charges that Elyot wrote thanking Cromwell for his "honorable and gentill report to the Kinges Majesty on Wednesday last passid in my favor." The letter is undated but was probably written early in 1537.[11] After the usual assurance of his loyalty Elyot said:

I perceyve that ye suspect that I savor not truely holy scripture. I wold Godd that the King and you mowght see the moste secrete thowghts of my hart. Surely ye shold than perceyve that, the ordre of charity savyd, I have in as moche detestacion as any man lyving all vayne supersticions, super-fluouse ceremonyes, sklanderouse jouglings, countrefaite myrakles, arrogant usurpacions of men callid spirituall and masking religious, and all other abusions of Christes holy doctrine and lawes. And as moche I injoy at the Kinges godly proceeding to the due reformacion of the sayde enormyties as any his Graces poure subject lyving.

Elyot's remark about More followed:

---

[9] P.R.O., St. Ch. 2/34/12, fol. 2.

[10] P.R.O., SP 1/115/95–102, 103–104, 105–106, 107–112, 113–114, 115, 116, 117, 119, 119a. He charged that Harcourt was paid by the abbot of Osney.

[11] Strype (op. cit., I, i, 405 ff.) dates it 1536; L.P. (XIII, ii, 854) suggests 1538.

I therefor beseich your goode lordship now to lay apart the remembraunce of the amity betwene me and Sir Thomas More, which was but *usque ad aras,* as is the proverb, considering that I was never so moche addict unto hym as I was unto truthe and fidelity toward my soveraigne lord.

And then came the request which Elyot had been leading up to:

I moste humbly desyre you, my speciall goode Lorde, so to bryng me into the Kinges moste noble remembrance, that of his moste bounteouse liberality it may like his highnesse to reward me with some convenyent porcion of the suppressid landes.

Elyot was not "married to abbots" if their loss could be his gain. He urged Cromwell to "forget not that neither of his grace nor of any other person I have fee, office, pencion, or ferme, nor have any maner of lucre or advauntage besydes the revenues of my poure lands, which are but small." And, to make his appeal more attractive, he offered Cromwell "the first yeres frutes" of "what so ever porcion of landes . . . I shall attayne by the Kinges gift."[12] Of this request, more later.

ELYOT'S REACTION to the English Reformation was the most interesting facet of his life after 1531. He was engaged, however, in a number of other activities: he bought land from Cromwell and from the Court of Augmentations; he was sued in Star Chamber by one of his tenants; he was named to the Commission of Sewers; he served as a justice of the peace, sheriff, and Member of Parliament.

We have seen that he endeavored to escape from the appointment as sheriff of Cambridgeshire in 1532.[13] He claimed that no one could be sheriff without losing 100 marks; he wrote Cromwell in November that he knew "no part of the contrary above thre myles from my house."[14] But his protests, repeated in a letter of December 8, were unavailing; he had to act as sheriff of Cambridgeshire and Huntingdonshire from November, 1532, until November, 1533.[15]

A single letter—and not an important one at that—pertaining to his duties as sheriff survives. Probably in May, he wrote Cromwell

[12] Elyot to Cromwell, "written at my house by Smythfeld this Moneday" [1537?].—Cotton MS. Cleopatra E. IV, fol. 260, B.M.

[13] See Chap. Six.

[14] Elyot to Cromwell, November 18, [1532], P.R.O., SP 1/72/36–37.

[15] *L.P.,* V, 1598 (10).

concerning the King's order that all men with lands worth 40 pounds a year should become knights. Elyot had submitted a list of such men, compiled by his under-sheriff, "wherein was named one Wawton whoes substance I knewe not and unneth [hardly] his personage." Subsequently Elyot learned that Wawton lacked 40 pounds in land "by a grete porcion." By his industry Wawton sent many sons to school ("very towardly" they were, too), and he would have to provide for the marriage of many daughters. These things were, in the sixteenth century as in the twentieth, "grete corrosives of a litle substance." Therefore, Elyot urged, "in as moche as the gentillman is poure and abasshful, but right wise and having sondry good qualities and accordingly bringith upp many his children, may it please you . . . to shew your gentill hart toward him in declaring how moche ye tendre the necessitie of poure gentillmen."[16]

Elyot's term as sheriff was not without its bright moment: at Michaelmas, 1533, the treasurer of the town of Cambridge recorded a payment of 53s. 4d. "to Sir Thomas Elyot, kt., for his friendship."[17] Elyot again served as sheriff from November, 1544, until November, 1545.[18]

Sir Thomas was a member of the Parliaments of 1539 and 1542; probably in both cases he sat for the borough of Cambridge. Our only knowledge of his membership in the Parliament that passed the Act of Six Articles and the act dissolving the last of the monasteries comes from Elyot's Preface to the 1539 edition of the *Castel of Helth*. Here he asked Cromwell to excuse the errors in the book, "myne attendance on the Parlyament, I being a member of the lower house, withdrawyng from me leysure convenyente to fynde . . . all the fautes."[19] Browne Willis, the eighteenth-century antiquarian, recorded that Elyot sat for Cambridge in 1542;[20] the official returns for the borough have disappeared, and Willis cannot now be proved right or wrong.

A number of routine responsibilities came Elyot's way. He was frequently named a justice of the peace in both Oxfordshire and Cam-

---

[16] Elyot to Cromwell, [May, 1533], P.R.O., SP 1/76/149.
[17] C. H. Cooper, *Annals of Cambridge* (Cambridge, England, 1842), I, 361.
[18] *L.P.*, XXI, ii, 472.
[19] *The Castel of Helth* (London, 1539), fol. A ii.
[20] Browne Willis, *Notitia Parliamentaria* (London, 1716–30), I, 190.

bridgeshire between 1531 and 1545, and in 1540 he was a member of the Commission of the Peace for the entire Eastern Circuit of the Assizes—Bedfordshire, Buckinghamshire, Cambridgeshire, Huntingdonshire, Norfolk, and Suffolk.[21] From 1541 until the time of his death he served on the Commission of Oyer and Terminer for the Eastern Circuit.[22] In 1542 he was a member of the Commission of Gaol Delivery for Cambridgeshire.[23] In 1540 and again in 1544 he was appointed to the Commission of Sewers for Cambridgeshire, Huntingdonshire, Lincolnshire, and Northamptonshire.[24] The commission had wide powers; Henry VIII's Statute of Sewers (1531) was one of the earliest examples of delegated legislative authority, since it gave commissions "full power . . . to make, constitute and ordain laws, ordinances, and decrees."[25] They had also taxing and judicial powers. In Cambridgeshire and Lincolnshire, where there were fens to be drained, the commissioners had even greater responsibilities than the usual ones.

Elyot was among the "knights and gentlemen to be servitors" at the coronation of Anne Boleyn in May, 1533; he was required to "attend upon the Queen's grace, the Bishop, and the ladies sitting at the Queen's board in the Great Hall at Westminster, the day of the coronation."[26] At a later and less happy stage in the King's marital career Elyot was among the knights and squires appointed to receive Anne of Cleves in 1540.[27] In 1543 he was ordered to provide ten foot soldiers for the army that Henry sent to Flanders in accordance with his treaty with Charles V, pledging mutual defense and a united invasion of France.[28] The next year he was charged with supplying twenty men

[21] Oxfordshire: 1531, 1532, 1536, 1537, 1541, 1542, 1545: *L.P.*, V, 119 (54), 278 (22), 1694 (ii); XI, 1217 (20); XII, ii, 157, 1150 (15); XVI, 678 (31); XVII, 714 (4); XX, i, 623 (vi).

Cambridgeshire: 1532, 1539, 1542, 1545: *L.P.*, V, 1694 (ii); XIV, ii, 619 (37); XVII, 1012 (52); XX, i, 623 (vi).

Eastern (Norfolk) Circuit: *L.P.*, XV, 282 (16).

[22] *L.P.*, XVI, 580 (18); XVII, 443 (24); XVIII, i, 226 (8); XX, i, 622 (ii, iv), 623 (ii, iv).

[23] *Ibid.*, XVII, 1154 (96).

[24] *Ibid.*, XVI, 107 (7); XX, i, 622 (vi).

[25] Committee on Ministers' Powers, *Report* (London, 1936), pp. 13 f.

[26] *L.P.*, IV, 562.

[27] *Ibid.*, XIV, ii, 572 (3, viii); XV, 14 (p. 6).

[28] *Ibid.*, XVIII, i, 832.

for "the vantguard,"[29] and in the last year of his life he was named to
the commission to take the musters for Cambridgeshire.[30] The county
was to provide two hundred men, but they may never have seen action,
for Henry made his peace with Francis I, not very advantageously, by
the Treaty of Camp, June 7, 1546.

HENRY VIII and Cromwell were confident enough of Elyot's loyalty
to make use of his services in the survey which preceded the dissolution of the smaller monasteries; in January, 1535, Sir Thomas was
appointed to the commission to visit monasteries in Oxford and Oxfordshire.[31] The visitation itself began in July and lasted just over six
months.[32] Most of the commissioners were lawyers, not country gentlemen as in the survey of the two hundred twenty doomed houses which
was made in 1536, and Elyot's experience with the Assizes and Star
Chamber may have been one reason for his appointment.

Probably shortly after New Year's, Elyot wrote Cromwell that he
had recently "travaylid aboute the survaying of certayne monasteries by
the Kinges commaundment, wherin my paynes shold appiere not unthankfull, if opportunity mowght happen for me to declare it." He
recalled that "at my last being with you at the Rolles" Cromwell had
given him "moste gentill wordes, to my grete comfort. I have often
tymes sens revolved theim in my remembraunce, setting in you onely
all my hole confidence."

Elyot saw in the dissolution an opportunity for the King to rectify
his oversight of Elyot's "importable charges and unrecuperable decay
of . . . living." He suggested to Cromwell that "it mowght please you
to devise with his highness for my convenient recompence toward my
said charges, either by landes now suppressid or pencion." He would
have discussed the matter with Cromwell personally "but that I dradd
to fynde you occupied with grete affayres, which of late hath causid
me to make many vayne journays." But Elyot wanted to "communicate
with you [Cromwell] some tokens of harty friendship; if it be your

[29] *Ibid.*, XIX, i, 274 (p. 159).
[30] *Ibid.*, XIX, i, 91 (Cambs.).
[31] *Ibid.*, VIII, 149 (52).
[32] Baskerville, *op. cit.*, pp. 127 f., 144 f.

pleasure that I shall attend on you at the Court to revyve your gentill remembraunce, I, that knowing, shall folow your commaundment and counsaile." Sir Thomas signed himself "yours with true affection."[33]

Elyot's request did not bear fruit immediately; he received none of the lands of the monasteries which were suppressed in 1536. But on December 5, 1539, after the possessions of the wealthier abbeys had fallen into the royal coffers, Thomas and Margaret Elyot were granted some lands in Cambridgeshire which had belonged, ironically, to the abbey of Eynsham, Oxfordshire. The grant included the manor of Histon Eynsham, the rectory and advowson of the parish church there, and the appurtenances of the manor in Histon Eynsham, Histon Denny, Hogington, Impington, Girton, Milton, and Landbeach. Elyot paid £437 15s. 4d. for the manor, and he was to give £4 annual rent to the Court of Augmentations.[34] At a Chancery Inquisition taken after Elyot's death these lands were reckoned to be worth £40 10s. yearly, so Elyot's payment was much less than the customary price of twenty times the annual value.[35] Henry VIII's grant must have been intended partly to compensate Elyot for his labors in the Council, in Germany, and in the Oxfordshire survey.

In 1538, Elyot bought the manor of Carlton, Cambridgeshire, from Cromwell. It adjoined lands which Elyot had inherited from Thomas Findern in 1523. A certain Henry Polstead was Cromwell's agent in arranging the sale; he asked £774 5s. for the properties, while Elyot offered £750.[36] By an indenture signed on March 14, Elyot agreed to pay Cromwell £789 14s. 6d. over a twenty-one-year period. In addition to the manor itself he received the patronage of the parish church at Carlton and the annexed chapel of Willingham and the advowson of the parish church of Weston Colville; these were worth just over £30. The manor included lands in Carlton, Brinkley, Carlton Barbedors, Weston Colville, and Willingham.[37]

Polstead had specified that Gilbert Claydon, a farmer at Carlton,

---

[33] Elyot to Cromwell, [1536], P.R.O., SP 1/104/248.

[34] *L.P.*, XIV, ii, 780 (4). At the Chancery Inquisition post Mortem the rent was said to be £4 6s.

[35] P.R.O., C 142/74/16.

[36] P.R.O., SP 1/129/56–57. The same Polstead was sued in Star Chamber for adultery with John Crowe's wife.

[37] P.R.O., SP 1/129/58–59.

was entitled to a fee of 40 shillings a year and the use of an acre of wood for fuel. Claydon had leased the manors of Carlton and Willingham from Cromwell, and Elyot had trouble getting him to vacate the properties. Claydon finally petitioned the King in Star Chamber for a settlement of his grievances, claiming that

Sir Thomas Elyot, Nicholas Stutevile, [Thomas] Laugton, with dyverse othere ryotouse persones to the nombre of viii^te or there aboute in moste ryotouse wyse agenst your graces peace, that ys to saie with billes and swerdes, entred as well into the said manors of Carleton and Welingham and other the premysses to your graces said subject demysed and letid as ys aforesaid, as also into the said mesuage and iiii acres of pasture callid Cranes, the first daie of November last past.[38]

We may discount Claydon's complaint about riots, swords, and bills or pikes, for these were stock legal terms thought necessary to bring the case within the jurisdiction of Star Chamber; but he alleged further that Elyot's action was contrary to the decision of a group of arbitrators (Sir Edward North, Philip Parish, Serjeant Townsend, Serjeant Hind, John Broke, and John Goswold) that Claydon "should peceably have hold, possede, and injoyed the said manours of Carleton and Welingham until the Feast of Thannuncyacion of Oure Lady" and that Elyot should pay him 100 marks "for the redempcion of the same lease and farme." Since Claydon was "a poore man and not able to sue for his remedie herin by thordre of the comon lawes," he asked for justice in the Star Chamber.

In reply, Elyot said that Claydon's bill of complaint was "uncerteyn and insufficient in the lawe, . . . and the matter theryn contayned for the mooste parte untrue and ffalsli . . . contryved." Besides, Claydon should have sued at the common law. Such purely formal protests are found in nearly all Star Chamber answers.

Elyot proceeded to explain the case. It was true that Claydon's father had held a messuage of four acres by copy of the custom of the manor, and it was true that Gilbert Claydon had leased the manors from Cromwell. But Claydon had confused "freehold" and "copyhold"; he had refused to render the customary services to the lord of the manor; he had enclosed "the comen ffeld of the said defendant"; he had

[38] P.R.O., St. Ch. 2/10/36, fol. 1.

rented out certain lands which he should have cultivated himself. A court held at Carlton on October 6 had decided that he had forfeited the right to his lands, and Elyot's bailiff, Thomas Laughton, had tried to occupy them. But Claydon made trouble because of his "most vengeable malice, hatred, and enmyte." Finally he agreed to submit to the arbitration of "Lord Awdley of Walden, highe Chaunncellor of England," but when Audley announced his decision Claydon "with prowde and most presumptuouse wordes . . . contemptuously refused" to abide by it.

Claydon thought that he would get a more advantageous decision from a group of local mediators. Elyot agreed to this; the arbitrators— those whom Claydon had listed—concluded that Claydon "should ymmedyatly surrendre, yelde upe, and utterly gyve over" the manors, and that Elyot should pay him 100 marks in compensation. Since Claydon had fourteen bullocks which he did not wish to sell immediately, Elyot agreed to rent him pasture until the Feast of the Annunciation, March 25. As surety that Claydon would pay the rent, Elyot's bailiff took ten of Claydon's bullocks to an open field "and ther dyd empounde theym and theym retayned untyll the sayd rent was to hym payde." It was not true that Claydon should have held the manors until Lady Day; he had in fact lost all right to them when he accepted the 100 marks. Elyot had been obliged to enter his land forcibly on November 1, but there was "no riott don agayne the Kynges peace as in the sayd byll ys surmysed."[39]

Claydon submitted the usual short "replicacion," asserting merely that his original charges were "not ymagined or contrivid."[40] There

39 *Ibid.*, fol. 2.
40 *Ibid.*, fol. 3. There was also an interesting and, in places, amusing suit (St. Ch. 2/24/345) between a Thomas Elyot and an Edward Stanbank, of Bray, Berks. A large number of Elyot's followers had pulled down Stanbank's house and barn and had "cutt downe and distroied . . . certen frute trees, as apple trees, peyre trees, warden trees, and other kynde of frute trees to the nombre of clx and above." Elyot asserted that he "was not therof nor of any parte therof gylty," and he explained that Stanbank had wrongfully enclosed a common field for his home and orchard. The Thomas Elyot involved here, however, was not our Sir Thomas, but rather a gentleman of Bray who died in 1558. His will was proved in the Court of the Archdeaconry of Berks.—See W. P. W. Phillimore (ed.), *Index to Wills Proved in the Court of the Archdeaconry of Berks., 1508 to 1562* (London, 1893).

is, as usual, no surviving record of the court's decision; we may suppose that it would almost certainly have been in Elyot's favor.

After Cromwell's attainder in June, 1540, the lands which he had sold to Elyot reverted to the Crown, but Henry granted them again to Thomas and Margaret on August 4. Elyot had paid Cromwell £500 and still owed £489 14s. 6d., which he was now to pay to the King.[41] At the time of Sir Thomas's death these lands were said to be worth £48 18s. a year; he had bought them at a little more than twenty years' purchase.[42]

A Chancery Inquisition post Mortem held at Newmarket on September 7, 1546, nearly six months after Elyot's death, examined the documents pertaining to his lands in Cambridgeshire. In addition to the estates which he had purchased from the King and from Cromwell, he had inherited the use of the Findern lands. Dr. Edmund Natures, master of Clare College, and a group of other men had originally been enfeoffed with the lands to Elyot's use, but the inquisition specifically stated that after the passage of the Statute of Uses (1536) Elyot and his wife were seised directly. The Findern lands included the manors of Weston Colville and Little Carlton (or Loppams), with lands in Weston Colville, Carlton, West Wratting, Babraham, Balsham, Willingham, and Wickham, which Elyot held from the Bishop of Ely in return for his fidelity, and the manors of Weston Moynes and Leverers, which he held from the Duke of Richmond for 6s. 6d. annually. These lands were worth £70 a year: that brought Elyot's annual income from lands in Cambridgeshire to £159 8s. The inquisitors found that Margaret Elyot was in possession of all the lands, and it was established that the next heir was Richard Puttenham, son of Elyot's sister Margery. Richard was then twenty-six.[43]

In addition to his lands in Cambridgeshire, Elyot held considerable estates in the West of England. The will which he wrote before he left England on his embassy in 1531 and which he confirmed three days before his death at Carlton on March 26, 1546, directed that they

[41] *L.P.*, XV, 1027 (16).

[42] P.R.O., C 142/74/16.

[43] *Ibid.*, printed in Croft, I, 322–327. The inquisitions in E 150/94/2 and Wards 7/2/119, P.R.O., are (as usual) copies of the Chancery Inquisition. All of these documents confirm that Elyot died on March 26 and not, as the *D.N.B.* states, on March 20.

should pass to his wife. He listed the manor of Fairwood, Dorset, with "landes and tenements, meadowes, pastures, rentes, rewersions, and frutes" in Fairwood, Gussage St. Michael's, Stower Eston, Stower Weston, Kinson, and "Ilande," the manor of Muscliff and land in Auscliff, Hampshire, and lands in Ebbesborne Wake, Willowbrook, and Chalk, Wiltshire.[44] He did not mention the manor of Long Combe, Oxfordshire, but there is no indication that he had sold it. With these lands in addition to his Cambridgeshire holdings Elyot must have had an income of well over £200 a year at the time of his death—a very considerable sum.

Interesting as the story of Elyot's governmental service and private life after 1532 is, these activities were of far less lasting significance than his literary endeavors. During the last decade of his life Elyot compiled his most ambitious scholarly work, an immense Latin-English dictionary, and wrote a number of other books. These must now claim our attention.

[44] Prerogative Court of Canterbury, MS. 14 Alen. Croft (I, clxxx) and the *D.N.B.* are in error in stating that Elyot died intestate. The error is puzzling, since Croft found and printed Sir Richard Elyot's will, also proved in the P.C.C. Thomas Elyot's will was proved July 2 at Lambeth on the oath of Dame Margaret Elyot, his wife, and Thomas Laughton, his bailiff.

CHAPTER TEN

Regarde to My Last Rekning

IN THE PREFACE to one of his works published in 1541, Sir Thomas Elyot reflected that he might have gained more wealth and risen higher in men's esteem had he not spent so much time reading and writing books. He defended his literary activities, however; the Scriptures, he said, had made him "take more regarde to my last rekning, than to any riches or worldly promotion."[1]

Making his own reckoning of his achievements, Sir Thomas set out a list of his works and showed the value of each. He mentioned his

Boke called the Gouernour, instructinge men in such vertues as shalbe expedient for them which shal have authority in a wele publike. The Doctrinal of princis, which are but the counsayles of wyse Isocrates, inducinge into noble mens wittes honest opinions. The Education of children, which also I have translated oute of the wise Plutarche, making men and women, which will folow those rules, to be wel worthy to be fathers and mothers. The litel Pasquill although he be mery and playne, teching as well servantes how to be faythfull unto their maisters, as also masters how to be circum-

[1] *The Image of Gouernance* (London, 1541), fols. A ii^v–iii^r.

163

spect in espying of flaterars. Semblably thoffice of a good counsellour, with magnanimity or good courage in tyme of adversity, may be apparantly founden in my boke called, Of the knowlege belonging to a wise man. In reding the sermon of saynt Cyprian by me translated, the devout reder shal fynde no litle comport in plages or calamities. The banket of Sapience is not fastidious, and in litle rome shewith out of holy scripture many wise sentences. The Castel of Helth being truly rad, shal longe preserve men (being some phisicions never so angry) from perillouse siknes.

He continued by describing three books which we shall examine in this chapter: *The Defence of Good Women*, which "not only confoundeth villainous report, but also teachith good wives to know well their duties"; *The Image of Gouernance*, which "shall be to all them which wil reade it sincerely a very true paterne wherby they may shape all their procedinges," and the "Dictionary declaringe Latyne by Englishe," which "shall not only serve for children, as men have expected it, but also shall be commodiouse for them which perchaunce be well lerned."

The most important product of the last decade of Elyot's life, and the most significant contribution to learning which he could claim at his last reckoning, was his Latin-English dictionary. It was first printed in 1538; it would have appeared earlier, although in a less adequate form, had it not been for the encouragement of Henry VIII. Or so Elyot said in his dedicatory epistle to the King:

About a yere passed I beganne a Dictionarie, declaryng Latine by Englishe, wherin I used lyttell study, beinge than occupied about my necessarye busynes, whiche letted me from the exacte labour and study requisyte to the makynge of a perfyte Dictionarie. But whiles it was in printyng, and uneth the half deale performed, your hyghnes being informed therof . . . mooste specially by the recommendation of the most honourable lorde Crumwell, . . . your hyghnesse in the presence of dyvers your noble men, commendynge myne enterprise, affirmed that if I wolde ernestely travayle therin, your highnes, as well with your excellent counsaile, as with suche bokes as your grace had, and I lacked, wold therin ayde me: with the which wordes, I confesse, I received a newe spirite, as me semed: wherby I founde forthwith an augmentation of myn understandynge, in so moche as I juged all that whiche I had writen not worthy to come in your gracis presence without an addition. Wherfore incontinent I caused the printer to cesse, and beginninge at the letter *M*, where I lefte, I passed forth to the last letter with a more diligent study. And that done, I eftesones returned to the fyrst letter, and with a semblable diligence performed the remnant.[2]

The form of the dictionary confirms Elyot's new spirit and more diligent study. Letters *A* to *L,* inclusive, are rather briefly treated, but the section *M* to *Z* contains more words and longer definitions. Then follows the addition, containing many more words belonging to the first half of the alphabet. If a reader fails to find the definition he wants in the first part of the dictionary, he must "repayre incontinente" to the addition.

Elyot's dictionary was not the first to be printed in England. Wynkyn de Worde had published a Latin-English dictionary, the [*H*]*ortus vocabulorum* or garden of words, in 1500, and between 1510 and 1528 he had also brought out about seven editions of the *Promptorium parvulorum,* the earliest extant English-Latin dictionary, written about 1440 and first printed by Richard Pynson in 1499. Both of these, however, were thoroughly medieval, based upon the works of such twelfth- and thirteenth-century writers as Hugh of Pisa, Joannes Balbus, John of Garland, and Alexander Neckam.[3] Elyot's dictionary was the first to bear the marks of the New Learning; it was intended for students of classical Latin, and, as Elyot told King Henry, it included "a thousande mo latine wordes than were together in any one Dictionarie publyshed in this royalme at the tyme when I fyrst began to write this commentarie, which is almost two yeres passed." Sir Thomas had included

propre termes belongynge to lawe and phisike, the names of divers herbes knowen among us: also a good number of fishes founden as wel in our occean, as in our rivers: moreover sondrie poysis [weights], coynes, and measures, sometyme used among the auncient Romaynes, Grekes, and Hebrues. . . . Nor have I omitted proverbes, callyd Adagia, or other quicke sentences which I thought necessarie to be had in remembraunce.[4]

His tables of weights and measures had required "moche study and incredible labour,"[5] but they would make the book useful to those who were studying Latin and the classics "withoute perfyte instructours,

[2] *The Dictionary of Syr Thomas Elyot* (London, 1538), fols. A ii^v–iii^r.

[3] D. T. Starnes, *Renaissance Dictionaries* (Austin, Texas, 1954), pp. 10–18, 31–37.

[4] *Dictionary,* fol. A iii^v.

[5] *Ibid.,* fol. Ll viii^v.

whyche are not many. . . . The cause I nede not reherse, sens I ones declared it in my booke called the Governour, whiche about viii yeres passed I dydde dedicate unto your hyghnesse."

Elyot's Dedication to the King did, however, rehearse some of the things which he had already said in the *Governor*, probably because Elyot could think of no better way to please Henry. "Truely I am and ever have bene of this opynion, mooste noble, moste puissaunt, and moste vertuouse prynce, that the royall astate of a kynge here in erth, next under God, is of men moste to be honoured, loved, and feared in an incomparable degree and facion." All natural things have one principal ruler. Even the polytheistic pagans assigned supreme power to Jupiter. There must be kings for "the commune distribution of justyce, wherby the people under their governaunce shulde be kepte and preserved in quiete lyfe, not exercysed in bestiall appetite." Considering this, all men must realize that "they whiche rebell agaynst kynges be ennemies to God, and in wyll confounders of naturall order and providence." Although Elyot had said the same thing in the *Governor*, the ideas seem to have more relevance to actual contemporary events after the Pilgrimage of Grace and the attendant civil disturbances. Elyot was probably still trying to combat the idea that he was a papist when he added that there was in Henry

a divine influence or sparke of divinitie: whiche late appered to all them that behelde your grace syttyng in the throne of your royal astate, as Supreme Heed of the Churche of Englande next under Christ, about the descision and condemnation of the pernicious errours of the moste detestable heretyke John Nicholson, callyd also Lambert.[6]

Nicholson had been accused of anabaptism, together with errors concerning the sacraments, the incarnation, and the interpretation of the Scriptures; soon after his trial he was dragged through the streets of London to a fiery death at Smithfield. It is significant that his heresy was of the left rather than of the right; Elyot would probably not have condemned a conservative dissenter from the Henrician regime.

The copy of the dictionary which Elyot presented to Cromwell is

---

[6] *Ibid.*, fol. A ii[r]. Nicholson was a Fellow of Queens' College, Cambridge; see H. C. Porter, *Reformation and Reaction in Tudor Cambridge* (Cambridge, England, 1958), p. 65.

preserved in the British Museum; there is a rather interesting manuscript letter, in Latin, on the flyleaf.[7] In it Elyot congratulated Cromwell on his appointment as "Minister ac Consiliarius"; Cromwell, though predestined to great honor, had won his position through the help of fortune and God's perpetual good will toward the people of England. Elyot valued Cromwell's friendship, he said, because of the rare fecundity of Cromwell's wit and the similarity of their studies, not because Elyot had any personal ambition; but he did remind Cromwell that (as Cicero had said) there was no worse crime than damaging the reputation of a friend or failing to protect him when he was in danger. No one, Elyot asserted, could be more loyal to Cromwell than he was; that he did not lie Cromwell could judge for himself if he would remember their first meeting nineteen years ago.[8] His last statement places the beginning of their friendship in 1519, when Elyot was still a clerk on the Western Assizes. Perhaps both were already under Wolsey's patronage then.

Although Elyot included marginal references citing such ancient authors as Plautus, Terence, Galen, Pliny, Livy, Columella, Cicero, Caesar, and Vergil, and although he referred to such Humanistic writers as Erasmus, Valla, Budé, and Perottus, the chief source for his *Dictionary* was another dictionary, the all-Latin *Dictionarium* of Friar Ambrose Calepine of Bergamo.[9] Calepine's compilation was first published in Reggio in 1502; sixteen editions of it issued from the great Aldine press between 1542 and 1583. Elyot mentioned Calepine only in passing, and then rather disrespectfully, but he took from the Friar not only a large number of definitions but also his method of arrangement. Both writers, preferring an etymological arrangement to a strictly alphabetical one, listed derivatives under their roots, and both included geographical and biographical entries in the main text rather than providing a separate list of proper nouns.

Already in the Preface to the 1538 edition of the *Dictionary*, Elyot admitted that his book had certain faults due to "to moche trust had

[7] B. M., class mark c.28.m.2.

[8] "Quod non mentior tute judicaveris primi congressus nostri memor, a quo hic quidem annus est undevigesimus."

[9] The discussion of Elyot's sources presented here is derived principally from Starnes, *Renaissance Dictionaries*, Chaps. VI and VII.

in Calepine." He endeavored to correct these in his *Bibliotheca Eliotae*, a considerably enlarged revision of the *Dictionary* published in 1542 and reprinted without significant change in 1545. Elyot again dedicated his work to the King, suggesting that it was Henry's favor which had spurred him to provide a more adequate book. In this Dedication Elyot repeated his stock comparison of the king to God and to the sun, adding that great kings have "most witty persones" among their counselors because the encouragement of kings "rendreth to theyr wittes a more sharpenesse, with a prompt dexteritee, armed with hardinesse." And yet—was not Elyot referring to himself?—"and yet sapience is often tymes hyd in those persones, whom either malicious wittes hateth, or envie pursueth, or fortune contemneth." But Henry had, Elyot said, commended his diligence in preparing the dictionary. And

the said comfortable wordes of your highnesse, continually resortyng unto my remembrance, ceassed not to provoke me to read over eftsoones and revolve my saied warke, fearing (as God shall judge me) lest by my negligence, either some woordes lackyng, or some interpretacion beyng misconceived, my labours shulde be not onely unprofitable unto the readers but also unwoorthy the moste benigne and favorable report of your excellent majestee.

I therfore most fervently stirred by your graces comfort, in perusing my saied Dictionarie, have proceded to the correction and amplificacion therof, in such fourme as hereafter foloweth. First sequestryng my selfe from all other businesse (that onely except, wherin I was bounden to serve your highnes) I assembled all suche authours as I thought shulde be necessarie for the achievyng of that, whiche I toke in enterprise, whose names do immediately folowe this proheme, and layng them before me, I not onely dyd seriously and diligently trie and examyne every woorde, which either in significacion or fourme of speakyng, called a phrase, mought make any doubt to them that shuld read it, and by the same authors dyd as truely correct it, as my learnyng wolde serve me: but also with a new spirite of hardinesse, received by the often remembrance of your gracious saide comfort, I . . . adventured to make a general collection by the ordre of letters of all notable countries, citees, mountains, and rivers, with their true descriptions, boundes, and commodities: the names and natures of sundry beastes, foules, serpentes, and fishes: the declaracion of a great number of herbes, trees, fruites, gummes, precious stones and metalles, whiche before me were never of any man (that I can here of) declared and set foorth in English: the true

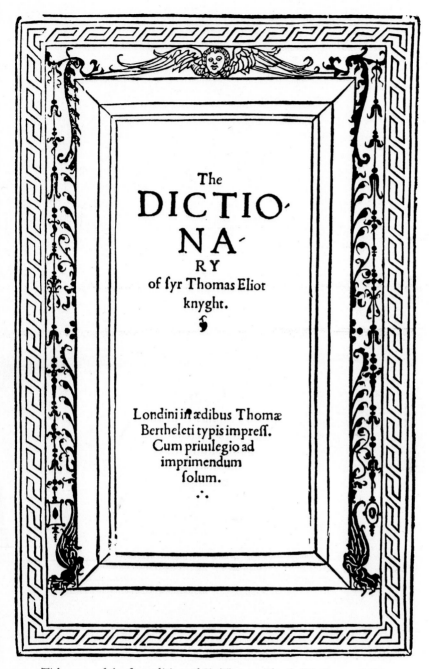

The
DICTIO-
NA-
RY
of ſyr Thomas Eliot
knyght.
§

Londini in ædibus Thomæ
Bertheleti typis impreſſ.
Cum priuilegio ad
imprimendum
ſolum.
∴

Title page of the first edition of Sir Thomas Elyot's *Dictionary*, 1538.
(From the copy in the British Museum)

The parish church of Carleton-cum-Willingham, Cambridgeshire.
(From a photograph by the author)

definicions of all sickenesses and kyndes of maladies, whiche commonly dooe happen to men, with the cause wherof thei procede: finally the names of moste notable personages, who from the firste man Adam until thre hundred yeres after the incarnacion of Christ dyd any thyng woorthy a speciall remembrance, expedient and necessarie to the moderacion of our actes and procedynges, with the histories or lives of the saied persones compendiously gathered.[10]

I have not omitted fables and invencions of painyms, for the more easie understandyng of poetes. I also thought it necessarie to enterlace the detestable heretikes, with their sundrie heresies, . . . to the entent that those heresies, beyng in this wise divulgate, maie be the sooner espied and abhorred in suche bookes where thei be craftily enterlaced with holsome doctrine. . . . As well in this parte as in the histories and fables, I have sette out the computacion of tyme called chronographie, wherin it appereth, how longe the persons were either before the incarnacion of Christe, or how long after.

He had also, as in the first edition, set out tables of coins, weights, and measures, explained adages, and defined the terms used in physic, surgery, "and other divers and sundrie artes and sciences. Moreover I have declared divers Greke woordes, which be usurped of Latine authors." Finally, he asked Henry to receive his new edition,

which I have eftsoones dedicated unto your highnesse, with like benignitee as you received my first edicion, whiche neither in diligence, nor syncere exposicion, nor in copie of woordes, nor in abundance of matter and sentence, is in any way to be hereto compared.[11]

The list of writers whom Elyot mentioned would be of considerable interest in revealing the breadth of his reading if we could be sure that he had actually studied all of the authors he names. In all he mentions a hundred nineteen authors, among them twenty-one historians, seven geographers, fifteen philosophers, eight sacred writers, thirteen medical authorities, eighteen grammarians, five writers of fables, four interpreters of laws, and seventeen "autores ambigui tituli." It is of particular interest to see which Renaissance writers Elyot claims to have

---

[10] It is interesting to note that the biographies end at A.D. 300. Doubtless Elyot thought that no medieval men merited attention, with the possible exception of kings of England.

[11] *Bibliotheca Eliotae* (London, 1545), fols. A ii^r–iii^v.

TABLE 3

Writers Consulted for the *Bibliotheca Eliotae*

Philosophers	*Authors of Sacred Works*	*Authors of Unclassified Titles*	*Physicians*
Plato	Moses	Varro	Hypocrates
Aristotle	The Hagiographers	Pliny	Galen
Xenophon	Eusebius	Solinus	Dioscorides
Theophrastus	Tertullian	Aulus Gellius	Paulus Aegineta
Plotinus	Jerome	Macrobius	Alexander Trallian
Porphyrius	Epiphanius	Vitruvius	Constantinus Affricanus
Proclus	Augustine	Vibius Sequester	Seraphio
Philo	Gennodius	Frontinus	Mesueh
Alexander Aphrodiseus		Vegetius	Jo. Ruellius
Xenocrates		Ludovicus Coelius	Jo. Manardus
Seneca		Hermolaus Barbarus	Antonius Musa Brascevola
Censorinus		Jovianus Pontanus	Jo. Agricola
Boethius		Erasmus Roterodamus	Georgius Agricola
Julius Firmicus		Gulielmus Budeus	
Hyginius		Lazarus Bapheus	
		Georgius Agricola	
		Robertus Senalis	

Phrases Collected from	*Historians*		*Geographers*
	Greek	*Latin*	
Cicero	Herodotus	Appian	Strabo
Julius Caesar	Thucydides	Helian	Pomponius Mela
Terence	Plutarch	Arrian	Ptolemy
Livy	Herodian	Polybius	Americus Vesputius

Salust
Cornelius Celsus
Junius Columella
Plautus
Vergil
Cornelius Tacitus
Quintilian

Dionysius of Halicarnassus
Diogenes Laërtius

Livy
Cornelius Nepos
Suetonius
Valerius Maximus
Quintus Curtius
Julius Capitolinus
Lampridius
Ammianus
Aemilius Probus
Justin
Eutropius

Peter Martyr
Antonius Sabellicus
Raphael Volaterranus

Grammarians

Suidas
Julius Pollux
Eustathius
The Interpreter of Homer
The Interpreter of Aristophanes
Priscian
Servius
Donatus
Porphyrio
Acron
Pompeius Festus
Pedian
Angelus Politianus
Pomponius Laetus
Beroaldus Bononiensis
M. Antonius Sabellicus
Vitellius
Baptista Egnatius

Writers of Stories

Homer
Hesiod
Ovid
Diodorus Siculus
Pausanias

Legal Interpreters

Authors of the Pandects
Andreas Alciatus
Uldericus Zasius
Claudius Cantiuncula

consulted; among them are Vespucci on geography, Poliziano on grammar, and, among the authors of unclassified titles, Erasmus, Pontano, and Ermolao Barbaro. Elyot's complete list is reproduced as Table 3.

Elyot was probably familiar with the works of all the authors whom he lists, but clearly he was not equally indebted to them all. Although he carries over a number of definitions taken from Calepine, he does not even mention the Friar in the *Bibliotheca*. He does say that he is "folowyng the example of Suidas the Greke" in including geographical and biographical data, and he actually took a good deal of material from Suidas's Greek *Lexicon*. Elyot is also rather heavily indebted to the works of three of his own contemporaries—the French Humanists Guillaume Budé, Étienne Dolet, and Robert (the Elder) Estienne. In fact it has recently been shown[12] that Estienne's *Dictionarium Latino-Gallicum* of 1538 was the principal source of the augmentation which makes Elyot's *Bibliotheca* so much more useful than his *Dictionary*. The extent of the augmentation may be suggested by the fact that there were, for instance, one hundred seventy-seven entries in the *Dictionary* under the letters *ER* to *EV*, inclusive. In the *Bibliotheca* there are forty-eight additional entries, and many of the original hundred seventy-seven have been lengthened with new definitions or illustrations. The 1542 and 1545 dictionaries are rearranged as well as augmented; Elyot apparently realized that an alphabetical pattern is more convenient, if less logical, than an etymological one.

Sir Thomas claimed that he had included "the names of moste notable personages," and it is true that there are a large number of biographical sketches in the *Bibliotheca*. In particular, he presented lives of Philip of Macedon, Phocion, Pericles, and Aemilius Paulus, all based on a Latin version of Plutarch; a sketch of Epimenides taken from Diogenes Laërtius; and, working from the *De poetis Latinis* of Petrus Crinitus, biographies of the Roman poets Horace, Plautus, Terence, Propertius, Ovid, Accius, Livius Andronicus, Ennius, Aemilius Macer, and Pacuvius.[13] For some reason Elyot did not appropriate Crinitus's sketches of Seneca and Vergil, among others, though they were two of his favorite writers.

Among the contents of the *Bibliotheca* are many proverbs, nearly

[12] By Starnes, *Renaissance Dictionaries*, pp. 58–61.
[13] *Ibid.*, pp. 63 f.

all derived from Erasmus' *Adagia*, and a number of definitions of botanical and zoological terms. It has been shown[14] that Elyot made use of the *Libellus de re herbaria novus*, by the great naturalist and dissident churchman William Turner, in revising his dictionary; Elyot and Turner frequently give the same English equivalents for Latin terms, and there were no earlier works from which both might have borrowed them. For his part, Turner made considerable use of Elyot's dictionary when he wrote *The Names of Herbes in Greke, Latin, English, Duche, and French* (1549), although his only direct reference to Elyot was one of disagreement—when he defined *Ligustrum* as "prim print or Privet, tho Eliote more boldely then lernedly defended the contrary."[15] Since there are two references in Turner's *Names* to "Coombe parcke," perhaps Elyot and Turner had discussed botany at Sir Thomas's manor of Long Combe. It is also quite possible that they met occasionally in Cambridgeshire, for Turner was a fellow of Pembroke College, Cambridge, until 1537, while Elyot made his principal residence after 1530 at Carlton. It is hardly likely that they were close friends, for Turner was a radical Protestant and Elyot clearly right of center in his view of religion.

After Elyot's death the dictionary was corrected and enlarged three times by Thomas Cooper, master of Magdalen College School, Oxford. Cooper was later master of Magdalen College, bishop of Lincoln, and finally bishop of Winchester from 1584 to 1594; he was lampooned in the Marprelate tract, "Ha' ye any work for the Cooper?" The title page of his revision of 1548 boasted that the book contained "above xxxiii thousande wordes and phrases, very nedefull for the knowlage of the latine tonge"; Cooper had corrected some of Elyot's definitions which were "greatly amisse by over muche folowynge of Calepine." The edition of 1522 was "the second tyme enriched, and more perfectly corrected," and the edition printed in 1559 stated that it was "the third tyme corrected, and with a great number of phrases enriched, as to him that conferreth the other aeditions, it may easely appeare." Material from the *Bibliotheca Eliotae* was also carried over into Cooper's *Thesaurus linguae Romanae & Britannicae*, which was

[14] By Canon C. E. Raven, *English Naturalists from Neckam to Ray* (Cambridge, England, 1947), pp. 43 f., 72 ff.

[15] Quoted in *ibid.*, p. 72.

printed in at least six editions between 1565 and 1587, and dictionaries as late as Robert Ainsworth's *Thesaurus linguae Latinae compendiarius* (1736) continued to use definitions derived ultimately from the Elyot-Cooper texts.[16] Elyot's lexicographical labors were thus of great lasting significance.

A brief history of Latin-English lexicography included by Francis Gouldman in the Preface to his *Copious Dictionary in Three Parts* (1664) gives Elyot credit for producing the first English dictionary of classical Latin:

> To come to our own Writers of Dictionaries: About the same time Sir Th. Eliot, an able Lawyer, and every way a famous Scholar in those days first brake the Ice as to our English Tongue, with great pains Compiling a Latine and English Dictionary, called his Bibliotheca, in the Reign of King Henry the Eighth, to whome it is Dedicated.[17]

How happy Sir Thomas would have been could he have heard such praise during his lifetime!

ELYOT FOLLOWED the first edition of his dictionary with a *Defence of Good Women*, published in 1540 and reprinted in 1545. Like the two Platonic dialogues of counsel which he published in 1533, the *Defense* is cast in the same genre; again this form was probably intended to veil Elyot's comments on English politics, for the book seems to present covert praises of Catherine of Aragon.

Perhaps because he wished to dedicate the *Defense* to Catherine's memory but thought that impolitic, Sir Thomas omitted his usual dedicatory epistle. Instead he began the work with a summary of its contents. His book was

> A Contencion betwene two gentill men, the one named Caninius, the other Candidus. Caninius, like a curre, at womens condicions is alway barkyng: but Candidus, whiche maie be interpreted, benigne or gentill, judgeth ever well, and reproveth but seldom. Betwene them two, the estimacion of womankinde cometh in question. After long disputacion, wherin Candidus (as reason is) hath the preheminence, at the last, for a perfect conclusion,

---

[16] Starnes, *Renaissance Dictionaries*, p. 346.

[17] Francis Gouldman, *A Copious Dictionary in Three Parts* (London, 1669), Preface; quoted in Starnes, *ibid.*, pp. 288 f.

Queene Zenobia (which lived aboute the yere after the Incarnacion of Christe 274, the noble Aureliane being emperour of Rome) by the example of hir life, confirmeth his argumentes, and also vanquissheth the obstinate mynde of froward Caninius, and so endeth the matter.[18]

Many ancient poets, of course, had condemned women; but Caninius and Candidus agree—in striking contrast to Elyot's praise of the poets in the *Governor*—to "geve no credence to poetes," since "the more part of their invencions consisted in leasinges [lies], or in steryng up of wanton appetites, or pouryng out, in railynge, their poison of malice."[19] None of the true philosophers thought that women were inferior to men—except Aristotle, who wrote that "a woman is a worke of nature unperfecte, and moreover, that her propertie is to delyte in rebukyng, and to be alway complainyng, and never contented." But Aristotle, rather surprisingly, is "not worthie to be of that numbre" of true philosophers, since he wrote with "cankred malice" and was not even "ashamed to rent with rebuke the immortall fame of Plato his master." He was "dissolute and also inconstant" because he made sacrifices to his mistress and regarded her as a goddess.[20] So Elyot disposes of Aristotle; again we see his preference for Plato.

Women are not inferior creatures, Candidus says, even though their bodies are not so strong as men's; perfection must apply to an end, and using his reason is man's proper end. And women do not lack reason. In fact, Candidus concludes, "women, which are prudent in keping, be more excellent then men in reason, whiche be onely stronge and valiaunt in geatyng. And where excellency is, there is moste perfection. Wherfore a woman is not a creature unperfect, but as it seemeth is more perfit than manne."[21]

Elyot supports this conclusion by giving examples of wise and learned women of antiquity. Most of his material comes from Boccaccio's *De claris mulieribus*, as does the life of Zenobia, whose noble example clinched Elyot's argument.[22] Sir Thomas was probably attracted to her by Boccaccio's praise of her learning: "She read and com-

[18] *The Defence of Good Women* (London, 1545), fol. A i^v.
[19] *Ibid.*, fols. A vii^v, v^v.
[20] *Ibid.*, fols. B iii^v, v^r–vi^r.   [21] *Ibid.*, fol. C v^{r-v}.
[22] Perhaps the subject was also suggested by Plutarch's *De mulierum virtutibus*, which Elyot probably knew although he did not borrow anything from it.

mitted to memory all the Latin, Greek, and barbarian histories with the greatest diligence."[23]

A number of the things Elyot said about Zenobia sound as if he had in mind the rejected first wife of Henry VIII rather than the widow of Odenatus of Palmyra; the *Defence of Good Women* seems to be in fact a veiled defense of Catherine of Aragon. The evidence that Elyot sympathized with her plight has already been noted; perhaps he thought that he could safely praise her, in a disguised form, four years after her death.[24] He locates his heroine's home in "Surry" rather than Syria; this is probably a rather broad hint that she lived in Richmond rather than Palmyra.[25]

Zenobia had been captured by the Romans and hence lost her queenly status, as had Catherine after the divorce; but, like Catherine, she dreaded infamy "more than ever I didde the losse of my libertie."[26] Zenobia was, Candidus thought, "one example amonge us, as well of fortitude, as of al other vertues."[27] Learned in languages herself, she saw that her children were also well educated. She had not married until she was "twenty yeres and above"—Catherine was twenty-three when she married Henry—and had spent the years between sixteen and twenty studying moral philosophy, in which she "perceived that without prudence and constanci, women mought be brought lightly into errour and foly."[28] Because of this knowledge, "duryng the lyfe

---

[23] *Ioannis Boccatii de Certaldo insigne opus de claris mulieribus* (Basel, 1539), fol. N iii[r].

[24] This view has been advanced by Foster Watson in *Vives and the Renascence Education of Women* (London, 1912), pp. 211 ff. He reprinted most of the *Defense* (pp. 213–239). He was in error in thinking that the book was necessarily written before 1538, that it was the first Platonic dialogue written in English, and that it was probably not printed until 1545.

[25] *Defense*, fol. C viii[r]. This was not the word which Elyot normally used; in the dictionary he defined *Palestine* as "a countreye in Syrie" and *Syrisca* as "a woman of Syria," not of Surry.

[26] *Ibid.*, fol. D i[r].   [27] *Ibid.*, fol. C vii[r].

[28] *Ibid.*, fol. D ii[r-v]. Catherine had been taught by two Humanists, Antonio and Alessandro Geraldini. She read "the Christian poets, Prudentius and Juvencus and their followers, the Latin fathers Ambrose and Augustine, Gregory and Jerome, the pagan sages, chiefly Seneca, . . . not a little Latin history, and something of the civil and canon law"; she was able to reply to ambassadors in fluent, classical, and correct Latin (Garrett Mattingly, *Catherine of Aragon* [London, 1942], p. 17). Catherine had taken pains to see that Mary's education was properly begun under the supervision of Vives and Linacre.

of my noble husband of famous memory, I was never herd or sene, saie or do any thynge, whiche mought not contente hym, or omytte any thyng, whiche shulde delite hym. . . . I retayned alway suche gravitie, that of any dyssolute appetyte, none could conceyve of me any suspicion."

After her husband's death, Zenobia found her knowledge of moral philosophy "a mervaylous treasure."

I determined . . . to susteine fortune at al times paciently. And to the intente that the name of a woman shulde not amonge the people be had in contempt, I used so my procedynges, that none of them mought be said to be doen womanly. Wherfore I sate alway abrode amonge my nobles and counsailours, and saied mine opinion, so that it seemed to theim all, that it stode with good reason. . . . Touchynge my servauntes I used such a diligent scrutiny that they were alway persones of singuler honestie. . . . Also, I acquired such magnanimitie, that nowe I kepe in as strait subjection al affections and passions, as the Romaines dooe nowe me and my children.

All of this was true, *mutatis mutandis*, of Catherine's life after her separation from Henry. Zenobia's "juste and politike governaunce" was so much admired that "diverse of our said ennemies, whiche againste the realme erst did conspire, . . . chase rather to leave their hostilitie, and to remaine in our subjection, than to retourne to their own countrey."[29] Was not Elyot saying that Catherine's steadfast, sober conduct had won sympathy and support even from those who had favored the divorce?

The noble example of Zenobia—or was it Catherine?—led Candidus and Caninius to agree that "women, beyng wel and vertuously brought up, do not onely with men participate in reason, but som also in fidelity and constancie be equall unto them. . . . The conclusion is good, where bothe partes are pleased, and if they bothe be wise, it maketh no matier though fooles be offended."[30]

"As I LATE was serching among my bokes," Elyot wrote in 1541, "I hapned to fynde certeyne quaires of paper, which I had writen about ix yeres passed, wherin were contayned the actes and sentences notable of the moste noble Emperour Alexander, for his wysedome and gravity

[29] *Defense*, fols. E iii^v–iiii^r, v^r–vi^v.
[30] *Ibid.*, fol. E vii^r–^{v}.

callid Severus." The Emperor's life expressed "of governance so perfite an ymage" that Eliot decided to publish his notes under the title *The Image of Gouernance.*[31]

A mystery surrounds his sources. Elyot claimed that he was translating a "boke . . . first writen in the Greke tung by [Alexander's] secretary named Eucolpius." This book had been lent him by a gentleman of Naples, one Pudericus, and Elyot was so "marvaylousely ravished" with it that he resolved to translate it into English. But he could not complete his work because the owner "importunately called for his boke," so he filled the gaps with material from "some other autours, as wel Latines as Grekis"—Lampridius and Herodian.[32] This is strange enough, but toward the end of the book there is an even more peculiar statement. "Hitherto," Elyot wrote, "is the reporte of Eucolpius" (if so, he had little to contribute, for most of the material is also in Lampridius and Herodian) ; "moche more he wrate, as it semed, for diverse quayres lacked in the booke. Wherfore to make some perfecte conclusion, I toke the residue out of other, which wrate also the lyfe of this Emperour."[33] Thus we have two apologies for the inadequacy of the translation from Eucolpius, each with a different excuse.

The historian Lampridius tells us that Alexander Severus did indeed have a secretary named Encolpius,[34] but he is not known to have written an account of the Emperor's life. It is perhaps significant that most of the statements which Elyot specifically attributed to Eucolpius (as he spelled the name) concern Alexander's attitude toward Christianity. For instance:

Eucolpius wryteth, that on a tyme [the Emperor] sayd to him, and to Philip his boundeman, I perceyve ye do wonder at the lernyng of Origene, wherby ye be induced to imbrace the Christiane profession. Trewely the humilitie and charytie of the Chrysten people, whiche I have herde of and do dayly beholde, doo moche more stere me to beleve that theyr Chryste is god than the residue of all his perswasion.[35]

It looks, then, as if Elyot either invented the comments which he

---

[31] *The Image of Gouernance* (London, 1541), fol. A ii^r-v.

[32] *Ibid.* Croft shows (I, cxlviii–cli) that there was a John Maria Poderico living in Naples in Elyot's time, but this proves nothing.

[33] *Image*, fol. 103^r.

[34] *Historia Augusti*, "Alexander Severus," II.

[35] *Image*, fol. 55^v.

ascribed to Eucolpius or else took them from the spurious account, now lost, of a medieval Christian writer. Considering Elyot's customary lack of originality, the second possibility is perhaps the more likely, though it is odd that no other reference to the pseudo-Eucolpius is known.[36]

Elyot's account of Alexander Severus's life is of no particular interest. He makes the Emperor appear a paragon of kingly nobility: he lived in accordance with the virtues recommended in the *Governor*. He was advised by learned men; he permitted free access to his person; he did not allow the sale of offices; he founded hospitals; he traveled about his realm in disguise to see the true condition of his people; he did not believe trumped-up charges of treason against his councilors.

Rather more significant is Elyot's long Preface, addressed to "al the nobilitie of this flouryshynge royalme of Englande." It was here that, with regard to his last reckoning, Sir Thomas gave the list of his works, adding that in none of them "a man shall finde any sentence against the commandmentes of God, the trewe catholyke faythe, or occasion to stere men to wanton devises. Wherfore I trust unto God, myn accompt shall of hym be favorably accepted, allthough some ingrate persons with ille reporte or mockes requite yl my labours."[37]

The last work which Elyot put to his credit was a devotional tract called *A Preservative agaynste Deth*. He wrote it, he said in his Dedication to Sir Edward North, chancellor of the Court of Augmentations, during Lent, 1545.[38] His last reckoning was still on his mind, and he thought that the work would please God. Preaching, he admitted, was the proper office of priests,

and yet no Christen man is excluded to gyve good counsaile in that which pertayneth to the lawes and commandementes of almighty God. And he

[36] According to a nineteenth-century view the *Image* is "only a compilation of what is suitable that he has drawn from Lampridius and Herodotus, to which he has added some of his own inventions." (*Dictionnaire de Biographie Universelle, Ancienne et Moderne* [Paris, 1855], XII, 426). It may be significant that Eucolpius, or Encolpius, is not identified in Elyot's dictionary.

[37] *Image*, fol. A iii[r-v].

[38] Elyot may have seen a good deal of North in the years just before his death. North had bought the estate of Kirtling near Newmarket and not far from Carlton. He was the father of Sir Thomas North, famous for his translation of Plutarch's *Lives*.

that can do it, and will not (though he be no priest) I dout not but he shall make a straite reknyng for byding his talent. A knyght hath received that honour not onely to defend with the swerde Christes faithe, . . . but also, and that most chiefly, by the meane of his dignitie . . . he shuld more effectually with his learnyng and witte assayle vice and errour, . . . havinge therunto for his sworde and speare his tunge and his penne. . . . Also forasmuche as I am a sheriffe, I think my selfe the more bounden to bee thus occupied.

Therefore he had "gathered togither out of holy scripture this litle treatise, whiche often tyme radde and kept in remembraunce, shall be a preservative against death everlasting."[39]

He added a rather curious comment: "Touchynge the readynge of this litle worke, if ye do rede it in the Masse while, for lacke of tyme more convenient, God will bee therwith nothynge offended." The mind often wanders during prayer; but meditation is more constant, and God will accept meditation on Elyot's treatise as a sincere prayer.[40]

The book itself is a medieval, other-worldly meditation in the manner of More's *Four Last Things* and *Dialogue of Comfort*. Elyot shows how the "divel" tries to ensnare us with the temptations of the flesh and the world. How foolish are those who follow him! "Nowe blow thou on that peyncted strumpette the Flesshe, that tempteth the, and thou shalte se nothynge but a mattier lothesome, corrupted and stynkynge, a mortall currayne [carrion] and bankette for . . . todes, serpentes, and other vile wourmes, who being than ashamed to behold the, will slyde awaie from the."[41] The pleasures of the world tempt us more sharply than those of the flesh, but they can be overcome by thinking about the incomparably greater joys of the world to come.

More interesting than Elyot's concern with other-worldliness are his criticisms of Protestant theology. He hit hard at the Lutheran view that every man is qualified to interpret Scripture for himself:

Saint Peter in his secounde epistle saieth, that Paule accordyng to the wysedom geven unto hym, hath written of thinges amonge the whiche are many thynges harde to be understande, whiche they that be unlerned and not constaunt doo pervert, as they doe the residue of scripture, unto their owne

---

[39] *A Preservative agaynste Deth* (London, 1545), fols. A ii^r–iii^v.
[40] *Ibid.*, fol. A iiii^r–v.
[41] *Ibid.*, fol. B iiii^r.

perdicion. This was spoken of the prince of the apostles, which is a sufficient testimonie that there be sundrie places in scripture whiche doe require bothe learnyng and a constaunt feithe to be wel understande. And
that thei whiche dooe lacke bothe the one and the other dooe often tymes
pervert it. Wherfore Lorde God, geve unto us an humble spirite with simplicitie, staunte feithe, whereby we maie be directed to enter boldely into
thy tabernacle, whiche is holy scripture, wherin resteth thy divine majestee.
Without those leaders we ought reverendly and fearefully to approche, lest
we be striken as Ozah was for settynge his hande to the arke of God, pre-
sumynge on the power of our propre wittes.[42]

His opposition to belief in an extreme form of predestination was
even greater. Sir Thomas pictured the Devil "lyke a great gyaunte
with an horrible visage" leading men into Protestant errors. The Devil
is speaking:

Presumest thou, ignorant foole, to atteyne to the kyngdome of heaven by
thy warkes? Thynkest thou that almes dede, fastyng, or prayer, or that fool-
ishenesse whiche thou callest vertue, have power to brynge the to any other
estate than God hath ordeyned the? Accordynge as he hath predestinate the,
so shalte thou be: He never chaungeth his purpose: his judgment is con-
staunte, lyke as his knowlage is from the begynnynge. If he hath ordeyned
the to be saved, dooe all thyng that thyne appetite lykethe the, and thou
shalte be cleane in his sight.

This was, Elyot said, "a sore assaulte, and an horrible ennemie." Elyot
refused to dispute about the mysteries of free will, although he did
write that God left man "in the power of his owne counsaile, whiche
is his free will"; he thought that simple faith is better than theological
subtlety. He concluded: "I feare not his predestinacion in me, sens I
seke not to knowe suche thynges as be above that I can teache, leste I
be oppressed with his majestee. But I feare his wrathe, whiche I have
deserved. And yet will I not cease to truste in his mercie."[43]

Although the *Preservative agaynste Deth* was the last of Elyot's
books to be published, he may have been at work on a history of England at the time of his death. Roger Ascham's treatise on archery, the
Toxophilus (1545), is our only source of knowledge about it. Ascham
wrote that he was "ones in company with Syr Thomas Eliote knighte,

---

[42] *Ibid.*, fol. D iiii^v.   [43] *Ibid.*, fols. D i^v–iii^r.

which suerlie for his learninge in all kinde of knowledge broughte muche worshippe to all the nobilitye of Englande." He asked Elyot whether he knew when the longbow was first used in England. Elyot replied

that he had a worke in hande which he nameth, *De rebus memorabilibus Angliae,* which I trust we shall see in print shortlye, and for the accomplishment of that booke, he had redde and perused over many old monumentes of Englande, and in seeking for that purpose he marked this of shootinge in an excedinge olde Chronicle, the which had no name, that what time as the Saxons came first into this Realme in Kinge Vortigers dayes, when they had bene here a while and at last began to fall out with the Britaynes, they troubled and subdued the Britaynes with nothinge so muche as with theyr bowe and shaftes, which weapon being straunge and not sene here before, was wonderfull terreble unto them.[44]

The work was almost certainly never printed, probably never completed; no manuscript is known to survive.[45]

SIR THOMAS ELYOT died at Carlton in Cambridgeshire on March 26, 1546. He had made a will in August, 1531, and, "sicke in boddye but hole and parfite of mynde," he had confirmed its provisions three days before his death.[46] He left all his lands to his wife, and it was determined at an inquisition held at Newmarket on September 7 that they should pass to Richard Puttenham, son of Elyot's sister Margery, after Margaret Elyot's death.[47] Elyot commended his soul "into the handes

[44] Roger Ascham, *Toxophilus* (London, 1571), fol. 28ᵛ.

[45] Croft (I, clxxv) is inclined to identify the work with "Sir Thomas Eliot, his Chronicle of the description of Brittaine," which was listed as one of the sources for a seventeenth-century MS. describing Chester. This MS. was formerly in the library of G. F. Wilbraham at Delamere House, Cheshire (*Fourth Report of the Historical Manuscripts Commission* [London, 1874], p. 416). This is possible, especially since the Delameres were related to Elyot; on the other hand there is no indication that Elyot had any special knowledge of, or interest in, Chester, so it is hard to see how his work—even if it survived to the seventeenth century—would have aided the historian of that city particularly.

[46] P.C.C., MS. 14 Alen; reprinted in Appendix II below.

[47] P.R.O., C 142/74/16. After Sir Thomas's death Margaret Elyot married Sir James Dyer, a serjeant-at-law and author of the famous Dyer legal reports. He had probably been a friend of Elyot's. On April 21, 1551, Dyer and his

and tuicion of my Saviour Christe Jesus" and directed that his body "be buried in the nexte xpen [Christian] buriall where I shall happen to depart, with somme image or stone sett in a wall next to my grave, wherin shalbe graven or carvide in Latten my name with the tyme of my deathe." He was buried in the parish church at Carlton. In accordance with his request, brass likenesses of Thomas and Margaret were erected, but they have disappeared, probably victims to a seventeenth- or eighteenth-century spree of iconoclasm.[48]

Unfortunately Sir Thomas left no catalogue of his library; he directed that all his books be sold, "the monney therof commynge to be distributed to poore scolars whiche be good students after the rate of six shillings eight pence to every scollarr." He left bequests to several of his servants, and he did not forget the usual charities; "one hundrede bedreden or veraye aged men and women" were to receive a shilling each at the time of his death, and four pounds was left to be "geven to some poore maidens towardes theire marriage."

Sir Thomas made no bequests to churches, as his father had done— an interesting illustration of the changed attitude toward ecclesiastical endowments. But he did direct his wife to see that prayers were said for him. "She shall kepe yerlie an obite at Weston [Colville] with tenne preestes which shall singe a solempne masse and ix lowe masses ffor the soules of Sir William Fynderne knyghte, Sir Richard Eliot knyghte and Alice his wiffe, and ffor my soule and all xpen soules"; she shall see that Sir Thomas is prayed for at Paul's Cross in London each term; every Friday she shall give "three pence to three poore men to praie for me, my father and mother." Barely a year after Elyot's death Edward VI's first Parliament dissolved the chantries: it was— said the act—mere superstition to believe that the Mass was a propitiatory sacrifice which could aid the souls of the dead. Sir Thomas Elyot cannot long have had the prayers which, with regard to his last reckoning, he had desired.

---

wife obtained Edward VI's permission to dispose temporarily of some of Elyot's manors (P.R.O., C 66/835, membrane 24). Margaret died in 1560 and was buried at Great Staughton, Hunts.

[48] Croft (I, clxxix) quotes a rather unhelpful description of the monument, written about 1632 by Layer.

WHAT ARE WE TO SAY in making our last reckoning of Sir Thomas Elyot's life and work?

None of his governmental services were of the first importance. By nature inclined to bookish pursuits, he cannot have been a brilliant diplomatist. The King's unrealistic expectations had made failure in his embassy to Charles V inevitable, but perhaps other ambassadors might have accomplished something more than Elyot did. As clerk to the Justices of Assize and to the King's Council, however, Elyot must have found his scholarly training an asset, and he probably gave greater satisfaction as a sheriff or justice of the peace than most men of his class. If he was not unusually keen-witted, he was surely diligent and scrupulously honest.

Of far greater significance were his contributions to English Humanism. These were twofold: his works bridged the gulf between Tudor England and antiquity, and they played an important part in the development of the English language. Elyot's talents may not have been of the very highest order—in wit, insight, and human sympathy he fell behind his mentor, More—and his works may lack originality. But they were of great value as intermediaries, bringing within the purview of all literate Englishmen ideas previously available only to the most advanced scholars. This was a service, Elyot believed, of profound utility: society could be improved if governors were educated in the classics and obeyed ancient moral precepts; health could be preserved or, if lost, regained by following the advice of the Greeks. Some physicians might cavil, but (as the frequent reprintings of his books show) many Englishmen gratefully accepted Elyot's offering.

His desire to make the ideas of the ancients available in the vernacular led Elyot to an interest in developing the English language. His conscious efforts to enrich it and to write clearly and fluently in it were, to a very considerable degree, successful. When he completed the revision of his Latin dictionary he had provided an English equivalent for virtually every important Latin word, and his translations from Latin and Greek proved that the vulgar tongue was quite capable of expressing the ideas of ancient writers. Elyot's prose style is a notable advance over More's: his sentences are more solidly constructed, more rhythmical, more lucid. However our minds may revere More, our ears must prefer Elyot.[49]

It is as well that Elyot died before the King whom he had served for so many years. Although he could stomach royal supremacy and the dissolution of the monasteries, it is clear that doctrinal innovations and alterations in the traditional religious ceremonies would have distressed him keenly. As it was, his services to government and Humanism complete, Sir Thomas Elyot was able to die in the confidence that he would join "the companie of the moste blessed spirites, abundyng in charitee, knowlage, and gladnesse, in beholdynge continually in the moste beaultifull presence of God, the wounderfull and inspeakable warkes of his majestee, in heven, erthe, and in hell."[50]

[49] Cf. C. S. Lewis, *English Literature in the Sixteenth Century* (Oxford, 1954), p. 276.
[50] *Preservative*, fol. E ii^v.

APPENDIX I

Forebears and Other Relatives of Sir Thomas Elyot

IT HAS RECENTLY BEEN SUGGESTED that the early Tudor Humanists, like other members of the new Tudor aristocracy, were "sprung from the commercial classes, without feudal connections. . . . Colet, the son of a knighted merchant who was several times lord mayor of London, and More and Elyot, the sons of leading lawyers, held prominent positions under Henry VIII." They thus rose from the commercial classes to governmental service.[1]

While it is true that Colet's father was a London merchant (though of a gentry family) and that More's father had been admitted to Lincoln's Inn only after years of faithful service as the Inn's steward, or butler, to say that Sir Thomas Elyot was a member of the new commercial aristocracy is to give a distorted picture of his position in Tudor society. Actually Sir Thomas's life was, apart from his literary activities, quite typical of that any member of the landed gentry might have lived at any time during the fifteenth or sixteenth century, and indeed it was much like the lives his ancestors had been leading for centuries. Many of his ancestors and other relatives had been West Country gentlefolk, and nearly all had served the Crown in some way. Although few held really important governmental appointments, the cumulative total of their public services is impressive. Sir Thomas's position under Henry VIII was neither new nor unusual. Not his was the rapid rise from complete obscurity to virtually absolute power enjoyed by Wolsey or Cromwell.

The deepness of Sir Thomas's roots in West Country gentry stock

[1] Paul N. Siegel, "English Humanism and the New Tudor Aristocracy," *Journal of the History of Ideas*, XIII (1952), 455.

can be appreciated only after a rather minute examination of the connections and activities of his relatives.[2]

His mother, Alice Delamere, was descended from the Finderns, originally an old Derbyshire family deriving its name from the village of Findern, about five miles from Derby, where the Finderns had held a manor in the early fourteenth century.[3] The particular line of Finderns to which the Elyots were related can be traced back to Sir William Findern, lord of a manor at Childrey, Berkshire, who died in 1444. His son, Sir Thomas Findern, was attainted of treason in 1461 for supporting the House of Lancaster and lost his lands and his life. We are more directly concerned with his son, again named Sir William: soon after Bosworth we find him in the king's favor. He was appointed in 1496 to a commission to survey walls and moats in parts of Lincolnshire, Huntingdonshire, and Cambridgeshire.[4] In 1489 and 1491 he was commissioned to secure archers and financial assistance from Cambridgeshire for the king's rather ludicrous expeditions to Brittany.[5] He was a member of the Commission of the Peace for Cambridgeshire from 1493 until 1515;[6] he served on the Commission of Goal Delivery for Colchester Castle in 1493 and for Cambridge Castle in 1493 and 1515;[7] he was on the Commission of Oyer and Terminer to inquire into and settle criminal cases in Cambridgeshire, Bedfordshire, Buckinghamshire, Huntingdonshire, Norfolk, and Suffolk in 1495.[8] In 1520, Henry VIII, apparently not knowing the Findern had died in 1517, named him one of the attendants for the Field of Cloth of Gold.[9]

This Sir William Findern had married Eleanor, daughter of Sir Thomas de Chelrey of Childrey, a village near Wantage, Berkshire, and widow of Sir John Kingstone, who held the manor of North Faw-

---

[2] See the genealogical table which accompanies this appendix. The family tree has been pieced together from various sources, each inadequate in itself. For this reason I generally have not given a citation for each relationship. Most of my information comes from family wills, which are the most reliable source available.

[3] Croft, I, xxxi.

[4] *Cal. Pat. Rolls*, I, 103.

[5] *Ibid.*, 281, 353.

[6] *Ibid.*, 482; II, 632; *L.P.*, I, 434 (4 m.4); II, 1196, 1131.

[7] *Cal. Pat. Rolls*, I, 434, 348; *L.P.*, II, 1187.

[8] *Cal. Pat. Rolls*, II, 31.   [9] *L.P.*, IV, 703.

ley near Childrey. Kingstone had a single son, also named John, who married Susan Fetiplace. She was, as we shall see, Richard Elyot's step-daughter. Young Kingstone died in 1514 and his wife retired to a nunnery.

Sir William Findern himself died in 1517; since his only son, William, had predeceased him, Sir William left his lands to his grandson, Thomas Findern. The Master of Clare College, Dr. Edmund Natures, was named trustee of the estate, and Richard Elyot was appointed one of the executors. Findern's will shows that he held a considerable amount of land, principally the manor of Carlton and land at Weston Colville and Duxford in Cambridgeshire, but also land at Little Horkesley, Widdington, and Saffron Walden, Essex, and at Depden, Suffolk. If his grandson died without heirs, Findern's lands were to pass to "Richard Elyot and my cosyn Alice his wife and the heires of their two bodies lawfully begotten." This provision became operative when young Findern died in 1523, and the lands passed to Thomas Elyot. William Findern also bequeathed the contents of his chambers in London—perhaps in the Middle Temple—to "Thomas, my cosyn Elyottes son."[10]

To understand the relationship, admittedly somewhat complex, between the Finderns and the Elyots, we must begin with Sir William Findern's first cousin Elizabeth Findern (d. 1494). She married Sir Thomas Delamere of Aldermaston, Berkshire, by whom she had two sons and a daughter, Alice.[11] Alice Delamere married twice; her first husband was Thomas Daubridgecourt. By him she had two children, Thomas and Mary. This Mary became the wife of Reginald Pym and thus the great-great-grandmother of John Pym.[12] Daubridgecourt died in 1485, and Alice was married again, probably about 1487, to Richard Elyot. She was Sir Richard's first wife and the mother of his two children, our Sir Thomas and Margery. Alice died in 1510.

Richard's second wife was a member of the Bessels (or Besiles) family. This family of West Country gentry can be traced back to the

---

[10] Will of Sir William Findern, P.C.C., MS. 36 Holder, and P.R.O., C 1/631/18, 449/59.

[11] Two grants in *Cal. Pat. Rolls* (I, 425; II, 533) make this part of the family tree clear.

[12] Chancery Inquisitions post Mortem, P.R.O., C 1/499/59, 501/29-34.

time of Edward I, when they held manors at Besselsleigh, Berkshire, and Brompton Regis, Somerset.[13] Our interest in the line begins with Richard Elyot's father-in-law, William Bessels of Besselsleigh. He served the Crown in numerous capacities: he was a member of the Commission of the Peace for Berkshire from 1494 until his death in 1515;[14] he served with Richard Elyot on the Commission of the Peace for Oxford town from 1510 until 1512;[15] he was a member of commissions to deliver the jails of Oxford Castle and Wallingford Castle.[16] He also served on *ad hoc* commissions to persuade Berkshire gentlemen not to retain felons, to inquire about prisoners escaped from Wallingford Castle, to look into offenses by persons enjoying the privileges of the University of Oxford, and, in 1513, to settle disputes arising from the authorized seizure of lands in Berkshire belonging to Scottish subjects.[17]

William Bessels and his wife Alice had a single child, Elizabeth. Her first marriage, to Richard Fetiplace, connected her with a neighboring Berkshire family which had held a manor at Childrey since the days of King John.[18] Richard was one of five brothers, sons of Peter Fetiplace, and probably the least important of the five. He held a manor at East Shefford and farm land at Petwick and Besselsleigh.[19] His only recorded public service was as a member of the Berkshire Commission of the Peace in 1510 and 1511.[20]

Richard's brother Anthony led a more exciting life. He was a squire of the body to Henry VII and Henry VIII, a service for which he received 20 pounds yearly after 1490 and 50 marks—apparently in addition—after 1497.[21] He was named Crown steward of land at Burford and of the park of Cornbury, Oxfordshire, in 1496.[22] In 1504 he

[13] John Collinson, *History of Somerset* (Bath, 1791), III, 504.

[14] *Cal. Pat. Rolls*, II, 130; *L.P.*, I, 1533.

[15] *L.P.*, I, 1542.

[16] Oxford Castle: 1487, 1504 (*Cal. Pat. Rolls*, I, 162; II, 407); Wallingford Castle: 1497, 1502 (*ibid.*, II, 116, 294).

[17] *Ibid.*, I, 71; II, 87, 286; *L.P.*, I, 2222 (16 Berks.).

[18] Daniel Lysons and Samuel Lysons, *Magna Britannia* (London, 1806), I, 178 f.

[19] Will of Richard Fetiplace, P.C.C., MS. 1 Fetiplace.

[20] *L.P.*, I, pp. 1534 ff.

[21] *Cal. Pat. Rolls*, I, 307; II, 110; *L.P.*, I, 94 (51).

[22] *Cal. Pat. Rolls*, I, 36, 137.

was granted the stewardship, doubtless profitable, of lands in Oxfordshire formerly held by Edmund de la Pole, Earl of Suffolk, the Yorkist claimant to the throne.[23] Suffolk had fled in 1501 to Maximilian, who was first his protector, then his jailor; he was brought back to England in 1506 only to be imprisoned in the Tower until 1513, when Henry VIII had him executed. The grant of his lands to Fetiplace as steward was renewed and extended in 1509, when Fetiplace was also made steward of Minster Lovell and Cogges.[24] Anthony Fetiplace was granted livery for the funeral of Henry VII and for the coronation of Henry VIII.[25] He served with Richard Elyot as an Oxfordshire justice of the peace from 1504 until his death in 1510. He was keeper of the lands of Sir John Kingstone and had the wardship and marriage of young John Kingstone.[26] It was only natural that he should arrange for John a marriage with one of his relatives, Susan, the daughter of his brother Richard Fetiplace and Elizabeth Bessels. Anthony held land in his own right at Swinbrook, near Burford, and was buried (1510) in the church there.[27]

Sir Thomas Fetiplace, another of the five brothers, held land at Abingdon, Compton Beauchamp, Shrivenham, Bray, and Stanford in the Vale of White Horse, Berkshire.[28] He was a member of the Commission of the Peace for Berkshire from 1495 until 1522 and of the Commission of Gaol Delivery for Wallingford Castle in 1504.[29] After attending the king at the Field of Cloth of Gold and at Gravelines, he died in 1524.[30]

John and William were the other brothers. John held a manor at Charnley, Berkshire, as well as lands at Stanford, Pewsey, Buckland, and Hanney.[31] He was one of the Berkshire justices of the peace from 1494 until 1506 and served on the Commission of Gaol Delivery for Wallingford Castle in 1494, 1502, and 1506 and for Oxford Castle in

[23] *Ibid.*, II, 356.
[24] *L.P.*, I, 94 (49, 51).
[25] *Ibid.*, 20, 82.
[26] *Cal. Pat. Rolls*, II, 107.
[27] Will of Anthony Fetiplace, P.C.C., MS. 36 Bennett.
[28] Will of Sir Thomas Fetiplace, P.C.C., MS. 32 Bodfelde.
[29] *Cal. Pat. Rolls*, II, 630; *L.P.*, I, p. 1533; II, 202, 430, 1247, 4445; III, 1522, 2415 (16); *Cal. Pat. Rolls*, II, 360.
[30] *L.P.*, III, 240, 345, 906.
[31] Will of John Fetiplace (d. 1510), P.C.C., MS. 32 Bennett.

1487, 1497, and 1504.[32] He died also in 1510. William Fetiplace, perhaps the eldest of the brothers, seems to have retained the family manor at Childrey.[33] His only recorded public service was as a Berkshire justice of the peace from 1512 until 1515;[34] he died in 1529.

Richard Fetiplace and Elizabeth Bessels appear to have had four sons and three daughters.[35] One daughter, Susan, is the girl who married young John Kingstone and to whom Thomas Elyot dedicated his translation of one of St. Cyprian's sermons. Of the sons—John, Edmund, Anthony, and Thomas—only John is of particular interest. Probably the eldest son, he received the manor of East Shefford at the death of Sir Richard Elyot, who had held it since the death of Richard Fetiplace in 1511.[36] John was also the heir and executor of his grandfather, William Bessels.[37] He was a Berkshire justice of the peace from 1512 until 1515 and was sheriff of Oxfordshire and Berkshire in 1523.[38]

The Fetiplace family continued to be large landowners in Berkshire until 1743, when the last male heir, Sir George Fetiplace (Phetiplace), Bart., died.[39]

There is no need to further labor the point that Sir Thomas Elyot, far from being a *nouveau riche* aristocrat, was descended from generations of gentry landowners. Surely this was the usual thing among Henrician Humanists and governmental officials; historians have too often been blinded by the dazzling but not typical careers of Wolsey, More, and Cromwell and have been led into unwarranted generalizations by them.

One sometimes sees the statement that Sir John Eliot was related to Sir Thomas Elyot. This rests upon the testimony of Browne Willis that Walter Eliot, one of Sir John's forebears, "as it should seem by the

[32] *Cal. Pat. Rolls*, II, 630; II, 87, 116, 491; I, 162; II, 118, 491.
[33] Will of William Fetiplace, P.C.C., MS. 6 Jankyn.
[34] *L.P.*, I, 1534 ff.; II, 202, 430, 1247.
[35] The will of John Fetiplace (d. 1524), P.C.C., MS. 28 Bodfelde, establishes this part of the genealogy.
[36] Will of Sir Richard Elyot, P.C.C., MS. 24 Maynwaryng.
[37] Will of William Bessels, P.C.C., MS. 6 Holder.
[38] *L.P.*, I, 1534 ff.; II, 202, 430, 1247; III, 3583.
[39] Lysons, *op. cit.*, I, 119. Elias Ashmole (*The Antiquities of Berkshire* [London, 1723], *passim*) gives a number of inscriptions from monuments to the Fetiplaces; his genealogical tables are, however, unreliable.

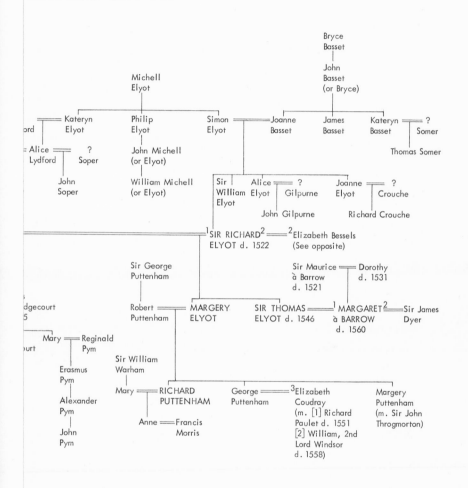

Bryce
Basset
|
John
Basset
(or Bryce)

Michell
Elyot

========Kateryn   Philip   Simon ========Joanne   James   Kateryn ====?
ord | Elyot   Elyot   Elyot   Basset   Basset   Basset | Somer

= Alice ====   ?   John Michell   Thomas Somer
  Lydford | Soper   (or Elyot)

       John   William Michell   Sir | Alice ==== ?   Joanne ==== ?
       Soper   (or Elyot)   William| Elyot | Gilpurne Elyot | Crouche
                                                Elyot | |
                                                          John Gilpurne   Richard Crouche

===[1]SIR RICHARD[2] ====[2]Elizabeth Bessels
                                                 ELYOT d. 1522   (See opposite)

                    Sir George   Sir Maurice ==== Dorothy
                    Puttenham   à Barrow   d. 1531
                                                  d. 1521

dgecourt   Robert ======MARGERY   SIR THOMAS========[1]MARGARET[2]====Sir James
5   Puttenham   ELYOT   ELYOT d. 1546   à BARROW   Dyer
                                                                    d. 1560

     Mary ====Reginald
urt   Pym   Sir William
                         Warham
     Erasmus
     Pym   Mary ====RICHARD   George ====[3]Elizabeth   Margery
                              | PUTTENHAM   Puttenham   Coudray   Puttenham
     Alexander | (m. [1] Richard   (m. Sir John
     Pym   Anne ====Francis   Paulet d. 1551   Throgmorton)
                                    Morris   [2] William, 2nd
     John   Lord Windsor
     Pym   d. 1558)

Arms, was ally'd to Sir Richard Eliot, . . . who was, as I take it, father to the famous Sir Thomas Eliot."[40] Willis, the eighteenth-century antiquarian, had married John Eliot's great-granddaughter, so he may have been repeating a family tradition. No firsthand evidence seems to exist; if Sir John and Sir Thomas were in fact related, the connection must have been remote.

[40] Browne Willis, *Notitia Parliamentaria* (London, 1716), II, 145.

Sir Thomas Elyot's Will*

IN THE NAME OF God the Father, the Sonne, and the Hollie Goste, three parsonnes and one Divyne Substaunce, in whome I do ffirmelie and puerlie beleve accordinge unto the universall ffaiethe lefte by the Hollye Appostles and Evangelistes, I, Sir Thomas Eliot knyghte the xxix^te daye of Auguste in the xxiii^te yere of the raigne of ower Soveraigne Lorde Kinge Henrie Theighte do declare my testamente and laste will of all my goodes, landes, and tenementes in manner and fourme followynge.

Firste I will that my boddye after the departinge of my soule, whiche I recommende into the handes and tuicion of my Saviour Christe Jesus, to be buried in the next xpen [Christian] buriall where I shall happen to departe with somme image or stone sett in a wall next to my grave, wherin shalbe graven or carvide in Latten my name with the tyme of my deathe. Also I will that at the daye of my death or ymediatelie after be geven one hundrede shillinges to one hundrede bedreden or veraye aged men and women. Also I will theire be geven to some poore maidens towardes theire marriage foure poundes. Also I will that every servante that longithe to me have a blacke cote, and everye one that goethe with me over the seae and abidethe have thirtene shillinges foure pence besides his wages. *Item*. I will that Thomas Laughton my servante shall have beside his wages fortie shillinges. Also I will that

---

* Prerogative Court of Canterbury, Somerset House, MS. 14 Alen. This will has never been printed and previous biographers of Elyot have been unaware of its existence.

194

Margaret Restwolde have to her marriage fortie shillings. Also I will that all my bookes be soulde and the monney therof commynge to be distributed to poore scolars whiche be good students after the rate of sixe shillinges eighte pence to every scollarr. Also I will that Robarte Putenham Esquier, my brother-in-lawe, be discharged of xvi^{li} xiii^{s} iiii^{d} parcell of twentie poundes whiche he oweth me uppon an obligacion so that he do not disquiet or trouble my wife or myne executrixe. Also I will that there be yerlie one obite kepte for me at Weston Colvile in the Countie of Cambridge. And twelve pence to be geven for the singinge therof. *Item.* I bequethe to my freende William Raynisforde twentie linkes of my chaine, and the beste geldinge in my stable.

The residue of all my goodes I bequethe to Dame Margaret my wife, whome I make and constitute myne executrixe to paie my debtes and doo dedes of charite for the weale of my soule, as she will answere at the daye of judgmente. *Item.* I will that my saide wiff after my deceas shall have and enjoye my mannour of Faierwood in the Countie of Dorset, and all my landes and tenements, meadowes, pastures, rentes, rewersions, and frutes in Faierwood, Gussage Sti. Michis [Sancti Michaelis: St. Michael's], Stower Eston, Stower Weston, Kinton, and Ilande in the countie aforesaid for terme of her liff. And after her deceas if I happen to die withoute heires of my boddye begotten I will the mannour landes and tenementes with thappurtenance shall remayne to my sister Margerye and to the heires of her boddye laufullye begotton. And for lacke of suche issue to John Eliot of Grewer and to theires males of his, of his boddye. And for defaute of suche issue to the righte heires of me the said Sir Thomas for ever.

Item. I will that my saide wiffe after my deceas shall have my mannoure of Musclyff in the Countie of Southampton and all my landes and tenementes in Ayuscliff in the Countie of Southampton. And also all my landes and tenementes in Ebbesborne Wake, Wellow Broke, and Chalke in the Countie of Wiltes for terme of her liff. And after her deceas I will the saide mannour of Ayuscliff and all other the saide landes in the saide counties of Southampton and Wiltes, if I departe withoute issue of my boddye, shall remayne to my saide sister and to theires of her boddye laufully begotton. And for defaute of suche issue to John Eliot of Greweyr aforesaide and to theires males of his boddye laufullye begotton. And for defaute of suche issue to theires males of

John Mychell otherwise called John Eliot of Frome in the Countie of Somersett. And for defaute of suche issue to the righte heires of me the saide Sir Thomas for ever.

Item. I will that my saide wiffe shall have and enjoye for terme of her liffe my mannours of Litle Carleton, Weston Colvile, Weston Moynes, and Leverers in the Countie of Cambridge with all rentes, reversions, and frutes with theire appurtenance in Carleton, Weston, Willingham, Brinkeleye, Westwratting, and Wykham in the Countie of Cambridge, for the which I will she shall kepe yerlie on obite at Weston with tenne preestes which shall singe a solempne masse and ix lowe masses, ffor the soules of Sir William Fynderne knyghte, Sir Richard Eliot knyghte and Alice his wiffe, and ffor my soule and all xpen soules. Also she shall cause me to be rehersed and praied for by mane at the crosse of Saint Paule every terme. And to geve every Fri-daye in the yere three pence to three poore men to praie for me, my father and mother. Provyded that my saide wiffe shall not sell above twentie acres yerlie of my woodes of Carleton and Weston. *Item.* I will that my saide wiffe shall have and receyve during her liffe my rente of my ferme in Chalke in the Countie of Wiltes, and therwith to kepe an obite.

Wittnes to this will and testaments Sir John Sharpe, curate of Combe, John Colles, Christofer Geffreye, Christofer Maye, and Robarte Newman.

Also for the coroboracion of the same, I, the saide Sir Thomas Eliot, sicke in boddye but hole and parfite of mynde the xxiii^te daye of Marche, the seven and thirtie yere of the raigne of ower Soveraigne Lorde Kinge Henrye Theighte by the grace of God Kinge of Englande, Fraunce, and Irelande, Defendoure of the Faiethe, and in earthe Su-preme Head of the Churche of Englande and Irelande, do affirme, con-firme, and stablisshe this to be my laste will and testamente. In the presens of Sir Giles Arlington kynghte and Thomas Elvington esquier withe other.

[Proved at Lambeth on July 2, 1546, by the oath of Thomas Laugh-ton and Dame Margaret Elyot, who was named executrix.]

Editions of Elyot's Works

I HAVE FOLLOWED A. W. Pollard and G. R. Redgrave, *Short-Title Catalogue of English Books 1475–1640* (1946), except where I know it to be in error. Additions to this work, herein referred to as *S.T.C.*, are marked by an asterisk. Editions known to have existed but of which no copy survives are shown in brackets. Except where otherwise stated, all editions were published by Thomas Berthelet. Works not certainly but probably by Elyot are listed in parentheses.

1. (*P. Gemini Eleatis Hermathena.* [*S.T.C.* 11719.] By Papyrius Geminus Eleates: perhaps Thomas Elyot. Published by John Siberch, Cambridge, 1522.)

2. (*A dialogue betwene Luciane and Diogenes . . . .* Trans. anon. *Ca.* 1528?.)

3. *The Boke named the Gouernour.* 1531; 1537; 1544; 1546; 1553; 1557; 1565, printed by Thomas Marsh; 1580, printed by Thomas East; ed. A. T. Eliot, 1834, Newcastle-upon-Tyne; ed. H. H. S. Croft, 2 vols., 1880, London; ed. Foster Watson, 1907, reprinted 1937, Everyman's Library; German translation by H. Studniczka as *Das Buch vom Führer,* 1931, Leipzig.

4. *The Doctrinal of Princes.* 1533?; 1548?.

5. *The Education or Bringinge vp of Children.* 1533?. (*S.T.C.* gives 1535?.)

6. *Pasquil the Playne.* 1533 (published anon.); 1540. (*S.T.C.* 7671, an edition of 1532 in Jesus College, Cambridge, appears to be a "ghost.")

7. *Of the Knowledeg which Maketh a Wise Man.* 1533; 1534; 1548?; 1552?* (B.M.); reprinted (in English) in Kurt Schroeder, *Platonismus in der englischen Renaissance*, 1920, Berlin; ed. E. J. Howard, 1946, Oxford, Ohio.

8. (*Howe one may take Profit of his Enemyes.* Trans. anon. 1533?.)

9. *A Swete and Devoute Sermon of Sayngt Ciprian* and *The Rules of a Christen Life made by Picus Erle of Mirandula.* 1534; 1539.

10. *The Bankette of Sapience.* [1534?]; 1539; 1542; 1545; 1557, printed by J. Daye; 1564, printed without license by H. Wykes; included with J. L. Vives, *Introduction to Wisedome* (trans. Sir Richard Morison), printed by Thomas East for Abraham Veale, 1575?.

11. *The Castel of Helth.* [1536?]; 1539; 1541, 8°; 1541, 4°;1544?; 1549?; 1559?; 1560?, printed for Thomas Powell; 1561, 1572, 1580, and 1587, all printed by Thomas Marsh; 1580?, printer unknown; 1595, printed for the Widow Orwin; 1610, printed for the Company of Stationers; ed. S. A. Tannenbaum, 1937, New York.

12. *The Dictionary of Syr Thomas Elyot.* 1538. Later editions called *Bibliotheca Eliotae*: 1542* (B.M. Bodleian); 1545; rev. Thomas Cooper: 1548, 1552, 1559. (*S.T.C.* gives 1542–1545 as one edition, but there were clearly two, with different title pages and with the introductory matter re-set. That Berthelet neglected to alter the colophon in the 1545 edition, which still read 1542, has caused the confusion.)

13. *The Defence of Good Women.* 1540* (unique copy in the Huntington Library; facsimile in the Bodleian); 1545; reprinted in Foster Watson, *Vives and the Renascence Education of Woman*, 1912, London; ed. E. J. Howard, 1941, Oxford, Ohio.

14. *The Image of Gouernance.* 1541; 1544; 1549; 1556, printed by W. Seres.

15. *A Preservative agaynste Deth.* 1545.

Bibliography

I. MANUSCRIPTS

A. *Public Record Office:*

SP 1/235/242. Elyot to Cromwell, March 25, 1528.

SP 1/72/36–37. Elyot to Cromwell, November 18, 1532.

SP 1/76/149. Elyot to Cromwell, [May, 1533?].

SP 1/104/248. Elyot to Cromwell, [January, 1536?].

SP 3/10/96. Elyot to Lady Lisle, December 3, [1533].

SP 1/75/81. Elyot to John Hackett, April 6, [1533].

SP 1/114/257–258. John Parkyns to Cromwell, January 21, [1537].

SP 1/115/32–33. John Parkyns to Fitzwilliam, January 24, [1537].

SP 1/115/95–102. John Parkyns to Cromwell, January 28, [1537].

SP 1/115/103–104
SP 1/115/105–106
SP 1/115/107–112
SP 1/115/113–114
SP 1/115/115 — John Parkyns to Cromwell, [January, 1537].
SP 1/115/116
SP 1/115/117
SP 1/115/119
SP 1/115/119*a*

C 142/74/16
E 150/94/2 — Inquisitions post Mortem concerning Elyot's lands
Wards 7/2/119 — in Cambridgeshire, September 7, 1546.

C 66/650, membrane 11. Elyot's patent to the clerkship of the Council.

C 66/835, membrane 24. Patent of April 21, 1551, permitting Sir James Dyer and his wife to dispose temporarily of certain manors which she had inherited from Sir Thomas Elyot.

C 142/78/144. Inquisition after the death of John Cheyne concerning the manor of Wanborough, Wilts.

C 1/405/1 ⎫
C 1/405/20 ⎬ Chancery proceedings involving Sir Richard Elyot.

C 1/499/59 ⎫
C 1/501/29 ⎪
C 1/501/32 ⎪ Chancery proceedings concerning Thomas Elyot's right
C 1/501/33 ⎬ to inherit the use of the manors of Little Carlton and
C 1/501/34 ⎪ Weston Colville from Thomas Findern.
C 1/631/18 ⎭

C 1/1016/62–64. Chancery proceedings concerning the guardianship of Erasmus Pym.

St. Ch. 2/10/36–38. Star Chamber proceedings, Gilbert Claydon *v.* Sir Thomas Elyot.

St. Ch. 2/34/11. Papers concerning the commission to inquire into John Parkyns's charges against the abbots of Eynsham and Osney, Oxon.

B. *Prerogative Court of Canterbury Wills, at Somerset House:*

William Bessels. 6 Holder.
Sir Richard Elyot. 24 Maynwaryng.
Sir Thomas Elyot. 14 Alen.
Richard Fetiplace. 1 Fetiplace.
Anthony Fetiplace. 36 Bennett.
Sir Thomas Fetiplace. 32 Bodfelde.
John Fetiplace (d. 1510). 32 Bennett.
John Fetiplace (d. 1524). 28 Bodfelde.
William Fetiplace. 6 Jankyn.
Sir William Findern. 36 Holder.

C. *British Museum:*

Henry VIII to Elyot, October 7, 1531. Cotton MS. Vitellius B. XXI, fol. 60.

Elyot to Norfolk, March 14, 1532. Cotton MS. Vitellius B. XXI, fols. 58–59.

Elyot to Cromwell, December 8, 1532. Cotton MS. Titus B. I, fols. 376–377.

Elyot to Cromwell, December 20, 1534. Cotton MS. Cleopatra E. VI, fol. 254.

Elyot to Cromwell, [1537?]. Cotton MS. Cleopatra E. IV, fol. 260.

Elyot to Cromwell, [1533] (Dedication to *Of the Knowledeg whiche Maketh a Wise Man*). Harley MS. 6989, fol. 33.

Elyot to Cromwell, dedicatory letter, MS. on flyleaf of *The Dictionary of Syr Thomas Elyot* (1538), class mark c.28.m.2.

Stephen Vaughan to Cromwell, December 9, 1531, Cotton MS. Galba B. X, fols. 23–25.

Stephen Vaughan to Cromwell, December 30, 1531, Cotton MS. Galba B. X, fol. 26.

II. Printed Books, Articles, and Typescripts*

Ascham, Roger. *Toxophilus: The Schole or Partitions of Shooting.* London, 1571.

Ashmole, Elias. *The Antiquities of Berkshire.* 3 vols. London, 1723.

Baumer, Franklin le Van. *The Early Tudor Theory of Kingship.* New Haven, Conn., 1940.

Benndorf, Cornelie. *Die englische Pädagogik im 16. Jahrhundert wie sie dargestellt wird im Wirken und in den Werken von Elyot, Ascham und Mulcaster.* Vienna and Leipzig, 1905.

Bennett, H. S. *English Books and Readers, 1475 to 1557.* Cambridge, England, 1952.

Berry, William. *County Genealogies: Pedigrees of the Families of Hants.* London, 1883.

Bouck, Constance W. "On the Identity of Papyrius Geminus Eleates," *Transactions* of the Cambridge Bibliographical Society, Vol. II, Pt. V (1958), 352–358.

Bush, Douglas. *"Julius Caesar* and Elyot's *Governour,"* Modern Language Notes, LII (1937), 407–408.

Caspari, Fritz. *Humanism and the Social Order in Tudor England.* Chicago, 1954.

Chambers, R. W. *Thomas More.* London, 1938.

Collinson, John. *History of Somerset.* 3 vols. Bath, 1791.

Conklin, Willet T. "Two Further Notes on Shakespeare's Use of Elyot's 'Governour,' " *University of Texas Studies in English,* X (1930), 66–69.

Cooper, C. H. *Annals of Cambridge.* 4 vols. Cambridge, England, 1842.

———, and Thompson Cooper. *Athenae Cantabrigienses.* 3 vols. London and Cambridge, 1858–1913.

Craik, Henry. *English Prose Selections, Vol. I.* London, 1893. Contains Alfred Aigner, "Sir Thomas Elyot," pp. 191–200.

* This bibliography excludes the printed works of Sir Thomas Elyot, which are treated separately as Appendix III.

Croft, H. H. S. (ed.). *The Boke named the Gouernour.* 2 vols. London, 1880.

Dictionary of National Biography. Ed. Sir Leslie Stephen and Sir Sidney Lee. 63 vols. London, 1885–1900.

Ellis, Sir Henry. *Original Letters Illustrative of English History.* 1st ser., 3 vols., London, 1824; 3d ser., 4 vols., London, 1846.

Elton, G. R. *Star Chamber Stories.* London, 1958.

Exner, Helmuth. *Der Einfluss des Erasmus auf die englische Bildungsidee.* Berlin, 1939.

Great Britain, State Papers. *Calendar of Letters, Despatches, and State Papers, Spanish.* Ed. G. A. Bergenroth (Vols. 1–2), Don Pascual de Gayangos (Vols. 3–7), M. A. S. Hume (Vols. 8–9), and Royall Tyler (Vols. 9–13). 13 vols., of which Vols. 2–8 (1866–1904) deal with the reign of Henry VIII.

———. *Calendar of Letters and Papers, Foreign and Domestic, Henry VIII.* Ed. J. S. Brewer (Vols. 1–4), J. Gairdner (Vols. 5–13), and Gairdner and R. H. Brodie (Vols. 14–21). 21 vols. in 37. London, 1864–1932.

———. *Calendar of Patent Rolls, Henry VII.* Ed. J. G. Black. 2 vols. London, 1914–1916.

———. *State Papers, Domestic, of the Reign of Henry VIII.* 11 vols. London, 1830–1852.

Grether, Emil. *Das Verhältnis von Shakespeares "Heinrich V." zu Sir Thomas Elyots "Gouernour."* Marburg, 1938.

Harpsfield, Nicholas. *The Life and Death of Sir Thomas More.* Ed. E. V. Hitchcock. London, 1932.

Hexter, J. H. "The Education of the Aristocracy in the Renaissance," *Journal of Modern History,* XXII (1950), 1–20.

Hogrefe, Pearl. "Elyot and the 'Boke Called Cortegiano in Ytalion.'" *Modern Philology,* XXVII (1930), 303–311.

Hopwood, C. H. (ed.). *Middle Temple Records.* London, 1904.

Kelso, Ruth. *The Doctrine of the English Gentleman in the Sixteenth Century.* Urbana, Ill., 1929.

Knowles, Dom David. *The Religious Orders in England, Vol. III: The Tudor Age.* Cambridge, England, 1959.

Lathrop, H. B. *Translations from the Classics into English from Caxton to Chapman, 1477–1620.* Madison, Wis., 1933.

Lehmberg, Stanford E. "Sir Thomas Elyot and the English Reformation," *Archiv für Reformationsgeschichte,* XLVIII (1957), 91–111.

Lewis, C. S. *English Literature in the Sixteenth Century.* Oxford, 1954.

Lysons, Daniel, and Samuel Lysons. *Magna Britannia.* 6 vols. London, 1806–1822.

McCoy, Samuel J. "The Language and Linguistic Interests of Sir Thomas Elyot." Unpublished Ph.D. dissertation, University of North Carolina, 1933.

MacGeagh, Sir Henry F., and H. A. C. Sturgess (eds.). *Register of Admissions to the Honourable Society of the Middle Temple.* 3 vols., London, 1949.

Major, John M. "Sir Thomas Elyot: Studies in Early Tudor Humanism." Unpublished Ph.D. dissertation, Harvard University, 1954.

————. "The Moralization of the Dance in Elyot's *Governour,*" *Studies in the Renaissance,* V (1958), 27–36.

Malone, Clifton J. "The Ideal Gentleman of Elyot's *The Governour* as a Reflection of Cicero's *De Officiis.*" Unpublished Master's thesis, University of Texas, 1931.

Palmer, H. R. *List of English Translations of Greek and Latin Classics Printed before 1641.* London, 1911.

Pocock, Nicholas. *Records of the Reformation.* 2 vols. Oxford, 1870.

Pollard, A. F. Communication to *The Times Literary Supplement* [London], XXIX, 592 (July 17, 1930), concerning Elyot's supposed embassy of 1535.

Pollard, A. W., and G. R. Redgrave (eds.). *A Short-Title Catalogue of Books Printed in England, Scotland, and Ireland and of English Books Printed Abroad 1475–1640.* London, 1926, 1946.

Raven, C. E. *English Naturalists from Neckam to Ray.* Cambridge, England, 1947.

Ro. Ba. *The Lyfe of Syr Thomas More,* ed. E. V. Hitchcock and P. E. Hallett. London, 1950.

Roper, William. *The Lyfe of Sir Thomas Moore.* Ed. E. V. Hitchcock. London, 1935.

Schlotter, Josef. *Thomas Elyots "Governour" in seinem Verhältnis zu Francesco Patrizi.* Freiburg im Breisgau, 1938.

Schroeder, Kurt. *Platonismus in der englischen Renaissance vor und bei Thomas Eliot, nebst Neudruck von Eliots "Disputacion Platonike."* Berlin, 1920.

Siegel, Paul N. "English Humanism and the New Tudor Aristocracy," *Journal of the History of Ideas,* XIII (1952), 450–468.

Sledd, James H. "A Footnote on the Inkhorn Controversy," *University of Texas Studies in English,* XXVIII (1949), pp. 49–56.

Stapleton, Thomas. *The Life and Illustrious Martyrdom of Sir Thomas*

More. Trans. P. E. Hallett. London, 1928. Translation of Part III of *Tres Thomae.*

Starnes, DeWitt T. *Renaissance Dictionaries: English-Latin and Latin-English.* Austin, 1954.

————, and E. W. Talbert. *Classical Myth and Legend in Renaissance Dictionaries.* Chapel Hill, 1955.

————. "Notes on Elyot's *The Governour,*" *Review of English Studies,* III (1917), 37–46.

————. "Elyot's *Governour* and Peacham's *Compleat Gentilman,*" *Modern Language Review,* XXII (1927), 319–322.

————. "Shakespeare and Elyot's *Gouernour,*" *University of Texas Studies in English,* VII (1927), 112–135.

————. "The Picture of a Perfit Common Wealth," *University of Texas Studies in English,* XI (1931), 32–41.

————. "Sir Thomas Elyot and the Sayings of the Philosophers," *University of Texas Studies in English,* XIII (1933), 11–12.

————. "Thomas Cooper's *Thesaurus,*" *University of Texas Studies in English,* XXVIII (1949), 15–48.

————. "Thomas Cooper and the *Bibliotheca Eliotae,*" *University of Texas Studies in English,* XXX (1951), 40–60.

————. "Sir Thomas Elyot and the Lanquet-Cooper *Chronicle,*" *University of Texas Studies in English,* XXXIV (1955), 35–42.

————. "Sir Thomas Elyot *Redivivus,*" *University of Texas Studies in English,* XXXVI (1957), 28–40.

Stenberg, Theodore. "Sir Thomas Elyot's Defense of the Poets," *University of Texas Studies in English,* VI (1926), 121–142.

Strype, John. *Ecclesiastical Memorials.* 6 vols. Oxford, 1822.

Vernon Harcourt, L. W. "The two Sir John Fastolfs," *Transactions* of the Royal Historical Society, 3d ser., IV (1910), 47–62.

Warren, Leslie C. "Humanistic Doctrines of the Prince from Petrarch to Sir Thomas Elyot: A Study of the Principal Analogues and Sources of *The Boke named the Gouernour.*" Unpublished Ph.D. dissertation, University of Chicago, 1937.

————. "Patrizi's *De Regno et Regis Institutione* and the Plan of Elyot's *The Boke Named the Governour,*" *Journal of English and Germanic Philology,* XLIX (1950), 67–77.

Willis, Browne. *Notitia Parliamentaria.* 3 vols. London, 1716–1730.

Wood, Anthony à. *Athenae Oxonienses.* 4 vols. London, 1813–1820.

Woodward, W. H. *Studies in Education during the Age of the Renaissance.* Cambridge, England, 1906.

Wortham, James. "Sir Thomas Elyot and the Translation of Prose," *Huntington Library Quarterly*, XI (1948), 219–240.

Yarbrough, Leta R. "A Comparative Study of Castiglione's *Il Cortegiano*, Budé's *De l'institution du prince*, Elyot's *The Governour*, and Villalón's *El scholástico*." Unpublished Master's thesis, University of Texas, 1933.

Zeeveld, W. Gordon. *Foundations of Tudor Policy*. Cambridge, Mass., 1948.

Index